W9-ADO-563

When four young men, slaves on Edward Gorsuch's Maryland farm, escaped to rural Pennsylvania in 1849, the owner swore he'd bring them back. Two years later, Gorsuch lay dead outside the farmhouse in Christiana where he'd tracked them down, as his federal posse retreated pell-mell before the armed might of local blacks—and the impact of the most notorious act of resistance against the federal Fugitive Slave Law was about to be felt across a divided nation.

Bloody Dawn vividly tells this dramatic story of escape, manhunt, riot, and the ensuing trial, detailing its importance in heightening the tensions that led to the Civil War. Thomas Slaughter's engaging narrative captures the full complexity of events and personalities: The four men fled after they were detected stealing grain for resale off the farm; Gorsuch, far from a brutal taskmaster, had pledged to release all his slaves when they reached the age of twenty-eight, but he relentlessly pursued the escapees out of a sense of wounded honor; and the African-American community in Lancaster County, Pennsylvania that provided them refuge was already effectively organized for self-defense by a commanding former slave named William Parker. Slaughter paints a rich portrait of the ongoing struggles between local blacks and white kidnapping gangs, the climactic riot as neighbors responded to trumpet calls from the besieged runaway slaves, the escape to Canada of the central figures (aided by Fredrick Douglass), and the government's urgent response (including the largest mass indictment for treason in our history)—leading to the trial for his life of a local white bystander accused of leading the rioting blacks. Slaughter not only draws out the great importance given to the riot in both

BLOODY DAWN

BLOODY
DAWN

THE CHRISTIANA RIOT
AND RACIAL VIOLENCE
IN THE ANTEBELLUM NORTH

Thomas P. Slaughter

New York   Oxford
Oxford University Press
1991

WINGATE UNIVERSITY LIBRARY

Oxford University Press

Oxford   New York   Toronto
Delhi   Bombay   Calcutta   Madras   Karachi
Nairobi   Dar es Salaam   Cape Town
Melbourne   Auckland

and associated companies in
Berlin   Ibadan

Copyright © 1991 by Thomas P. Slaughter

Published by Oxford University Press, Inc.,
200 Madison Avenue, New York, New York 10016

Oxford is a registered trademark of Oxford University Press

All rights reserved. No part of this publication may be reproduced,
stored in a retrieval system, or transmitted, in any form or by any means,
electronic, mechanical, photocopying, recording, or otherwise,
without the prior permission of Oxford University Press.

Library of Congress Cataloging-in-Publication Data
Slaughter, Thomas P. (Thomas Paul)
Bloody Dawn: the Christiana riot and racial violence
in the antebellum North / Thomas P. Slaughter.
p. cm.   Includes bibliographical references and index.
ISBN 0-19-504633-1
1. Riots—Pennsylvania—Christiana—History—19th century.
2. Fugitive slaves—Pennsylvania—Christiana—History—19th century.
3. Violence—Pennsylvania—Christiana—History—19th century.
4. Christiana (Pa.)—Race relations.   5. Afro-Americans—
Pennsylvania—Christiana—History—19th century.   I. Title.
F159.C55S58   1991
974.8'15—dc20   90-22901

9 8 7 6 5 4 3 2 1

Printed in the United States of America
on acid-free paper

This book is dedicated to the memory of
James E. Chaney, Andrew Goodman, and Michael H. Schwerner,
who died near Philadelphia, Mississippi, on June 21, 1964
—another tragedy in the ongoing story
about race, violence, and law.

Contents

Introduction

THIS BOOK TELLS THE STORY of a riot that erupted on September 11, 1851, at Christiana, Lancaster County, Pennsylvania, and of the people whose lives were changed forever by that violent event. Shortly after dawn on that day, Lancaster's African-American community rose up in arms against attempted enforcement of the Fugitive Slave Law of 1850; and, in the course of saving four men from the federal posse charged to re-enslave them, rioters killed the Maryland farmer who was trying to reclaim his human chattel.

Nine years before the War between the States, the events described in the following pages were proclaimed in screaming banner headlines that prophesied the bloody cataclysm to come. "CIVIL WAR, THE FIRST BLOW STRUCK," captured for many, especially in the South, the true meaning of what came to be known on both sides of the Mason-Dixon Line as the "Christiana Tragedy." The murder of Edward Gorsuch by men he claimed to own was not the only, the first, or the last death to result from the border warfare over fugitive slaves. The timing and circumstances of this particular riot were, however, of immense significance on the national scene.

Whether Americans could reach a rapprochement on the issue of slavery was not at all clear, and the Christiana Riot challenged the government's ability to mediate the demands of politics and law. The line between riot and rebellion was shifting during the antebellum period, leaving the definition of political crime open to broad construction. Federal prosecutors seized this imprecision in constitutional law to charge thirty-eight men on 117 separate counts of "levying war" against the government for their alleged roles in the Christiana Riot, making this the largest mass indictment for treason in the history of our nation.

Abolitionists, pro-slavery secessionists, and politically aware Americans in between those two poles anticipated the resulting trial as a test case for the Compromise of 1850. Some people in the South saw energetic enforcement of the new Fugitive Slave Law, which was one of eight parts of the intersectional compromise proposed by Senator Henry Clay, as a condition of their continuing loyalty to the Union. The previous federal law of 1793 provided no protection to alleged fugitives, no right to a jury trial or to testify in their own behalf. Unscrupulous kidnappers exploited the situation in a variety of ways, including taking free blacks by force and selling them into slavery on the pretense that they were fugitives. In response, as opposition to slavery grew in the North, some states passed personal-liberty laws designed to remedy abuses.

From the perspective of Southerners, the new laws went much too far, making it increasingly difficult for masters to locate and return fugitives who were their lawful property. Under one such law, Pennsylvania convicted Edward Prigg of kidnapping in 1837 for his actions in seizing a woman and her children and returning them to her Maryland owner. Prigg's lawyers appealed to the Supreme Court, which issued a complex decision in 1842 ruling the Pennsylvania anti-kidnapping law of 1826 unconstitutional, upholding the fugitive slave law of 1793, but declaring that enforcement was a federal responsibility. Pennsylvania, among other Northern states, vitiated the Court's decision in the *Prigg* case by passing new personal-liberty laws that barred the cooperation of state officials or the use of state jails for the holding of fugitive slaves.

As a consequence, Southerners still had a difficult time pursuing their escaped human chattel. The Fugitive Slave Law of 1850 was designed to alleviate that problem by putting the burden of proof on captured blacks, but giving them no legal power to prove their freedom. A claimant could bring an alleged fugitive before one of the new federal commissioners provided for by the law. In support of his case, the claimant could produce white witnesses or introduce an affidavit from a Southern court. If the commissioner decided in favor of the claimant, he received a ten-dollar fee; if he ruled in behalf of the alleged fugitive, his fee was five dollars. In either case, the costs of the slave-catching enterprise were drawn from the federal treasury.

The discrepancy in the fees was purportedly in recompense for the additional paperwork involved in remanding slaves, but anti-slavery advocates saw the additional five dollars as a bribe, which gave the commissioners a pecuniary stake in ruling against the alleged fugitives who already had the legal cards stacked against them. In fact, the Fugitive Slave Law did function in the slave-owners' behalf. During the first fifteen months that it was in force, eighty-four alleged fugitives were remanded South by commissioners, and only five were set free. Over the course of the de- cade, 332 African-Americans were enslaved under the provisions of this act, and only eleven were released by federal commissioners.[1]

The Union itself seemed to hinge on enforcement of this controversial law, and tensions were high in 1851 as both sides in the controversy over slavery tested how the Compromise would work. Armed resistance at Christiana to a federal marshal with a warrant issued under the new Fu- gitive Slave Law presented a challenge of immense political significance. In the eyes of pro-slavery Southerners, and ultimately of federal prose- cutors, treason was the crime committed here, and the traitor was a white man named Castner Hanway, who allegedly directed the black mob in its attack on the federal posse. If the laws of the nation could be resisted with impunity, if citizens were free to "levy war" against the government as embodied in its legislative enactments and law-enforcement officials, then the very survival of the Union was at stake. Nothing less than con- viction and execution of *white* abolitionist "leaders" would satisfy the honor of Edward Gorsuch's family, the State of Maryland, and Southerners who identified with the slain slave owner who died what they saw as a hero's death defending their rights under law. Nothing less than acquittal of all the rioters on all counts would appease the most radical abolitionists, who appealed to a higher law and a superior justice than that found in the Constitution and the Fugitive Slave Law of 1850.

So the lines were drawn in a fashion that pushed the Christiana Riot and the government's response to center stage in the national political drama. No other fugitive slave case, neither Jerry's in Syracuse nor those of Shadrach and Thomas Simms in Boston, had the same political signifi- cance at the time. Whatever the comparative importance of these other cases in law, whatever effect they had on firing the abolitionist movement and drawing the lines of conflict over the fugitive slave issue, no other fugitive episode struck the raw nerve of Southern honor so painfully or had the same impact on public opinion throughout the nation.

Indeed, no single event before John Brown's Raid contributed more to the decline of confidence in the nation's ability to resolve the contro- versy over slavery without wholesale resort to arms. Were we to search for parallels between the events leading up to the American Revolution, this nation's first civil war, the Christiana Riot corresponds in some re- spects to the Stamp Act crisis in the same way that John Brown's Raid does to the Boston Tea Party. Neither the Stamp Act resistance nor the

Christiana Riot caused the wars that followed them by nine years; however, each galvanized public opinion in ways that made it increasingly
difficult to resolve differences amicably. Neither resulted in a decisive
victory for law and order; indeed, each encouraged those who acted outside the law to think that they could do so with impunity. Both were later
remembered by contemporaries as the beginning of a violent process that
became a war.

Here the parallel ends. The Christiana Riot has not been treated by
historians of the Civil War with the same regard accorded the Stamp Act
crisis by the Revolution's chroniclers. It is seen more as a footnote than
as a prologue to war. To the extent that the riot has had its historians,
and it certainly has over the past century and a half, they have tended to
focus on it for the dramatic qualities that its sources embody, for its significance as a local event, or for its contribution to the history of fugitive
slave law. So the riot has its legions of local historians, its playwrights, its
legal historians, and two compilers of documents who argue convincingly
that the historical record speaks eloquently for itself. In all regards, these
authors have served the memory of the Christiana Riot well. My purpose
in retelling the story is not to correct or to supplant the contributions of
other scholars and history buffs. Without them, this book would have
been much more difficult to research. I am simply telling a story different
from theirs.[2]

The setting and events selected for discussion here are less "typical"
than they are illustrative of historical experiences in other places and at
other times. I chose the Christiana Riot as a focus of analysis because it
was the subject of attention in its own day. For that reason, the riot provides an opportunity to comprehend wider contexts of meaning. The politicians, political activists, newspaper writers, ministers, jurists, and lit-
erary figures of the time decided that these particular themes were
important and that the historical setting depicted here was a significant
one. I, drawing on their testimony and that of less historically articulate
participants, have reinterpreted meaning for them, for me, and, I hope,
for some of you.

At the time and since, this riot has been popularly known as the
"Christiana Tragedy." The "tragedy" represents a white man's perspective that was not necessarily shared by all African-American participants.
Incontestably, the riot was a tragedy for the family and friends of Edward
Gorsuch, who died at the hands of his fugitive slaves. Just as certainly,
officials of the State of Maryland and moderate pro-slavery Southerners
throughout the region were horror-struck by both the riot and the outcome in the courts. The tragedy was felt by both Northern and Southern

moderates who valued the rule of law and who prayed for the peaceful resolution of interregional tensions. Many—indeed most—abolitionists felt the tragedy to their cause and tried, unsuccessfully in the eyes of others, to disassociate their movement from the violence of the riot. The riot was a political tragedy for Pennsylvania moderates, the state's sitting Whig governor, and all those citizens who hoped to see the Commonwealth pursue a liberal course in the slavery controversy.

Perhaps least obvious, the riot was a tragedy for African-American residents of the region—if not for those who fled to Canada in the days immediately following the violence, and for men and women who sought to escape from slavery across the Maryland border. Free blacks and those who pursued their freedom were the victims of white Marylanders' vengeful rage, a general decline of faith in the rule of law, and an environment even more conducive to violence. White residents of Pennsylvania were even more suspicious, less sympathetic, and less tolerant of their black neighbors than they had been before. The racism, the poverty, and the other hardships associated with "free" black life were also parts of that continuing tragedy. The pains of dislocation were no less real for those rioters who found it necessary to abandon family and friends in order to avoid possible prosecution for what they saw as defensive acts. And the Civil War was no less a tragic outcome of the tensions exacerbated by the Christiana Riot, despite the positive consequences of that bloodbath.

The Christiana Riot is significant not just in its own right but also as a window on the culture of violence in the place where it occurred. The intense light of national interest in the case created a written record unsurpassed for its rich documentation of the perspectives of all parties to the ongoing struggle over slavery and race. The testimony of illiterate men and women recorded by newspaper reporters, lawyers, and court stenographers provides insight into a world normally lost to modern eyes. The commonplace thoughts of literate people, who were not normally prone to preserving their ideas about violence and race, are also revealing. This episode enabled Americans to articulate their fears in concrete terms, and they did so in voluminous detail.

A retelling of the Christiana Riot's story allows me to recapture some of the emotions that led to so much violence and to so many tears. It assists me in looking at the controversy over slavery as it was acted out in the lives of ordinary people, in watching them act under the stresses of an extraordinary event, and in comprehending better the perspectives of all sides in the controversy over ownership of other human beings.

The book looks more broadly at some of the ways that law functions as an expression of culture and how it represents the interests of some groups against perceived threats posed by others. Sometimes the line between politics and law is unclear; the treason trial resulting from the Christiana Riot is one such case. Law is always affected by social prejudices that are embodied in legislation and the actions of judges and juries. Tolerance for particular kinds of violence, the presence or absence of sympathy for victims, and the degree of identification with perpetrators all play roles in communities' responses to violent acts. The riot helps me to find additional meaning in the everyday actions of people, to discern the motives that we do not normally examine thoughtfully in ourselves and that we almost never explain.

The story told here illustrates some of the ways that sufferance of violence responds to broader social patterns. I explore connections between physical brutality toward other humans and the way we define who really belongs to our community and who does not—"us" and "them"—through the example of one rural Pennsylvania county and the state and nation of which it is a part. I use the Christiana Riot—including its short-term background and causes and its immediate consequences—to illustrate these themes, and I look at some of the same motifs in greater analytical detail over the decades preceding the Civil War.

The story is about black participants in an ongoing battle for freedom, and it is about the general problem of violence among different races and classes and across gender lines. The book is about relations among people and about perceptions they had of each other. It considers the meanings of social, legal, and political relations within one county and across territorial borders.

The poverty, racism, and savagery in my story are scourges that transcend the people, events, times, and places treated here. Some readers will be saddened or angered or have their sensibilities irritated by the violence portrayed in these pages. Some may detect the potential in this book for an unpatriotically bleak interpretation of our national history. Such readers could assert, quite rightly, that this is only a partial picture of our collective past. It would be a mistake, however, to see the episodes depicted here as exceptions to the ways in which we conduct public business. Only when we confront our national myths and begin to recognize these truths can we realistically hope to achieve the sort of kinder, gentler nation that we all wish we had. If this book has one goal, it is to play a part in this process of owning our violent past.

BLOODY DAWN

Their story, yours, mine—it's what we all carry with us on this trip we take, and we owe it to each other to respect our stories and learn from them.

WILLIAM CARLOS WILLIAMS

So it has been for many of us—going back, way back, to the earliest of times, when men and women and children looked at one another, at the land, at the sky, at rivers and oceans, at mountains and deserts, at animals and plants, and wondered, as it is in our nature to do: what is all this that I see and hear and find unfolding before me? How shall I comprehend the life that is in me and around me? To do so, stories were constructed— and told, and remembered, and handed down over time, over the generations. Some stories—of persons, of places, of events— were called factual. Some stories were called "imaginative" or "fictional": in them, words were assembled in such a way that readers were treated to a narration of events and introduced to individuals whose words and deeds—well, struck home.

ROBERT COLES,
The Call of Stories: Teaching and the Moral Imagination

[1]

The Escape

EDWARD GORSUCH WAS A GOOD FARMER, and 1849 was a good year for his farm. By November, bacon, potatoes, and cider filled the basement for the winter. His slaves had put up jelly, preserves, and pickles in the pantry, where they also stored sweet potatoes and a keg of molasses. Gorsuch's forty or so cows (including the bull and several calves), fifty pigs (counting the shoats), thirty sheep, and uncounted ducks and chickens mooed, snorted, bleated, quacked, cackled, and crowed the prosperity of the farm. The dozen horses and six plows had done their season's work, and the corn house full of wheat (Figure 1.1) was a testament to the hard and successful labors of the animals and slaves who worked them.

Well, the granary had been full, but Gorsuch noticed that some wheat was missing and unaccounted for. It was not enough to be a serious financial loss or to affect the diet of the humans and animals for which Gorsuch was responsible as the patriarch of Retreat Farm in rural Baltimore County, Maryland, but as a careful husbandman, he made a mental note of the mystery. The lost grain could be a symptom of what might become a larger problem. The bin was about five bushels low, too much to be the quick work of rodents, and there was no evidence of a break-in by larger creatures. So the perpetrator or perpetrators of the robbery must have been human.[1]

Perhaps the slaves were obvious suspects. Most slaveholders of Gorsuch's day accepted petty thievery as a fact of life as unalterable as the weather. Indeed, there was a well-known ethic among slaves that "taking" from masters was not stealing in a moral sense. After all, if they were hungry or wanted for clothing and other essentials it was a consequence

FIGURE 1.1. The Gorsuch corn house *(with permission of the Lancaster County Historical Society)*

of masters' irresponsibility to their people. They were only using what was rightfully theirs; and what they took was only a pittance by comparison to what masters stole from them. As Frederick Douglass recalled from his youth as a Maryland slave,

> considering that my labor and person were the property of [my] Master
> . . . and that I was by him deprived of the necessaries of life—necessaries obtained by my own labor—it was easy to deduce the right to supply myself with what was my own. It was simply appropriating what was my own to use of my master, since the health and strength derived from such food were exerted in *his* service.[2]

Edward Gorsuch would have been surprised to find members of his slave "family" reasoning like Douglass or acting upon such logic. In his own eyes, Gorsuch fed his slaves well and was a kindly master. What is more, he had made provisions to free his slaves as each of them reached the age of twenty-eight years. He owned a total of twelve slaves, four of whom were adult males who plowed his fields and carried most of the heavy load of farm labor. Noah Buley and Joshua Hammond were in their early twenties. Later, after the tragedy, members of the Gorsuch family would describe Buley as a copper-colored mulatto with a "treacherous disposition." Nelson Ford and George Hammond each had eight or nine years left to serve Edward Gorsuch, who, according to the master's family, gave Ford only light work as a teamster because of his "delicate" physical condition. In 1849, Gorsuch thought his "boys" respected him; they certainly wanted for no essentials in his opinion, and their freedom was on the immediate horizon.[3]

Gorsuch was no Simon Legree. By all accounts, he did not beat his slaves. He tried to rule his household as a New Testament father, by love and mercy, seasoned, of course, with firmness and a dash of the Old Testament patriarch. To be sure, for the time and place in which he lived, Gorsuch had reason to see himself as a benevolent father, whose children—biological and legal, white and black, free and slave—should love and respect him for the character that he tried always to display among them. He was a man of honor and liberality in his own eyes and in the eyes of his neighbors, of his church, and of his sons. Neighbors brought him disputes to arbitrate because he was such a fair man. Gorsuch thought that his slaves saw him that way, too.

There was no law that dictated the manumitting of his slaves; there was no communal imperative that drove Gorsuch to make the financial sacrifice of freeing his chattel laborers. But, in retrospect, we cannot take at face value the master's testament to the unmixed humanitarian origins of his personal effort to gradually abolish slavery on his farm. After all, he did not free the slaves outright or offer them compensation for their labors in his behalf. What is more, there is good reason to believe that his moral concerns about slavery, which were certainly real, were fertilized by an economic calculation that many of his neighbors had already made. Gorsuch was not the first, or even among the first, in Baltimore County to see the light on this perplexing moral issue. In 1849, when Gorsuch's wheat disappeared, only 5 percent of northern Maryland's population was enslaved; and no other slave state had a comparable portion of free blacks within its borders.[4]

The ideology of the American Revolution, revivalism, and evangelical religion had certainly all played a role in this process of emancipation. Gorsuch's Quaker ancestry and Quaker neighbors perhaps also had some moral influence, as did the teachings of the liberal Methodist Episcopal Church, which he attended regularly and in which he was a "class leader." But given the timing and circumstances under which Gorsuch's slaves were to be freed, it seems clear that the movement away from tobacco production and toward the growing of wheat played a determinative role in the conclusion of Gorsuch and his neighbors that slaves were no longer a necessary, or even a financially desirable, feature of northern Maryland farming.[5]

The rhythms of tobacco production could keep slaves occupied throughout the seasons, while wheat called for intense labor at harvest but left little for a permanent work force to do the rest of the year. The keeping of animals and growing grain as a cash crop were not so labor-intensive that they justified slavery in economic terms, so Gorsuch really did not "need" his slaves in the same way that his ancestors had. But he could have sold the slaves South rather than setting them free. By 1840, 12 percent of Maryland's slave population ended up on the auction block per annum, many of them sold out of state. He might have kept some of the slaves, those he could use as agricultural laborers, and gotten rid of the others. Instead, he set his slaves free as they turned twenty-eight and offered them seasonal employment and a place to live if they wished to continue working on the farm. Some of them, at least, accepted the offer.[6]

Gorsuch was a good man, not a great one. He took what seemed at the time a responsible middle course, thereby failing, with the great mass of mankind, to transcend the evils of his day. Gorsuch was also a stubborn, foolhardy, and hot-tempered man, but such traits were no cause for celebrity in his own day any more than they are in ours. He also misjudged his slaves, repeatedly and with fatal consequences.

Gorsuches had, by 1849, lived and died on the land of rural Baltimore County for almost two hundred years. The original ten-thousand-acre grant had shrunk by subdivision over the generations, but the adjacent tracts of "Retreat" and "Retirement" in the far northern end of the county were still substantial working farms. Edward inherited Retreat, renamed for its historic role in the War of 1812, from his Uncle John in 1845. The heir was fifty years old when he came into his legacy, a mature man with five grown children. Rightly proud of his new status as patriarch of Retreat, he determined to manage the farm and slaves inherited from his uncle in a manner that sustained the honor and wealth of this substantial Southern family.

Gorsuch was among the larger slaveholders in Maryland. Only 10 percent of the state's slave owners held eight or more slaves. His farm was in the most prosperous agricultural region of the state, where the value of market produce in the twelve months preceding June 30, 1850, amounted to one and a half times that for the rest of Maryland. Laborers harvested twice as much hay in the region as in southern Maryland and the Eastern Shore combined. Northern Maryland, where the Gorsuches farmed, produced 70 percent of the rye and buckwheat and over half the oats and wheat grown in the state. The per-acre value of farms in the region was consequently higher than elsewhere in Maryland. So Edward Gorsuch was a prosperous farmer, indeed, and had good reason to be proud of the estate that he husbanded.[7]

FIGURE 1.2. Retreat Farm, home of the Gorsuches *(with permission of the Lancaster County Historical Society)*

The house in which Gorsuch and his wife lived on Retreat was partly constructed of logs, reflecting its frontier origins, but had been expanded by a stone addition from its original one and a half stories to three (Figure 1.2). The cellar windows still had the iron bars installed in a previous century to keep out the wolves and panthers that roamed the forests before the white settlers could eradicate such threats to a civilized landscape. The previous owner had added a number of outbuildings, including a sheep fold, ox stable, blacksmith shop, spring house, corn houses, hog house, and slave quarters. In 1841, he also built a brick-and-fieldstone barn, which resembled those in southeastern Pennsylvania constructed at about the same time.[8]

In November 1849, the barn was a busy place, full of life and the sounds, smells, and textures of people at work on a communal task. The farm's laborers—slave and free, women, men, and children, too—gathered each evening to cut and top the corn. Laboring in concert, the slaves blended elements of work and play. The harmony was that of work—muffled tones of sharp corn knives in the calloused hands of women whose lifetimes of experience made the tools extensions of their unconscious will—cutting and tearing the husks from the cobs, corn hitting corn as the ears were tossed to the finished pile. The older children, helping as befit their ages, were certainly less agile with the knives, more determined, more focused, working harder and accomplishing less than the adults.[9]

The melody was that of play—joking, singing, teasing, voices glad to be working at this task rather than others, pleased to see and feel and hear the rhythms of the agricultural cycle slowing to a more tranquil winter's pace. What songs did they sing, what jokes did they tell, what dreams did they dare to dream aloud for themselves and the toddlers around them? Almost certainly the walls echoed the old Maryland slave song "Round the Corn Sally," which provided a rhythmic accompaniment to the task at hand and articulated a not so subtle escape fantasy:

Five can't ketch me and ten can't hold me,
Ho . . . round the corn, Sally!
Round the corn, round the corn, round the corn, Sally!
Ho, ho, ho, round the corn, Sally!

With the seasonal change in the air, it was also a likely time for "The Winter," with its less cheerful metaphoric expression of the wish, the prayer, that the worst was over:

O the winter, O the winter, O the winter'll soon be over, children . . .
Tis Paul and Silas bound in chains, chains, chains,
And one did weep, and the other one did pray, other one did pray . . .
I turn my eyes towards the sky, sky,
And ask the Lord, Lord, for wings to fly.
O the winter, O the winter, O the winter'll soon be over, children . . .[10]

Perhaps they sang the hymn that expressed the dream—"We are Free"— which was a safe way to unburden the heart within earshot of the master. The younger children were surely playing against the tide of labor and song, climbing on the piles, exploring, testing the limits of their freedom, caught up in the festive spirit. But we must not exaggerate the joy or mistake the light-hearted banter for contentment.

There was also anger and concern and anticipation of unsettling change. But those were softer tones not heard, or at least not comprehended, by the master when he stuck in his head to see that all was well with his people, that the work proceeded apace, that the play was not interfering with the work that was the business of the farm. We do not know how often the still relatively new master of Retreat Farm checked on his employees and slaves as they labored in the barn. We cannot recover how his appearance affected the pace of work, the cacophony of sounds, or the joy of the task at hand. We do know that the slaves successfully hid what was in their hearts from the master as they went about their chores.

Occasionally, another sound would intrude: the low rumbling noise of wood on wood as male slaves rolled an ox cart full of unhusked corn across the floor and dumped it on the dwindling pile of work yet to be done. The dust raised by the crash was illumined during the day by light filtering through the door and the four large brick ventilators, one on each wall of the new barn. At night, and husking was principally an evening chore, lanterns would cast different, perhaps more haunting, shadows across the room. What did the male slaves talk about as they shoveled corn into the ox cart toward the end of this long work day? Perhaps we can guess, because they knew who took the missing wheat from Master Gorsuch's corn house, and they thought they were going to be caught. They were making plans for the dangerous, but exhilarating, new lives that they were about to begin.[11]

Rumor had it among the slaves that the master knew who took the grain. Nothing had been said yet, but they were waiting for the boot to drop. The miller had gotten suspicious when Abe Johnson, a free black man, offered to sell him five bushels of wheat. Johnson had no fields of his own, no obvious source for the grain. Johnson might have lied to the miller or declined to answer his question, but he trusted Elias Mathews, who was a Quaker, and told the white man the truth. The source for the wheat was several of Edward Gorsuch's slaves, Johnson told the miller. They brought the grain to him because "the person who had been in the habit of receiving from them had closed up"; in other words, this was not the first theft by the slaves. Their usual channel for disposing of stolen goods was unavailable, and they were forced to try something new. Perhaps they should not have trusted Abe Johnson. Johnson certainly misjudged Elias Mathews.[12]

No other information survives about the miller. If he agonized over the decision to betray the slaves to their master, it was an agony suffered in his heart, not one expressed on paper. If he shared the moral burden of other Quakers in the region, it could not have been an easy choice, and yet it was one consistent with the general character of Quaker relations with slaveholders in northern Maryland.

The Society of Friends, first in Philadelphia and then in London, had taken the lead in opposing slavery in America and the slave trade throughout the British Empire. Maryland Quakers, too, were influenced by the moral impulses that led the Philadelphia Yearly Meeting slowly, by stages, during the eighteenth century to renounce the ownership of other people. By the 1790s, the Baltimore Yearly Meeting had also effectively determined that no one could be a Quaker and an owner of slaves and tried its best during the first half of the nineteenth century to alleviate the worst suffering of African-Americans, slave and free, who lived in the neighborhood.[13]

To be sure, in the eyes of Quakers in London and Philadelphia, the Maryland Quakers could have done more. And in the course of a long and sometimes heated correspondence among the London, Philadelphia, and Baltimore Yearly Meetings, the Maryland Quakers tried to explain and defend the less strident stand they took in the movement to abolish slavery from the English-speaking world. "Our belief is," the Maryland Quakers wrote during the 1840s, "that unless we are careful to move under a lively sense of duty in each particular case, such is the extreme delicacy of the subject, that we are in danger of retarding instead of advancing the work of deliverance to this people."[14]

Their religious brethren would have to recognize that "the circumstances which surround us are peculiar, and our situation and difficulties are hardly to be appreciated by Friends at a distance." In their own eyes, they were not lukewarm on the issue, but their numbers were few and to unite with the Northern abolitionists, who "*have* done injury to the cause," would be counterproductive. What is more, their concern for the souls of the masters, as well as the slaves, required that they maintain the confidence of the masters. To circulate abolitionist literature or take public stands against slavery in Maryland would, in the opinion of the Baltimore Quakers, be a mistake,

> *because* we think it would have a tendency to lessen our future usefulness and would probably close the door of access we now have to the slave-holders, who know we oppose slavery on conscientious grounds, that we have not selfish views in our opposition, that we are lovers of peace and that we are friends both of the master and the slave.[15]

For the Quaker miller Elias Mathews to collude with Abe Johnson and the slaves at Retreat would be a breach of faith with Gorsuch and other slaveholders in the region. Not only would he risk losing the white-men's business—and perhaps that was his greatest concern—but he would sacrifice any influence that he had with the owners of slaves and be less effective in efforts to assist the black inhabitants of the neighborhood. The fact that Johnson trusted the miller with his story suggests that Mathews was known to be sympathetic to the blacks and had treated them honestly and with regard in the past. But Johnson expected too much from the white man. He asked for more than a Quaker in northern Baltimore County was likely to do for a black. He was asking the miller to stand alone in opposition to the moral standards of the white community. Like Edward Gorsuch, Elias Mathews was a good man, not a great one.

As Gorsuch told the story:

The miller immediately called to see me and gave me the . . . information. I went with him to see the wheat, and believed it to be mine it perfectly corresponding with some that I had just before in my granary, and of which I had missed a quantity. I said nothing to my coloured boys about it but had a state warrant issued for said Abraham Johnston [*sic*], but Johnston finding out that they were after him secreted himself for a few days.

So the whites were looking for the free black man who could implicate Gorsuch's "boys" and assumed, wrongly, that the slaves did not know what was going on. In fact, the slaves were probably hiding Johnson, while making their own plans for what to do next.[16]

It was November 6, 1849. Noah Buley, Nelson Ford, and George and Joshua Hammond talked quietly, and no doubt nervously, as they shoveled corn into the ox cart. One of them casually asked a white carpenter who worked on the farm whether "the Boss is going to husk corn tonight?" Another one announced a bit more publicly than was normal or necessary that he was setting his rabbit trap before sunset, because it was "going to be a very dark night." Having done their best to act "normal," under cover of that very dark evening the four male slaves escaped through a skylight in the back building, climbed down a ladder, and sneaked away from the farm. We cannot know whether they ran simply because they feared the consequences of being discovered as thieves or whether stealing the grain was to raise money for an escape that they had planned all along. But run they did, with the help of Alexander Scott, "a tall yellow fellow," who was also one of Gorsuch's slaves. According to a black resident of Lancaster County interviewed long after the fact, Scott said that he brought Buley, Ford, and the two Hammonds in a wagon to Baltimore, where he put them on a northbound train.[17]

Another account indicated that the fugitives fled on foot, using the York Road as their path to freedom. This is much more likely than the other story, because four black men could not board a northbound train in Baltimore city without some challenge by local authorities. As William Still reported in his first-person narrative of Underground Railroad experiences:

Baltimore used to be in the days of Slavery one of the most difficult places in the South for even free colored people to get away from much more for slaves. The rule forbade any colored person leaving there by rail road or steamboat, without such applicant had been weighed, measured, and then given a bond signed by unquestionable signatures, well known.[18]

So the Baltimore train story was undoubtedly a ruse. There were good reasons to be cagey about the methods and directions of escaped slaves in flight. Circulating two contradictory stories about the route they took was one way of keeping opportunities open for those who might flee on another day. Stories told later, long after the event, still reflected the necessity, and the habit, of such deception. Descendants of the master believed into the twentieth century that the four slaves left on foot; while the oral tradition among local blacks still maintained that the men rode the above-ground railroad to freedom.[19]

In any event, such diversions were apparently unnecessary in this particular case, because Gorsuch never suspected that his "people" would run away. No special provisions were made to secure the slaves in their quarters. The master was shocked and his pride wounded the next morning when his son Dickinson shouted up the stairs that "the boys are all gone." Gorsuch blamed the free black man Johnson for enticing the slaves and deluding them with false hopes about the nature of life across the Pennsylvania border to the north.[20]

Free blacks were indeed a thorn in the side of Maryland's slave owners. As a foreign traveler observed in the 1790s, "house robberies are frequent in Maryland. . . . The judges attribute the multiplicity of robberies to the free negroes, who are very numerous in the state." A series of laws during the nineteenth century was intended to control the free black population, denying them the right to own dogs or firearms or to purchase liquor or ammunition without a special license. Free blacks were supposed to secure written certification of ownership before selling tobacco, grain, or meat. Nonetheless, the white community continued to feel plagued by thefts, which they blamed on free blacks. Whites did make one special exception to the rule against slaves testifying in court: in the cases of free blacks accused of stealing, slaves could give witness *against* them. Still, the stealing continued. By 1850, free blacks represented about 13 percent of the county population but a little more than one-third of those incarcerated in Baltimore's jail.[21]

The free blacks were not only thieves, according to Maryland's whites, but burdens on society in a host of other ways as well. They lived on the economic fringes, as the seasonal fluctuations of black men, women, and children in the county's almshouse attest. These free blacks also stood as models of an alternative life for the slaves. They were, in the eyes of whites, tutors in crime, receivers of stolen goods, and "kidnappers" of slaves. They lent their "free" papers to slaves, who sought the short-term liberty to travel the countryside visiting relatives or friends. They cajoled, goaded, and tricked slaves into lives of crime; or, worse yet, they misled them into believing that there was a better life for them outside their masters' farms.

In 1790, Maryland had the second largest free black population in the country; by 1810 it was first, where it remained until Emancipation. By 1850, seven out of every ten Baltimore County blacks were free; ten years later only one-quarter of the county's black population was enslaved. This had happened despite the efforts of slave owners to prohibit immigration of free blacks from outside the state and despite adequate numbers of proletarian whites in the city to carry the burden of free labor on their backs. The mushrooming of the free black population occurred in the face of laws restricting the movement and activities of free blacks, laws which proved impotent against the tide of black crime that whites saw as the consequence of black freedom.[22]

The whites tried laws that mandated the incarceration and sale of "idle" blacks into temporary servitude, banished from the state free blacks convicted of crime, and tightened the rules for manumitting slaves. The legislature regulated the times and conditions for worship services attended by free blacks, made it a felony for them to seek or possess abolitionist literature, and relaxed the normal laws relating to search and seizure to permit authorities freer access to their homes. On a number of occasions throughout the years, the assembly saw fit to restate the rule that no court of law could accept the testimony of blacks against a white person for any reason or pertaining to any crime. Better to let a white murderer go free than to grant blacks any measure of power across racial lines. These free blacks represented a threat to capital accumulation, a menace to slavery, and a challenge to the way of life that Baltimore County's prosperous white farmers and Baltimore city's mercantile entrepreneurs sought to enjoy. But still they were there, as difficult to eradicate as mosquitoes in the countryside or rats in the city, and no more desirable a presence than other vermin to many white citizens of Baltimore County.[23]

Seeing his slaves as victims of the free black Johnson, incapable of asserting their own will and lacking the initiative and capacity for setting their own course, was the only explanation that made any sense to Gorsuch. He saw the slaves as passive, complacent, incompetent, and incapable of making their own way in the world. He worried that they would starve to death. He reasoned that they had no good cause to run away and believed for a long time that they would come wandering back any day begging for the forgiveness which he, as a New Testament father, would bestow on the prodigal slaves. The fugitives, who were all between the ages of nineteen and twenty-two, were to be freed in a scant few years in any event. What exactly had they to fear from such a benevolent master as himself? Even as the days passed into weeks, months, and then a year without their return, Gorsuch continued to believe that his "boys" really wanted to come back, that if he could just talk to them, tell them he intended no punishment for the crime they had committed, they would return gladly to Retreat. On the other hand, Gorsuch wanted to see Johnson, the free black "instigator" of the robbery and escape, punished severely by the law.[24]

Gorsuch tried his best to locate Johnson and the four "boys" the free black had "led" away. First, Gorsuch sought and received an official requisition from the governor of Maryland to assist in the capture and extradition of Johnson from Pennsylvania. Then, when he thought that he knew where the slaves were living, he procured the same sort of document to buttress his legal right to bring them back home. When Gorsuch's son Dickinson traveled to Harrisburg with the legal papers, however, he found Pennsylvania officials with whom he discussed the case unsympathetic. Clearly, they were not going to help, and likely they were going to resist any efforts to recapture and extradite the black men.[25]

Despite such obstacles, Gorsuch persisted, never giving up hope that he could find his slaves and bring them back to Baltimore County. His motivations are not obvious. Gorsuch never really explained why he poured time, money, and eventually his own blood into the attempt to re-enslave these four men. At first, to be sure, he thought that the men would willingly come home if only he could talk to them himself. Perhaps he persisted in a paternalistic concern that the "boys" were in trouble and needed his help. An economic explanation does not entirely account for the master's behavior during the two years following the escape. Gorsuch, like his neighbors, had already calculated that on balance slavery was an economic drain on his farm. He had already promised the four men in question their freedom upon reaching the age of twenty-eight, so as the years passed without their return, the amount of labor to be extracted from them was becoming less and less valuable.[26]

Available evidence about Edward Gorsuch's personality points in another direction. It was a matter of pride, of "honor," for him to recapture his slaves. The slaves' desire to run away and their ability to escape his dominion were an embarrassment, perhaps a humiliation, to the Maryland slave owner. Gorsuch saw himself as personally diminished in the eyes of his neighbors, his family, and the rest of the slaves on his farm. He felt betrayed by the slaves who had left and threatened by, perhaps even vulnerable to, the slaves who remained.[27]

As Bertram Wyatt-Brown has observed, honor was perhaps the central motivating force behind the public actions of Southern white men during the antebellum era. Whether behavior was rational, "wise, or fraught with risks" was of little moment to men whose greater concern was "the necessity for valiant action." In Edward Gorsuch's mental world, "fellow whites—as well as blacks themselves—would have despised a squeamish slaveholder who was unable to make his will felt." His good name, and that of his family and ancestors, was at risk. Gorsuch, like other Southern men of his day, would sacrifice his wealth, and even his life, to salvage the honor lost by the escape of his slaves. If it was the "threat of honor lost, no less than slavery," that led the South toward secession and Civil War, it was the same concern that propelled Edward Gorsuch down the road to his personal destruction. It was because Gorsuch symbolized the region's lost honor on the issue of fugitive slaves, embodied the values that motivated other Southern white men, and died a martyr to the cause that his death would become a cause célèbre in the South.[28]

Still, Gorsuch grossly underestimated the potential for violence in the confrontation that he sought to provoke between himself and the four escaped slaves. He did not, at least initially, intend to martyr himself on a field of honor. Southern masters had a difficult time imagining that their slaves could ever do them harm. This was partly an assessment of slave personality, a vision of African-Americans in bondage as "tamed" by the institution of slavery. Such attitudes were also a function of the masters' general belief that slaves felt a familial attachment to the whites who ruled over them. In some cases, this was true. But the unlocked doors, remarked on by surprised foreign travelers in the South, and the free access that slaves had to the houses of their masters, day and night, belied the reality of slave violence, which the masters psychologically suppressed. As Edward Ayers discovered in his study of Southern violence, "although whites considered most blacks to be thieves and knew that some blacks had killed whites, [they] did not generally consider slaves violent people." It was Gorsuch's valuation of honor and his assumptions about the personalities of the black men he had once enslaved and their affection for him that lay behind this master's single-minded pursuit of the fugitives.[29]

It is no less difficult to recover the perspective of the slaves than of the master. We cannot really know how the men who stole the wheat and made their escape perceived enslavement on Gorsuch's farm, except to reason from their actions that slavery was a greater burden than the master believed. Hypothesizing again from what we can learn about the perspective of other slaves who shared similar experiences, it seems that a master's lenity or the promise of freedom at some future date was no guarantee of contentment among the enslaved. Indeed, according to

Frederick Douglass, who had both generous and harsh masters during his youth as a Maryland slave, the more solicitous a master was about their welfare, the more likely human chattel would be to seek out their freedom. "Beat and cuff your slave," Douglass advised,

> keep him hungry and spiritless, and he will follow the chain of his master like a dog; but, feed and clothe him well,—work with him moderately—surround him with physical comfort,—and dreams of freedom intrude. Give him a *bad* master, and he aspires to a *good* master; give him a good master, and he wishes to become his *own* master.

Even a walk in the country, along a stream, or in a forest or field was likely to inspire a thirst for freedom in the slave for whom hope, rather than despair, was the guiding light. Freedom requires an act of imagination followed by an act of will. A master who gives sustenance to his slave's imagination should, according to Douglass, expect flight rather than gratitude. "The thought that men are made for other and better uses than slavery," Douglass remembered, "thrives best under the gentle treatment of a kind master." Promise him liberty tomorrow, and he will crave it today. Such is human nature. Such is the psychology of the slave.[30]

At best, the attitude of the young male slave toward the kind master was one of ambivalence and distrust. Male slaves, no less than their masters, were products of cultures in which honor and shame defined identity, determined a sense of self-worth, and dictated assertive action when the will and the body were not crushed by the weight of oppression. It was power that complicated the honor-shame paradigm for slaves. It was circumstance that determined how, where, and when they gave vent to the pent-up emotions repressed in the face of "the boss."[31]

According to Wyatt-Brown, the slave had options that permitted honorable subservience to the master. Some slaves, of course, became socialized to subordination, accepting the circumstances that brought them their shame. Others, more assertive and with greater self-esteem, found that technical compliance with their masters' orders left room for the maintenance of honor in a slowed work pace, intentional misunderstandings and mistakes, or the willful loss and destruction of tools. Adopting the guise of Sambo—the dumb, smiling, foot-shuffling fool—represented a third alternative that denied the system of honor and substituted a mask of shamelessness. Whatever choice the slave adopted, however, he paid a psychic price that was recoverable only by direct confrontation with the master or running away. Each required a compromise with the system, with the master, and with himself. It was the slave of some sensitivity, what Douglass termed "imagination," who faced the greatest dilemma: how, in the words of Wyatt-Brown, "to maintain dignity in the face of shamelessness by masters and even by fellow slaves." Again, it was these sensitive slaves, precisely the sort that Douglass saw as the products of life under a "good" master, who might be expected to take flight. These were the slaves least able, in an emotional sense, to live with the shame of involuntary servitude.[32]

So, the perennial question, why did not more slaves run away? Frederick Douglass offered several observations on this point, which historians have supplemented with several more. In the first place, as Douglass mentioned in the passage previously quoted, many slaves were so psychologically battered, so full of despair, that they were incapable of seizing the initiative to strike out on their own. The message delivered by their masters, and by society at large, that they were incompetent, dependent, born and bred to a servile status was received and, at some level, believed by many slaves. As Douglass suggested, those who lived under the worst conditions were most likely to be seized by a sense of utter hopelessness that kept them from acting in their own behalf.

Then, too, there were the ties to friends and family that kept many or most slaves in the environs of their servitude. "It is my opinion," Douglass contended, "that thousands would escape from slavery who now remain there, but for the strong chords of affection that bind them to their families, relatives, and friends." Only one of the four men who ran away from the Gorsuch farm was married, and there is no indication that he had any children. The four young men were at an age when kinship responsibilities did not yet outweigh the desire to do the best they could for themselves.[33]

It would be a mistake to underestimate the danger involved in an escape attempt or the degree to which the violence of the slave system functioned to discourage challenges to the regime. As Eugene Genovese has noted, what is most remarkable about challenges to the antebellum slave system is not that there were so few but that in the face of such daunting odds there were so many slaves who risked their lives for liberty's sake. About a thousand African-Americans took the risk each year during the 1850s, even after the federal Fugitive Slave Law added another hurdle to their race for freedom. Gorsuch's slaves were four among the 279 who escaped from Maryland during the twelve months preceding June 30, 1850; this was the highest number of losses for any slave state.[34]

The runaways from Gorsuch's farm were typical in a number of ways that help us to comprehend the meaning of their actions. Like 80 percent of those who ran to freedom, Gorsuch's ex-slaves were males between the ages of sixteen and thirty-five. They also conformed to the normal practice of fleeing in a group and in response to a specific incident for which they feared retribution. Like so many others who made their way surreptitiously to the North, Buley, Ford, and the two Hammonds fled a comparatively kind master, a comparatively lenient form of enslavement, the upper rather than the lower South, and the country rather than the city.[35]

Compared to the great mass of those who stayed behind, these runaways were confident men who had gotten a whiff of freedom on a breeze from the North. Just as the others who struck out across the border, these four men probably underestimated the trouble that lay ahead and the limits of freedom for African-Americans in a Northern state. Still, that is not to say that had they known all that lay before them the fugitives would have taken another course. Freedom is certainly its own reward, whatever the tribulations of independence, but that is not something that they could have easily explained to the master whose pride they had injured by running away. It had been a long time since the Gorsuches braved an Atlantic crossing and challenged a wilderness to realize their personal liberty. Perhaps they had forgotten what it meant to be unfree.

Rumor had it that Ford, Buley, and the Hammonds were somewhere in southeastern Pennsylvania, perhaps living a distance apart in Berks, Chester, or Montgomery County. Over the next two years, Gorsuch pursued every rumor, seized every opportunity to try communicating with the fugitives, but had difficulty pinning down exactly where they were. Perhaps the ex-slaves moved around to avoid detection, possibly the network of anti-slavery activists was better organized than those who worked against them, but it took time and money to determine with certainty where the men lived. The federal Fugitive Slave Law of 1850 removed impediments thrown up by officials in Pennsylvania, but the master still had to find the slaves.

A letter from an informant in Gorsuch's employ dated Lancaster County, 28 August 1851, removed this major obstacle to bringing the fugitives home. "Respected friend," the letter began,

> I have the required information of four men that is within two miles of each other. Now, the best way is for you to come as a hunter, disguised, about two days ahead of your son and let him come by way of Philadelphia and get the deputy marshal, John Nagle I think is his name. Tell him the situation and he can get force of the right kind. It will take about twelve so that they can divide and take them all within half an hour. Now, if you can come on the 2nd or 3rd of September come on & I will meet you at the gap when you get there. Inquire for Benjamin

Clay's tavern. Let your son and the marshal get out [at?] Kinyer's [sic] hotel. Now, if you cannot come at the time spoken of, write very soon and let me know when you can. I wish you to come as soon as you possibly can.

Very respectfully thy friend
William M.P.

This was exactly what Gorsuch had been waiting for. He must have been thrilled. Immediately, he began to make plans for the journey, recruiting several friends and relatives for the trip north. We do not know what the master of Retreat Farm was thinking as he prepared to meet his slaves. Gorsuch's actions suggest that he no longer believed the fugitives really wanted to come home, that he no longer was confident he could convince them to return to his farm. Edward Gorsuch packed guns, and so did the rest of his party.[36]

Black Images In
White Minds

RELATIONS BETWEEN PEOPLE OF DIFFERENT RACES had
changed in the North during the century preceding the escape of Edward
Gorsuch's slaves. The abolition of slavery was central to this process, and
the influx of fugitive slaves put an additional strain on the tolerance of
whites for the blacks who lived in their midst. By the time the runaways
from Retreat Farm crossed the Susquehanna River in late 1849, Pennsylvania's gradual emancipation law of 1780 had completed its work.[1] In Lancaster County, there were 348 slaves in 1790, 178 a decade later, 55 in
1830, and 2 in 1840; the last one died only a few years before Ford,
Buley, and the two Hammonds arrived. Even in 1790, free blacks
outnumbered slaves in Lancaster's population 545 to 348, and African-
Americans represented about 2.5 percent (1.5 percent free, 1 percent
slaves) of the county's inhabitants. At its antebellum peak in 1850, the
number of blacks reached 3,614 (about 3.7 percent of the county's population). From there the number of African-Americans in Lancaster declined to 3,459 (just under 3 percent of county residents) ten years later
as fear heightened by the Fugitive Slave Law drove hundreds to emigrate
farther north to Canada.[2]

Perhaps the four fugitives had not believed the self-interested portrait
of Northern white bigotry and free black poverty drawn by their master.
Possibly they were surprised, as European visitors were during the 1830s
and 1840s, that the "prejudice of race" was at least as bad in the North as
in the slave states. "The Negro is free," Alexis de Tocqueville observed,

> but he can share neither the rights, nor the pleasures, nor the labor,
> nor the afflictions, nor the tomb of him whose equal he has been de-
> clared to be; and he cannot meet him upon fair terms in life or in death.

"Singular is the degree of contempt and dislike in which the free blacks are held in all the free States of America," Frederick Marryat recorded in his diary; "is this not extraordinary in a land which professes universal liberty, equality, and the rights of man?"[3]

Tocqueville hypothesized a causal connection between African-American freedom and white bigotry. "In the South," he reasoned,

> the master is not afraid to raise his slave to his own standing, beause he knows that he can in a moment reduce him to the dust at pleasure. In the North the white no longer distinctly perceives the barrier that separates him from the degraded race, and he shuns the Negro with the more pertinacity since he fears lest they should some day be confounded together.[4]

There is some truth in Tocqueville's diagnosis of racial intolerance in the North, but he lacked the sort of longer-term historical context for his observations that shows local relations between the races in a different light. In the eighteenth century, before the American Revolution, before Pennsylvania's gradual emancipation law even began to take effect, and before the influx of fugitive slaves from the South, there existed an inveterate prejudice against people of African ancestry who lived in the colony. Changes in the attitudes of whites toward blacks were subtle and slow, and for one brief period at the end of the eighteenth century there was even the promise of some improvement. But over the long term, the trend was certainly not from good to bad, from tolerance to intolerance, from sufferance to disdain.

Pennsylvania's first colonial law mentioning its black population did not distinguish between those who were free and those who were slaves. To white legislators in the Quaker-dominated assembly, race transcended class or status in a way impossible for blacks to overcome. Special "Negro courts" heard all cases concerning African-American defendants beginning in 1700 and meted out punishments significantly harsher than those reserved for white criminals. Blacks—free and enslaved—were whipped rather than fined for property crimes. None could be a witness against whites in criminal cases, which meant that blacks were fair game for white rapists, thieves, and assassins.[5]

A special law of 1726 made a legal distinction between free blacks and slaves for the first time, but for the purpose of placing additional restrictions on the movements of "free" blacks. According to the new law's preamble, experience had shown whites that "free negroes are an idle, slothful people, and often burdensome to the neighborhood and afford ill examples to other negroes." Therefore, the act sought to limit the size of the free black population by imposing a £30 indemnity on masters who manumitted their slaves. What is more, any able-bodied free black who, in the opinion of a magistrate, misspent his time could be returned to bondage for as long as the jurist saw fit.

Such unique burdens on African-Americans have led one historian to conclude recently that "the legal treatment of *free* blacks in colonial Pennsylvania appears to have been as restrictive and discriminatory as in any other colony." And according to A. Leon Higginbotham, Jr., "in one significant respect Pennsylvania treated free blacks even more harshly than did any of the southern colonies." Standard legal doctrine dictated that the children of free women of any race were also free, but in colonial Pennsylvania the children of *all* free blacks or mulattoes and *all* blacks freed by their masters before reaching the age of twenty-one years in the case of women and twenty-four for men were to be bound into the service of a white master until they reached those ages.[6]

Children of mixed racial unions endured an even harsher fate. These children were bound to white masters until reaching the age of thirty-one years. Clearly, the children were being punished for the "sin" of their parents. As embodiments of the racial amalgamation most feared by whites, these children were a marginal people in between the two races, who were no doubt singled out for more forms of harassment than this one law reveals. In such legislative enactments the fears and prejudices of white legislators are visible, and some of the limits on freedom for people of African and mixed racial heritage are revealed.

Another student of the African-American experience concludes that "slavery in Pennsylvania was not unique in its mildness," contrary to the colony's reputation among historians for racial liberalism. Merle G. Brouwer notes the harshness of punishments based on race and the prejudices of even the best white friends of black Pennsylvanians as evidence supporting this conclusion. A free black convicted of fornicating with a white was, according to law, sold into servitude for seven years, while the guilty white faced a maximum sentence of one year in prison and a fine of £50. Until a new law of 1706, black men condemned for attempted rape of white women were to be castrated; death was the punishment for blacks convicted of raping a white woman. A white man found guilty of raping a white woman was subject to a maximum of thirty-one lashes plus seven years in jail, and according to Brouwer, the punishment of white men was considerably more lenient than the law allowed.[7]

Beyond the laws, a few surviving court cases, and the comments of some comparatively liberal white men, we know little about the daily lives of African-Americans during the eighteenth century.[8] We do know that whites feared blacks and believed them capable of terrible violence—that is clear from the highly restrictive laws intended to limit their numbers and control those already in Pennsylvania. The records reveal few instances of blacks attacking Lancaster County whites over the course of the century.[9]

We can safely conclude that blacks despised their status as slaves, if only because so many malingered, broke tools, ran away, or even killed themselves to escape the service of their masters. We can be sure that Pennsylvania's African-Americans coveted their freedom, whether it came by flight, manumission, self-purchase, or after 1780 by the slow-working liberty of the state's gradual abolition law. Over 250 slaves fled from rural southeastern Pennsylvania between 1730 and 1755 alone, and only about fifty-three of them were ever caught. That tells us something about the attitude of Lancaster's slaves toward their status; it reveals something about their courage and their ingenuity in getting away.[10]

We cannot know how extraordinary was the experience of a slave who escaped in 1761 despite the iron collar around his neck, the handcuffs on his wrists, and the six-foot chain that encumbered him further. We can only imagine with horror what it must have been like for a free black to be imprisoned on suspicion of being a slave, to languish in jail while advertisements were placed to see if any master came forward to claim his "property," and if no "master" showed up, to be sold into bondage, nonetheless, until the "free" black worked off the costs of his incarceration. The humiliation, anger, fear, and despair that must have swept over black Pennsylvanians in waves is pretty much lost to us, even though we try, and inevitably fail, to picture ourselves in the same place.[11]

Imagine the experience of James Daniel, a free black man who had fought in the American Revolution under General Nathaniel Greene. In 1782, Daniel was impoverished after he got out of the army, so he indentured himself to a Lancaster County farmer. The farmer, in turn, kidnapped Daniel, transported him across the Maryland line, and sold him into slavery. Daniel escaped, ran North, and arrived at the office of the Pennsylvania Abolition Society with his "master" in hot pursuit. Daniel was eventually set free, but after a harrowing ordeal. We can only guess how many similar incidents from Lancaster County and elsewhere in the state did not turn out so well.[12]

Some historians believe that in the first half of the eighteenth century the ownership of slaves in Pennsylvania was more a means to display one's wealth than to become richer still. As house servants, liverymen, and carriage drivers, slaves became one among other affectations of style for an emerging provincial elite. According to Alan Tully, "it was the rich who, along with the silver watch, the showy pacing horse and the expensive personal wardrobe, acquired the Negro slave," at least up until the late 1750s. The initial outlay of cash to purchase a slave (£45 Pennsylvania currency) exceeded the total personal estate of over one-third of the region's taxable residents and added to the yearly tax assessment of the owner. The law also required that, at the time of manumission, masters post a substantial bond (£30) against the possibility that a freed black would become a burden on the community. So the ownership of slaves was beyond the means of most white Lancastrians up to the middle of the century and was not perceived as economically desirable before that time.[13]

After 1758, and into the 1760s, labor shortages brought an increase in local purchases of slaves, which were often financed by loans, to the point where more than one in every six southeastern Pennsylvania households was involved in slaveholding. But still, most masters never owned more than one slave, usually a field hand or a household servant, less frequently a craftsman's assistant or an innkeeper's maid. Over time, most African-Americans in rural southeastern Pennsylvania worked on farms. Slaves, and then free blacks, were also significant in the early years of the region's iron industry; and after emancipation, as before, they continued to work in some trades, particularly leather and building, and as house servants.[14]

For Lancaster County, the eighteenth-century record is thinner than for Philadelphia and for Pennsylvania at large; but there is no reason to believe that slaveholders were any more lenient or racial prejudice any less virulent in this rural county than throughout the colony and then Commonwealth. Race rather than status or class fixed the quality of life for Lancaster's black residents. African-Americans were segregated in church services and cemeteries, and even Quakers isolated blacks in their Meetings. John Woolman, the New Jersey Quaker and anti-slavery reformer, thought of African-Americans as "far from being our kinsfolk" and "of a vile stock." Benjamin Franklin, who was not a Quaker and did own slaves though president of Pennsylvania's reconstituted anti-slavery society in the 1780s, believed the majority of blacks were "of a plotting disposition, dark, sullen, malicious, revengeful and cruel in the highest degree." And these were two of the best white friends that black people had in the Delaware Valley during the eighteenth century.[15]

There were, to be sure, instances of humanity by white Pennsylvanians to black ones during the colonial period, but historians Brouwer and Higginbotham believe that those were the exceptions, even among Quakers and other more racially tolerant whites. The likes of such white men as Anthony Benezet, the Quaker reformer and educator of African-American children, were not the rule. Brouwer finds no evidence that Quaker slave owners were "particularly noted for leniency," even though "humane exceptions can be found in every age and every place where slavery has been practiced."[16]

As Pennsylvania Quakers came, by stages, to see the light on the issue of slavery, they ceased to engage personally in the buying and selling of slaves, manumitted their own chattel laborers, and a number of them worked to meliorate the condition of free blacks. Some—apparently most—bestowed a freedom settlement on ex-slaves, which they calculated by subtracting the costs of purchase and sustenance from an estimated value of labor over the period of enslavement. And it was not unusual for blacks in southeastern Pennsylvania to continue working on a salaried basis for their ex-masters, with whom they enjoyed amicable relations. Even after 1776, however, when the Philadelphia Yearly Meeting reached the conclusion that one could not be both a member of the Meeting and an owner of slaves, some Quakers resisted such enlightened goals. Noah Dixon told a visitation committee from the Uwchlan Monthly Meeting in 1777 that, in his opinion, slavery "is a good thing. It keeps them apart so they will not do misdeeds." The 1797 edition of the Society's *Rules of Discipline* reminded members that they must release all their slaves and that their charitable responsibilities toward blacks did not end upon manumission. The 1806 version pointed out that hiring slave labor was also inconsistent with the Society's testimony against trafficking in slaves.[17]

The limits of empathy across racial lines, even among this socially enlightened religious group, were quite clear. Just as in Baltimore County, where the Quaker miller betrayed Gorsuch's slaves to their master, Pennsylvania's Quakers would go only so far—individually and collectively—in their relationships with blacks. African-Americans were more or less welcome to attend Quaker Meetings, as long as they sat in special sections reserved for members of their race. Full membership in the Society of Friends was another matter, however, and that is where Meetings generally drew the line on their brotherly feelings for blacks.[18]

Throughout the antebellum period, Quakers testified publicly and privately against slavery and in behalf of the interests of free blacks. Over time, however, the Society became re-absorbed in its own internal problems and resisted any affiliation with the radical abolitionist movement, leaving the fight against racial injustice primarily in the hands of individual members. And the prejudice against African-Americans, which the Quakers shared in kind if not in degree with other whites, grew rather than abated over time.

John Chandler, a British Friend traveling through Pennsylvania in the early 1840s, was among those who commented on the racism of Quakers he met. Chandler believed that Philadelphia, the City of Brotherly Love, merited the name "more in its origin, when it rose fresh from the wilderness, than it does now." It was not just the working-class whites, according to Chandler, but also the better educated who harbored a "great dislike to their Coloured fellow-citizens":

> The members of our religious society form a numerous body in the city, and many of them are wealthy, and have proportionate influence; but the general prejudice of the community on this head is too deeply rooted for them, individually or unitedly to overcome. In fact, they make no effort to overcome it. . . . They are kind to the coloured people: they relieve their necessities; they visit their sick; they educate their orphan children, and perform to them many disinterested acts of love and mercy; but still they seem to consider them as aliens—as a people who have no right to a possession in the land that gave them birth.[19]

The limited sufferance described by Chandler was the best that any African-American could expect from a white person in Pennsylvania; and the worst was much worse, indeed. Blacks would have to rely on themselves, supplemented by aid from the few whites who bore them goodwill as the nineteenth century began. African-American institutions—churches, schools, clubs, and self-protection associations—would have to pick up where white philanthropy and the protection of the laws left off. We do know that prior to 1817 whites permitted Lancaster's African-Americans to worship in St. James Episcopal and Trinity Lutheran churches. As late as 1820, blacks could still be buried in special sections of the county's "white" cemeteries, although the practice was controversial by that time.[20]

The possibility, and the limitations, of such amicable integration across racial lines is suggested by the earliest graphic depiction of an African-American from this region of rural Pennsylvania (Figure 2.1). Local artist Lewis Miller drew on a childhood memory for the scene inside York's Lutheran Church on a Sunday morning in 1800. Among the hundreds of congregants shown in the picture, in the corner farthest removed from the central focus of attention is a lone black man huddled in humble supplication. Whites are passing him on the stairs as they climb to the balcony; he is apparently all but invisible to them and others gathered for the worship service.

The posture, location, and lone presence of the black man in Miller's painting are revealing. There is literally no room for even this one

FIGURE 2.1. Lewis Miller, "In Side of the Old Lutheran Church in 1800, York, Pa." *(with permission of the Historical Society of York County)*

African-American in the crowded pews of the church. What would happen if several more African-Americans sought even such marginal inclusion as that claimed by the solitary figure on the back stairs? They would be noticed; they would be in the way; it would become clearer that they did not belong.

Over time, growth of the African-American population, fueled in part by an influx of Southern blacks—both fugitives and recently manumitted slaves—tested even this limited tolerance of whites for people who were racially and culturally different. The interracial accommodation of eighteenth-century Lancaster, which was based on the total subordination of blacks, crumbled under the stresses of change. As historian Winthrop D. Jordan noticed on the national scene:

> Whatever their behavior . . . free Negroes constituted a threat to white society which . . . arose within the white man as a less than conscious feeling that a people who had always been absolutely subjected were now in many instances outside the range of the white man's unfettered power.[21]

Violence involving African-Americans increased over time in response to such bigotry and to social upheaval, which included growth of the black population, the threat to white identity posed by economically successful African-Americans, and the impoverished conditions in which a growing number of blacks continued to live.

The fugitives from Gorsuch's farm, as others before and around them, found that white Lancastrians had a limited range of images to which they expected blacks to conform; what they could not know is how such depictions had changed over time. Some assumptions about the character and capacities of African-Americans came from personal acquaintance with blacks, but even then cultural stereotypes filtered information about who a black person was, or could be. Jordan suggests that "in all societies men tend to extrapolate from social status to actual inherent character, to impute to individuals characteristics suited to their social roles."[22]

During the late eighteenth century, there were several black personae that supplement those in Lewis Miller's painting. Lancaster's newspapers provided readers with portrayals of African-Americans drawn from local, regional, national, and international sources. In part, these were selected by editors from a wider array of stories involving African-Americans. Advertisements for runaway slaves also included behavioral descriptions that reflected cultural stereotyping. Both news stories and advertisements for fugitives were generally, but not always, drafted by writers who lived outside the county and then reprinted in local newspapers.

For the purposes of this chapter, the question is not so much whether the likenesses were "true," although it would be interesting to know how "facts" were transformed—selected, interpreted, and perhaps even re-cast—in the hands of writers and editors for a variety of ends and in light of their own assumptions about African-American character. Of more significance here is the cumulative sense in which readers were exposed to a fairly narrow range of African, African-Caribbean, and African-American images, and how those narrowed, sharpened, and changed over time.[23] Such portrayals give us clues about the attitudes toward blacks in the white community and also to the ways that information from outside the region contributed to changing local impressions of African-Americans.

All of the negative qualities assigned to blacks during the eighteenth century continued to appear in the Lancaster press through the Civil War, although images of African-American violence and stealth became more frequent. The most generous portrayals of the mental capacities of blacks— and here opinion was divided between biological determinists and environmentalists—were often transformed into hostile depictions of African-Americans' talent for outwitting naive and trusting whites. To simplify the process only a bit, the image of the loyal and sometimes brave black servant—who was always outnumbered in white minds by African-American cowards, drunkards, fools, thieves, and murderers—was replaced over time by two all-encompassing types: the black victim and the black perpetrator of violence. The guise of the faithful domestic came to be seen as a disguise. Even many of those writers and editors who continued to speak out for the abolition of slavery, for the rights of blacks, and against the worst abuses of Northern bigotry, believed African-Americans to be alien beings who ought to return to Africa.[24]

There were, of course, unsavory white characters in the newspapers as well. Neither editors nor readers were so bigoted or so blind as to believe that African-Americans monopolized all of humanity's vices. White murderers, thieves, drunkards, and fools also appeared in the press. But the disproportionate share of negative images were of blacks, in a region where they constituted a tiny fraction of the populace. And more important, the few positive depictions of African-Americans in Lancaster's newspapers (and even fewer over time) were eclipsed by a significantly wider cast of white characters, many or most of them admirable for the very qualities that the blacks seemed to lack. For every Toussaint L'Ouverture—"a truly great man. . . . [of] sound judgement, a penetrating mind, a correct observation, great industry, and unbounded energy"—

and there was only *one* from the late eighteenth century through the Civil War, there were scores of white statesmen, philanthropists, reformers, men of science, medicine, letters, and law presented as models of their race. For every loyal and faithful African-American servant or slave in the news, and there were a few before the second decade of the nineteenth century, there were dozens of black robbers and assassins; Lancaster's newspaper editors found very little to admire about black people during the thirty years after 1830.[25]

The earliest surviving images of African-Americans in Lancaster's newspapers from the 1790s often came in advertisements for escaped slaves, which presented them as foolish or "simple," incompetent, sneaky—"a very artful fellow"—impudent—"very impertinent, and a great liar"—evil— "an arch villain and very cowardly"—and prone to excessive drinking— "very quarrelsome when in liquor." Masters sometimes described African-American fugitives by their behavior in the company of whites— "he has when spoken to a very simple look with his eyes" or a "down look" or is "very apt to laugh" or is "embarrassed when spoken to."[26]

Masters often remembered their escaped slaves as thieves and otherwise dishonest, and there were numerous stories in the press that supplemented this image, reinforcing the stereotype and giving it texture and hue. The emphasis in reports of robberies by blacks was more on the violence perpetrated by African-American thieves than on the financial losses sustained. The stock images were of random violence, unsuspecting travelers waylaid on the road, or innocent white families who had the locked doors to their homes battered down by wild-eyed blacks. There were stories about African-American strangers beating householders senseless and abusing horrified wives who came to their husbands' defense, all for a pittance of cash and goods that the victims would have surrendered peacefully if given the chance. The *Lancaster Journal* also carried stories about African-American mail robbers, the attempted murder and hold-up of a toll keeper on the Lancaster highway by two black men, and dozens of anecdotes about small but frequent pilfering by black servants and slaves from as far away as Louisiana and New York.[27]

More often, murder rather than plunder seemed the sole goal of the African-Americans depicted in the press. Arson, poisoning, and slave insurrections were news staples from the late eighteenth century through the Civil War. A frequent theme highlighted in such stories during the late eighteenth and early nineteenth centuries was that of betrayal by servants and slaves who were ill-treated by whites. The *Lancaster Journal* printed in full, for example, the confession of "Negro Chloe," condemned to death in nearby Carlisle for murdering two daughters in the white family she served. "The reason I killed them," her white amanuensis recorded,

> was not because I had any spite or malice against them; on the contrary, I loved them both. My motive in the first place was this; I knew that the children were compelled by my mistress to give information respecting some parts of my conduct; for which I was severely corrected, far beyond the demerit of the fault. To cut off this means of information was the first end I promised myself; but my second and greatest motive was, to bring all the misery I possibly could upon the family, and particularly upon my mistress.

In a backhanded way, this "confession" was an anti-slavery appeal and a plea for greater kindness, fairness, and sympathy for blacks. As such, it was the product of a time and place wherein people saw slavery as evil but harbored more fear than affection for African-Americans. The image projected by the rest of the story, in which the murders were recounted in horrible detail, was one of an unbounded capacity for violence harbored in the breast of even the seemingly meekest and most loyal of family servants.[28]

Most of the murders by blacks described in the press were similar to Chloe's in the sense that they were committed by slaves against members of the white families they served. Slave insurrections throughout the South and the Caribbean were, of course, common fare and were reported in Lancaster's newspapers in livid detail. Women were more often the victims than men in the cases of individual murders, and when the perpetrators in such cases were black men, editors played the imagery of threatened white womanhood to the hilt. "HORRID!" was the screaming headline, and unrequited lust was the motive, in a story about the attempted rape and murder of a New York woman by a sixteen-year-old slave on her farm. According to the *Journal*, revenge against a Kentucky master led to the brutal murder of his daughter by a slave. African-American women were also quite capable of violence, as Lancaster readers learned not only from Chloe's "confession." The *Journal* reported that two female field slaves murdered their mistress, whose corpse was later chopped into at least eight pieces and floated down the James River. More often, female slaves—and male cooks as well—used poison as the chosen instrument of death; but since dosage was critical—too much could be tasted or induce immediate vomiting, too little would bring on painful symptoms, but nothing more—the poisoners written up in the newspapers almost always failed. Occasionally, a slave harbored the mistaken belief that if she could wipe out the whole white family at one meal, there would be nobody left to own her, and she would be free. More often, revenge for a particular injustice was apparently the goal, although accumulated rage was sometimes enough to trigger a mass-murder attempt.[29]

The numerous failed poisonings also reflected another characteristic of African-Americans as portrayed in the press. In addition to being violent, blacks also seemed thoughtless and inept to reporters, editors, and no doubt readers as well. Sometimes the "incompetence" of blacks saved whites from the most violent intentions of the African-Americans around them, but it could also result in occasionally fatal accidents. The *Journal* reported, for example, that a slave girl accidentally swallowed about thirty sewing pins, from which she died slowly and in excruciating pain. There were a number of stories over the course of sixty years about black children injuring themselves or accidentally killing others while playing with guns, and not one about similar accidents among whites. Given the expected incidence of such calamities in a gun-toting society and the newspapers' interest in violence from across the continent and around the world, the race specificity of these stories must have been a matter of selection by the editors rather than a mere reflection of available news. And accounts of African-American servants clumsily breaking household items (which we should suspect were often not accidents), losing control of horse-drawn carriages because of inattention, drowning or catching themselves on fire—despite numerous warnings to take better care—were much more frequent than similar stories about whites.

There are no doubt a number of mutually reinforcing explanations for the focus on mishaps involving African-Americans in a population that was preponderantly white. It is possible that such events did involve blacks out of proportion to their numbers in the population. We should not be surprised if African-Americans bore a disproportionate share of the dirtiest, most dangerous, and least desirable work; or that their judgment, balance, and skill were more often affected by dietary deficiencies, physical debilities, consumption of alcohol, and lack of sleep. Surely, as historians of slavery tell us, many "accidents" by slaves, including some in which blacks incapacitated themselves, were willful acts of destruction that reflected either an attempt to avoid work or to "punish" the master in ways that were comparatively safe. Beyond such possible explanations, it is still striking that newspaper editors found so few comparable stories about whites or deemed them less newsworthy. At least in part, the explanation must include the stereotypical roles assigned to blacks by this culture and the purposes for which the stories were intended. Reports of self-destruction by blacks were clearly presented as moral tales, and were perhaps even read aloud by the master of the household as injunctions to his careless servants.[30]

The slant of such stories is often revealing, as in the case of the slave girl who caught her clothes on fire when she reached for something on the mantlepiece. According to the account reprinted in the *Lancaster Intelligencer*, when the young woman, whose clothes were ablaze, ran for help, the fire spread from the slave to her mistress's curtains. The white woman's immediate reaction was to extinguish the flames on her furnishings, by which time the slave was beyond help. The mistress's priorities provoked no comment by the reporter or the editor who reprinted the account from a Norfolk newspaper, and the moral of the story was clear from the title—"An Awful Admonition to Careless Servants."[31]

Lancaster's newspapers reprinted numerous such stories about the inadvertent destruction of property by blacks; but arson and interpersonal violence were often undeniably intentional and of even more interest to Lancastrians. Though stories about accidental self-destruction were more common, the papers also reported spectacular suicides by blacks much more frequently than similar stories about whites. The *Journal,* for example, reported that a black woman threw her children and then herself down a well; and that a slave in nearby York, Pennsylvania, hanged both her infant and herself.[32]

The few African-American characteristics presented in a positive light during the late eighteenth century included musical skills—"inclined to play on the fiddle"—deference, strength, and good health—"bidable, strong and healthy." Most of all, whites seemed to respect those African-Americans whose loyalty included the willingness to sacrifice their own lives to save their masters. Stories about a black servant rushing back into a burning house to attempt a bold rescue and about a slave who threw himself between his master and *white* assassins were the most striking examples of this type.[33]

Then, in the early nineteenth century, things changed in the selection and reprinting of stories about African-Americans. Negative characteristics gained even greater precedence—in frequency and kind—over any positive portrayals of blacks, and the perception of the African-American capacity for loyalty almost disappeared from the newspapers. In the era of slave revolts, in Haiti and the Southern United States, stories about black arsonists entirely supplanted those describing heroic acts by loyal African-American servants. There was greater consistency in the negative images of blacks over time. Anecdotes, news stories, and advertisements continued to project images of carelessness, incompetence, foolishness, thievery, and stealth, but these were supplemented, and in some senses transformed, by portrayals of blacks as shrewd, calculating, and evil. Numerous stories of attempts to poison white families suggested that African-Americans' apparent affection for the white children they raised was only a ruse.

Although many of the portraits of violence by blacks came from outside the region, their selection by editors for republication in Lancaster's newspapers reflected not just changes in the available news but also growing local fears as the county's free black population increased. The York arson conspiracy of 1803 appeared to Lancaster's residents as a local symptom of the wider problem of African-American violence that they read about in stories from as far away as New Hampshire, South Carolina, and the West Indies.[34] Over a period of three weeks during February and March, six fires of suspicious origin occurred in the town without any suspects coming to light. Then, according to the local press, a black girl misunderstood her instructions, tried to burn down a barn at noon rather than midnight, and was caught in the act. Based on her (no doubt coerced) confession, townsmen arrested twenty-one African-Americans and several whites suspected of participating in the arson ring; eventually six blacks went to prison for the crimes.

The *York Recorder* was the main source of public information about the fires, which it diagnosed as a consequence of anger among the town's blacks over the conviction of an African-American woman for trying to poison two whites. In a search for systemic causes of the conflagration, the court also noted that the borough was "infested with some disorderly houses," which served as rendezvous for enslaved and free blacks. Besides closing down such illicit gathering places, magistrates would try to keep better track of black residents—who they were, where they lived, and whether they belonged. Basically, the problem appeared to be one of control, of bringing order to a disorderly population of vagrants and outsiders whose cheap labor was useful but whose presence constituted a threat to the safety of the community.[35]

Violence perpetrated by African-Americans seemed an increasing threat. Only a short time before—during the brief thaw in race relations that accompanied the American Revolution and brought about the state's gradual emancipation law—newspapers had portrayed some blacks as passive sufferers of brutality. But now again, as during the colonial period, African-Americans appeared quite frightening to whites. The pictures in Lewis Miller's sketchbook reflect such changes, as the prayerful supplicant (Figure 2.1) is replaced over time by gun-toting, fist-fighting blacks (Figures 2.2 and 2.3). How much of the changing depiction of African-Americans in the newspapers and paintings was a matter of white percep-

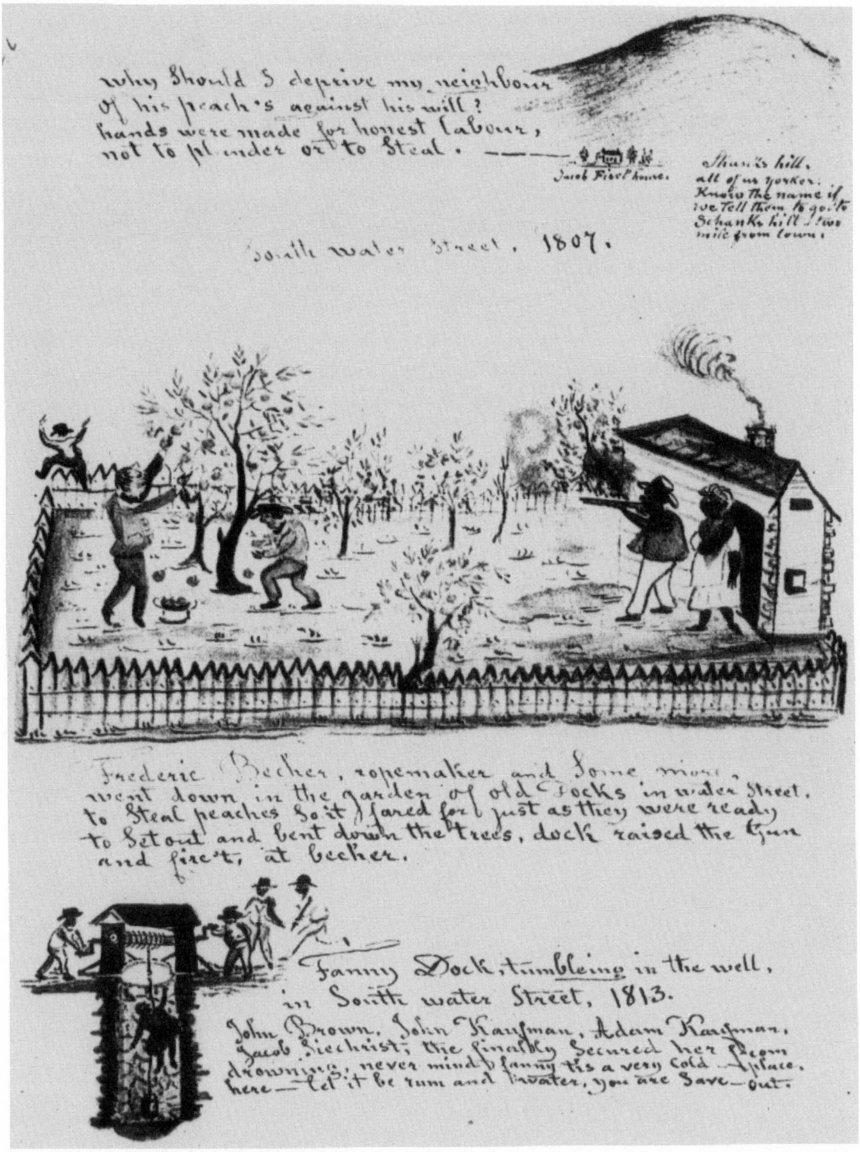

FIGURE 2.2. Lewis Miller, untitled, men stealing peaches from "the garden of old Docks," and "Fanny Dock tumbleing [sic] in the well" (with permission of the Historical Society of York County)

FIGURE 2.3. Lewis Miller, "A Fight on the Common" *(with permission of the Historical Society of York County)*

tions, and how much was real is impossible to say. We cannot know, for example, whether justice was done in the York arson case, whether the conspiracy was simply a figment of white fears and a coerced confession from a frightened young girl. But the flames and the linkage of local blacks to a conspiracy to burn down the town provide some indication of the suspicions—and perhaps the violent reality—that affected race relations early in the nineteenth century, as more African-Americans became free, more free blacks moved into the region, and news of violence by peoples of African heritage in other places was reported more frequently and in greater detail.[36]

Lancaster city's black population was increasing at a rate three times greater than that of the white between 1790 and 1810—126 percent compared to 43 percent—a trend that continued into the 1820s. To some whites, at least, it seemed like a flood and was about as welcome as a deluge. The growth was from a very small base; by 1820, after an increase of another 42 percent in the black population, there were still only 308 African-Americans among the 6,633 residents of the town—less than 5 percent—but whites noticed the change.

Beginning in the 1820s, white citizens from Lancaster and Pennsylvania's other southern counties continually petitioned the state legislature to stop the immigration of blacks from the South. Bills to this end did not receive the support of both houses in the same year, but in 1829 state lawmakers did agree to a statement that removal of African-Americans would be "highly auspicious to the best interests of the country," and they endorsed the efforts of the American Colonization Society to bring that about. There were other testaments to increasing fear and hostility toward blacks. The revised state constitution of 1837 limited voting to whites and was the specific outcome of a Bucks County election in which African-American ballots were believed decisive in a closely contested poll. Again, as long as there was only a meaningless handful of black voters, their presence could be tolerated, indeed pointed to with pride as symbols of the community's liberality; but when the numbers of black freeholders rose, made a difference, put African-Americans in a position even to make demands for fair treatment, then they became a threat that whites wanted quashed.[37]

It was during the 1820s and 1830s in Lancaster, as throughout the North, that the increased presence of blacks led whites to try to make them less visible, less threatening, and less part of "their" world. While once everyone had understood the rules of racial segregation, and whereas the presence of a small number of inconspicuous blacks could be tolerated because it went almost unnoticed, now whites found a need for even greater control, and the price was further restrictions on the lives of "free" blacks. In Lancaster city, it was fire and fear accompanied by the increased numbers of African-Americans that led to greater vigilance. In January 1820, the *Intelligencer* reported the devastation of Savannah, Georgia, by fire. Two months later, the *Journal* suggested a connection between the Savannah conflagration, a rash of local fires of suspicious origin, and the formation of two fire companies in Lancaster.[38]

The next step, as in York seventeen years earlier, was to begin more systematic surveillance of the black population. A city ordinance adopted in May 1820 required all "free persons of color" to register with the mayor. One consequence was creation of the "Negro Entry Book," which local historian Leroy Hopkins has transcribed and published. The 340 entries constitute an African-American city directory for the years from 1820 to 1849 and provide a wealth of information that otherwise would be lost to us. The entry book reveals that there was no concentration of blacks into ghettos during this period and that ownership of homes by them was rare. The unsurprising evidence that African-Americans generally occupied the lowest rung of the city's economic ladder is supplemented by information about the skilled and semiskilled black middle class. Beginning, as it does, at a moment of profound change in local race relations, the entry book also helps us to chart that process.[39]

The entry on James Clendenin, for example, tells us something about the emergence of propertied black leaders in this local setting and helps us put faces on the statistics about economic change. The Lancaster tax list for 1797 identified Clendenin as the first black property owner in the borough and as a painter by profession. By 1800, he was no longer paying any ground rent, which meant that he owned his house and land outright. The assessment valued Clendenin's property at two hundred dollars. By 1820, he had become more prosperous still. According to the registry book:

> James Clendenin, a mulatto enters that he is about sixty-five years of age, resides in Mussertown in the City of Lancaster, is a householder, by occupation a painter and glazier, has a wife named Elizabeth but no children, has a bound mulatto boy named William Clendenin about 10 years of age, learning said trades, and a mulatto girl about seven years of age, named Hannah Clark.[40]

This kind of moderate economic success brought new standing to some members of the black community during the early nineteenth century. It also exacerbated white fears of amalgamation and made working-class whites jealous of African-American economic achievements, which heightened interracial violence (see Chapter 9). Throughout the antebellum North, according to Leon Litwack, the economic achievement of blacks brought down upon them "even greater hostility and suspicion" from whites:

> Northern whites had come to accept irresponsibility, ignorance, and submissiveness as peculiar Negro characteristics, as natural products of the Negroes' racial inferiority. Consequently, those who rose above depravity failed to fit the stereotype and somehow seemed abnormal, even menacing.[41]

Although whites believed that black transients had to be watched and better controlled—that "troublemakers" who stole, started fires, and threatened the peace of the city generally came from outside the area— many also feared the likes of James Clendenin for what he was and for what he symbolized about the possibilities for African-Americans to challenge and break the stereotypical roles in which they were cast. One or two propertied blacks could be tolerated, just as the lone black on the back stairs in Lewis Miller's painting could be suffered to stay. But a rising black middle class was a different matter and, as we shall see in Chapters 8 and 9, became the focus of violence in Lancaster County more than once.

These middle-class blacks were a socially critical group, instrumental in the formation of African-American churches and, with the sufferance and assistance of whites, in the establishment of the local anti-slavery society. Historian Carl Oblinger found that only the wealthiest of these blacks had "recent, observable contact with the white Quaker abolitionists"; so such men as James Clendenin, Stephen Smith, and William Whipper were interracial mediators, in addition to their other roles. And it was the African-American chimney sweeps, skilled and semiskilled artisans, and barbers in Lancaster and Columbia boroughs who, in concert with other black property owners, helped in shadowy and now mostly lost ways to assist fugitives from slavery.[42]

Middle-class blacks were also different from the fugitives in a number of ways. Nearly all of them were mulattoes—less black—than those who arrived in Lancaster County hungry and scared. Over 80 percent descended from families that had lived in the region for more than one generation, while fewer than 10 percent of the laboring-class blacks had resided in the county for more than twenty years. Since only one-eighth of all blacks worked as skilled or nonmanual laborers in 1850, and only one-tenth could say the same in 1860, this was truly an elite, and one whose numbers were in decline at the time of the Christiana Riot. Along with the fugitives and the other local free blacks, African-Americans of property and standing also were scared—frightened of their white neighbors (and probably of the black laboring classes as well), of slave catchers to whom one kidnapped black was worth as much as another, and of the new Fugitive Slave Law. It was an era of change, some of it good, but most of it bad; and wealth provided little insulation from injustice, violence, and death. As a consequence, the most successful of Lancaster's blacks moved away in the 1850s, leaving even fewer philanthropic resources to assist a growing indigent population.[43]

The rest of the black community was even more exposed to the rough knocks of the marketplace, the bigotry of whites, and the shortcomings of justice under the law from the 1830s onward. The consequences included severe economic instability for working-class blacks. Day-laboring jobs left them unemployed for at least a hundred days a year. Class stratification accelerated within the black community; there was a visible and growing gap between the 5 percent at the top and the 70 percent that fell into what Oblinger terms the working- and under-classes during the 1840s. An increasingly large pool of itinerant workers traversed the area, evoking racial hostility and committing petty property crimes. Although African-Americans represented only $\frac{1}{34}$ of Pennsylvania's population, they made up one-third of the prisoners in the state's jails. During the 1840s and 1850s, Irish workers were competing successfully for jobs as carters and porters, which were once the sole province of blacks. Economic hard times in the late 1840s resulted in even greater hostility between Irish and black laborers and an increase in work-related violence. In 1842, Irish coal miners battled with African-Americans who competed for their jobs; in 1853, armed blacks replaced striking Irish railroad workers. According to Oblinger, between 1800 and 1860, at least a fourth of the black population . . . fell into poverty and disappeared either through death or transiency. This downward pressure on the black population increased towards mid-century, and only eased in the 1860's. The black poor were in a desperate condition. Ignored by the community, particularly after the mid-1820s, their death rates skyrocketed. The main community effort was directed at their removal either through fugitive aid or indentureships with farmers.[44]

Between 1830 and 1860 over five thousand African-Americans arrived in the region; about 20 percent of these fugitives and freed blacks from the South died within five years after securing their freedom. The death rate for impoverished blacks in southeastern Pennsylvania was better than a hundred out of a thousand, compared to forty-five per thousand for indigent whites. During the 1850s, increasing numbers of black children were growing up on the streets of Lancaster's towns, unsupervised by parents and often drawn to juvenile gangs that were responsible for much of the region's petty crime. This was the nature of freedom for fugitives who crossed the Mason-Dixon Line at about the same time as the four men from Edward Gorsuch's farm.[45]

Life for those blacks who were born in the region was also getting worse. During the 1840s and 1850s, people of African descent were losing the skilled work that members of their community had held for generations. Many were thrown out of their jobs and saw their sons denied apprenticeships in their trades.[46] Such changes were part of transformations in the craft system that were unsettling for white artisans as well as for black; they were also partly a consequence of competition from immigrant groups in trades that had once been monopolized by African-Americans.[47] But the story is much more complicated than that.

The changes that began earlier in the century and became increasingly visible from the 1820s to the 1850s were more than reflexive responses to an expanding market economy. They were also a product of white reactions to the increasing numbers of African-Americans in the region and of a diminishing tolerance for the presence of blacks. The unsavory images of African-Americans predated these changes, as local newspapers reveal, and were only enhanced by the arrival of so many poor, ignorant, and culturally alien fugitives during the antebellum decades. At the same time, there was a backlash—local and national—against the perceived social and political threats from radical abolitionism beginning in the 1820s, which occurred in the context of new "scientific" theories of racial inferiority.

In the nation at large, the persuasive powers of environmentalist philosophy—the belief that racial groups were products of their surroundings and that blacks would become more like whites in America over time—began to erode during the second decade of the nineteenth century. By the 1830s there was a wide-ranging debate between environmentalists and biological determinists, which by the 1840s and 1850s was, for the most part, resolved in favor of biology. According to historian George M. Fredrickson, the biological school "saw the Negro as a pathetically inept creature who was a slave to his emotions, incapable of progressive development and self-government because he lacked the white man's enterprise and intellect." In 1838, a writer for the *Lancaster Intelligencer* contributed a series of essays intended to demonstrate that blacks were unalterably inferior to whites. "Climate and its consequences," he asserted, "may effect them exteriorly, but it never can operate to change them to a different species of mankind. . . . It is well known that Africans, in their own country, left to their own unaided exertions, have not, in a long course of ages, made one single step in intelligence, industry or enterprize; one single progressive movement in refinement or any of the arts that render society agreeable, or life a blessing." The thrust of his argument, according to "Vindex," was not hostile toward African-Americans, just realistic:

> In attempting to show the mental inferiority of the negro to the white or Caucasian race, it is not my intention to make the fact an excuse for oppression or injustice towards them; but simply to make use of it to show the utter impracticability of Abolitionists elevating them to an equality with the whites. They are not only mentally but physically incapable of enjoying such privileges.[48]

The alternative view of African-American character, by mid-century, was a form of "romantic racialism," classically expressed in Harriet Beecher Stowe's *Uncle Tom's Cabin*. Even Stowe, however, saw African-Americans as fundamentally, and unalterably, different from whites—as childlike, innocent, and good-natured, qualities that white civilization had lost. Even such humanitarian liberals tended to believe, just as "Vindex," that colonization was in the best interest of blacks and that for their own good, African-Americans should be removed from an environment in which whites would always take advantage of their good nature.[49]

Whatever the intentions of nineteenth-century philosophers of race, the consequences of such attitudes toward African-Americans, coupled with demographic changes, included more violence on the streets of Lancaster beginning in the 1820s and 1830s. As Winthrop Jordan aptly put it, "the

Negro's color attained greatest significance not as a scientific problem but as a social fact." Even those whites who had once been supportive of blacks increasingly focused their humanitarian concerns on the local branch of Pennsylvania's Colonization Society, which had as its goal the exclusion of blacks from the community and their "repatriation" to Africa. As a result, blacks became even more isolated from whites among whom they lived and worked. They endured local and statewide attempts to exclude them from public places, as well as legislative efforts to expel them from the state.[50]

There were still white abolitionists in the county when Buley, Ford, and the two Hammonds arrived, and some of them worked diligently— attending meetings, giving speeches, and donating money to the cause. But for the most part, their efforts were aimed at the eradication of slavery and repeal of the Fugitive Slave Law, not the betterment of local conditions for African-Americans; on a day-to-day basis, Lancaster's blacks generally found themselves on their own. They still had white "friends," but African-Americans knew that if it came to a fight—as it increasingly did—it was a battle that blacks would have to fight on their own. So violence, isolation, and poverty drew blacks together. Their shared experiences, fears, and no doubt their dreams were the foundation upon which they built a community separate from whites. They had each other and their freedom (such as it was), and that counted for much.

What united Lancaster's whites across class, religious, moral, and political lines was a shared sense that African-Americans were aliens who worked in the region but were not truly members of the communities in which they lived. This vision of blacks as outsiders defined the limits of white tolerance, even among those considered "friends" of ex-slaves. It was possible to sympathize with the general plight of African-Americans, to give individual blacks some food, hire their labor to bring in the crops, pass on used clothing, and even harbor and assist fugitives from slavery without believing that blacks really belonged. Over time, as the numbers of African-Americans in Lancaster County increased and as they became more integrated into the local economy, they made claims to membership that enraged some local whites. And the violence that we see in the eighteenth-century court records now crossed racial lines perhaps more frequently, at least more visibly to us. It was in this new world of violent interracial relations, which grew from local cultures of violence established during the eighteenth century, that the four fugitives from Edward Gorsuch's farm lived for almost two years preceding the fall of 1851.

[3]

The Chase

1851 WAS A VERY BAD YEAR FOR FARMS from the Atlantic to the Mississippi. Unseasonably cold weather in the spring resulted in late plantings, which got everything off to a slow start. Then, throughout the summer, an almost unprecedented combination of heat and drought wilted crops in the fields and stunted their growth. The blazing sun baked and cracked the clay soil of northern Maryland and southeastern Pennsylvania. As August mercifully came to an end, it was clear that this season's corn, wheat, and tobacco crops would be two-thirds, or less, of the normal yield. When September began, farmers could only pray for some relief from the heat for themselves and their animals, a break in the weather that would give some hope for fall plantings. In early September, the topic for discussion whenever farmers met was rain—the lack of it, whether anyone could remember a worse summer, or prospects for a change. Conversation at Retreat Farm certainly included the weather, but the Gorsuches also talked about slaves, especially the four who were not there to suffer and work along with the rest.

Across the York Pike from Retreat Farm, to the east, was an inn that served as a meeting place for the area's white propertied class. Owners of large farms, doctors, lawyers, and even a liberal minister or two would stop for a drink, to exchange pleasantries, to discuss the weather or business transactions, or just to eat a good meal with family and friends. Located on land adjoining the extended Gorsuch family's other estate, Retirement Farm, the roadhouse was the largest in the area, and its proprietor was also, not surprisingly, a Gorsuch. Captain Joshua Gorsuch retired from his seafaring profession and built the hostelry in 1810. The brick building also housed a store, where country women could purchase imported fabrics, frocks, and hats and could browse among shawls, fans, perfumes, jewelry, teas, coffee, spices, and trinkets from around the world. The gentry also found imported liquors, snuff, watches, and sundries in addition to the commonplace domestic products sold by other local merchants.

Weary travelers knew the tavern for its fine food and drink, comfortable rooms, and the gracious hospitality of its host. As an additional service, the innkeeper provided accommodations for any slave traveling with the paying guests. There were cells with barred windows in the basement, where slaves could be securely locked for the night. This enabled the masters, who were perhaps on their way to or from the slave market in Baltimore or were simply on the road with a slave work crew, to dine at leisure and rest without concern for the loss of their human chattel.[1]

It was the matter of slaves that brought members of the Gorsuch clan together in Captain Joshua's tavern during the first week of September 1851—not the slaves in the basement, of course, or the slaves back at Edward Gorsuch's farm, but those who had run away almost two years before, at least three of whom had now been located in Lancaster County, Pennsylvania. None of the family doubted the informant's reliability. The "William M. P." who signed the letter of August 28 was William Padgett, a young man who, although born and raised in Lancaster, had lived for a time in the Baltimore area. Not exactly a family friend, as he had asserted in the letter, Padgett did know the Gorsuches, apparently recognized their escaped slaves on sight, and had assisted others in this sort of matter in the past.

Back in Lancaster, Padgett had a less savory reputation among those unsympathetic to the stalking of fugitive slaves. Local people later remembered him as a "miserable creature," who used his clock repairman's trade as a cloak for his labors as an informer. Once inside a customer's house, Padgett seized the opportunity to hunt out his unsuspecting victims. "During the fall months," a resident later recalled, "he pretended to be gathering sumac tops for the dyeing of morocco. By these means he became aware of every cow path and by-road, and could keep a close watch wherever he suspected a victim might be concealed and thus make an accurate report." Padgett reputedly had a talent for ingratiating himself with local blacks for the purpose of locating fugitives.[2]

Whatever the finer points of his personality, Padgett played an essential role in the attempt to recapture Gorsuch's slaves. He was also reputedly a member of the notorious "Gap Gang," a loosely organized band of working-class whites who terrorized the black community of Lancaster County. This gang of toughs took its name generally from the Gap Hills in the eastern part of the country, where many of them lived and worked, and specifically from the Gap Tavern, which served as a hangout and rendezvous for many of their endeavors. During the twelve months preceding September 1851, such kidnappers had used the Fugitive Slave Law as license for terrorist acts against black residents of the county. "Spies and informers were everywhere," a white Lancastrian recalled many years later:

> Every peaceful valley, as well as populous town, was infested with prowling kidnappers on the watch for their prey. . . . Quiet homes and peaceful communities were constantly threatened with midnight incursions of manhunters, with their treacheries, stratagems, their ruffian outrages and bloody violence, and menacing the defenseless people of color with a "reign of terror."[3]

The distinction between lawful and illegal attempts to capture black residents of Lancaster County was a subtle one, whose meaning was often lost on those unversed in the language of governments and courts. Illiteracy could leave a man more vulnerable to those who waved "legal papers" before his face, or it could make him wary of anyone who claimed to enforce the law. The authority of pistols and clubs could be comprehended by all, but weapons demanded quick, perhaps unreasoned, judgments in an atmosphere of violence and fear. So, in practical fact, the Fugitive Slave Law escalated a war between those who had tasted freedom and those who would try to deprive them of liberty's sustenance.

To the "kidnappers" of Lancaster County, the difference between a free black and a fugitive slave was often without meaning. African-Americans, especially men, were marketable commodities whatever their past and no matter what was the law of the land. To the black residents of the county, a kidnapper was a kidnapper, to be feared and resisted at whatever cost. These were the realities of life on the border between slavery and freedom; there were no laws in this war, except for the laws of nature that govern relations between hunter and hunted—the rules of survival and self-defense. Long after the Civil War, Josiah Pickle remembered one such kidnapping, which occurred on his father's farm:

> The Negro was a post and railer by trade and very industrious. One evening after dusk a couple of men in a wagon drove up to his house and asked his wife if John was home. She replied that he was not, but was working for a neighbor and probably was coming up the road. They drove away and met him, talked for a while, and one knocked him down and then threw him into the wagon when they drove rapidly away. A scream, when he was attacked, was the last that his wife and family ever

heard from him, and no doubt a large sum was received for him by his captors in some southern market.

According to David Forbes, who interviewed Pickle over forty years after the kidnapping occurred, "this is only one of the hundreds of such cases of the stealing of human beings at which the unscrupulous made a living, and there are several people still surviving, unless wrongly accused, who accumulated much of their wealth in this questionable manner."[4]

Skirmishes were frequent, with the hunters often seizing the advantages of surprise and darkness to pounce on their quarry. Kidnappers of the illegal variety succeeded in taking what the newspapers described as "an old colored man" in March 1851. In the middle of the night, the house was invaded by a party of whites who were unknown to the residents, displayed no warrants, and did not bother the courts with affidavits or testimony to the black man's status as a slave. According to the papers, "the old man and his wife made all the resistance they could, but were overpowered—the woman knocked down and the man captured."[5]

Earlier this same year, the legal capture of a fugitive slave in Columbia, Pennsylvania, provoked a riot. A farmer from Havre-de-Grace, Maryland, claimed the escaped slave named Stephen Bennett was his property. During the battle that ensued between lawmen and African-Americans who came to Bennett's assistance, the sheriff's arm was shattered by a bullet. Eventually, the constabulary assembled in sufficient numbers to recapture the fugitive and fight back the crowd. Residents raised seven hundred dollars—the asking price—to purchase Bennett's freedom, and the town settled back into a semblance of order.[6]

Those who were hunted responded in one of two ways to the threat posed by kidnappers and the new federal "kidnapping" law. Flight was the path of choice for countless hundreds, who decided that the odds were against them any place south of the Canadian border. The exodus of blacks from Lancaster County in the months surrounding adoption of the Fugitive Slave Law was described locally as a wave of emigration. Not all were sorry to see them go, but even the most virulent racists among the propertied white community had to admit that the cheap seasonal laborers would be missed by the local economy. Unbeknownst to Edward Gorsuch, at least one of his four escaped slaves had chosen this option months before the posse assembled at Captain Joshua's tavern.

Others, including either two or three of the fugitives from Gorsuch's farm, chose to stay and fight for their freedom, even if it meant death in the battle. The African-American residents of Lancaster County were not defenseless. They often gave as good or better than they got in this war for survival. They were not passive victims but a determined, self-led people who relied first and foremost on themselves for protection against those who threatened their liberty and their lives. All the blacks who remained in the county, somewhere in excess of three thousand souls, lived in fear; they worked, ate, prayed, played, loved, and slept in constant vigilance against the day that the kidnappers would come for them. Fear drove the black community even closer together than shared circumstances had bound them before. Two decades earlier they had formed a mutual protection association—a gang to combat the Gap Gang—which took an aggressive stance against all who threatened the life and liberty of any member of their community.[7]

William Parker led this self-defense organization. He was a man of courage, intelligence, bravado, and justifiable pride, who was admired by Lancaster's black residents, and some of its whites, and rightly feared by those who wished ill to him and his cause. By all accounts, Parker was a tall, thin, well-muscled mulatto man, whom his African-American neighbors knew as "the preacher" during his twelve years in Lancaster County. He was about twenty-nine years old in September 1851. According to a local historian, Parker had "a reputation among both the colored people and the kidnapping fraternity for undaunted boldness and remarkable power." He was the one above all others whom the slave catchers "wished to get rid of." A white abolitionist from the region remembered that Parker was as "bold as a lion, the kindest of men, and the most steadfast of friends." He was the sort of man who made an impression, even on those who met him only once. Parker "could have commanded an army had he been educated, and he challenged the universal respect of all of them who did not have occasion to fear him," another white man recalled. Local blacks "regarded him as their leader, their protector, their Moses, and their lawgiver all at once."[8]

Parker's life paralleled that of Frederick Douglass's in a number of ways. Parker, too, was born into Maryland bondage and secured his freedom by running away. Indeed, the two men had known each other as slaves; they were reacquainted in freedom; and later, in the fall of 1851, their paths would cross yet again. The violence of slavery had shaped Parker's nature, like Douglass's, at a tender age. "My rights at the fireplace were won by my child-fists," Parker would write in his memoirs; "my rights as a freeman were, under God, secured by my own right arm."[9]

Like the four fugitives from Edward Gorsuch's Baltimore County farm, Parker had a "good" master, who would not "allow his hands to be beaten or abused, as many slave-holders would." Although he was convinced of the evils of slavery, although the comparative lenity of his own enslavement bred the courage and imagination that persuaded him that he must be free, Parker, like Gorsuch's slaves, needed an impetus—an excuse— to propel him to freedom. Just as most others who ran away, Parker chose not to go alone; like the others, he ran away from a farm rather than the city and from a "good" master rather than a bad one. Unlike Gorsuch's slaves, Parker self-consciously created the event that "justified" running away:

> Much as I disliked my condition, I was ignorant enough to think that something besides the fact that I was a slave was necessary to exonerate me from blame in running away. A cross word, a blow, a good fright, anything, would do; it mattered not whence nor how it came. I told my brother Charles, who shared my confidence, to be ready; for the time was at hand when we should leave Old Maryland forever. I was only waiting for the first crooked word from my master.[10]

When the "crooked word" did not come, at least not in a timely fashion, Parker refused one day to work in the fields. When the master asked him why he did not labor with the others, the slave replied that it was raining, he was weary, and he did not want to work on that day. According to Parker, "he then picked up a stick used for an ox-gad, and said, if I did not go to work, he would whip me as sure as there was a God in heaven." The slave had succeeded in provoking his master, wounding his pride, challenging the system, and making the master look bad in the eyes of those who would see a black man setting his own hours in defiance of the master's rule. "Then he struck at me," Parker recalled; "but I caught the stick, and we grappled, and handled each other roughly for a time, when he called for assistance. He was badly hurt. I let go my hold, bade him good-bye, and ran for the woods." Parker was about sixteen years old at the time.[11]

Parker and his brother made their way north under cover of night, eventually crossing the Susquehannah River to Columbia, Lancaster County, Pennsylvania. Since they had grown up in the country, town life was of little appeal to the Parkers; so they sought agricultural employment. "Those were memorable days," Parker later recalled; he felt free as a bird; "instead of the darkness of slavery, my eyes were almost blinded by the light of freedom." The reality of life in the North soon intruded on Parker's idyll, and he found "by bitter experience, that to preserve my stolen liberty I must pay, unremittingly, an almost sleepless vigilance." The injustice of life in the North, the ubiquitous racism, and his status as prey of the economic system and of those who would try to return him to slavery were worth it, though, compared to the life he had escaped in Maryland:

> I thought of my fellow-servants left behind, bound in the chains of slavery,—and I was free! I thought that, if I had the power, they should soon be as free as I was; and I formed a resolution that I would assist in liberating every one within my reach at the risk of my life, and that I would devise some plan for their entire liberation. [12]

As Parker knew well, gaining freedom was one thing and keeping it another; helping one fugitive was a small step toward overthrowing the institution of slavery. But those were his goals, and Parker was not alone in his ambitions. One way to think about what Parker and his African-American compatriots were about in Lancaster County is to draw a parallel between the way that the black mutual-protection organization functioned in the early 1850s and the way that communities of escaped slaves, known as maroons, undermined slavery going back to the sixteenth century. [13] Like the maroons who lived in forests and swamps bordering the "civilized" South, Lancaster's blacks challenged the slave system by providing a visible alternative to the lives of northern Maryland's slaves. There was constant communication among blacks, slave and free, on either side of the Mason-Dixon Line; the Northerners provided aid and sustenance to those who ran away and engaged in guerrilla warfare against slave masters and their agents who dared to confront them in pitched battle. [14]

Eugene Genovese's explanation of the slave-maroon relationship and the function of maroons in undermining the slaveocracy applies in interesting ways to the interaction across Pennsylvania's southern border. The Commonwealth's free black communities served a transitional role in the history of slavery just at the time that Genovese finds the maroons' alliance with slaves suffering strain. Where the maroons were the obvious source of inspiration and aid for the slave who would be free during the seventeenth and into the eighteenth century, the free blacks of southern Pennsylvania served the same function for slaves such as Douglass, Parker, and the four fugitives from Gorsuch's farm during the antebellum decades. [15]

Power defined the differences between the ways that northern Maryland's slaves and the freemen of Lancaster County related to the injustice of slavery. "If a people, over a protracted period, find the odds against insurrection not merely long but virtually certain," Genovese reasoned, "then it will choose not to try." In light of such a calculation of risks, the boldest of Maryland's slaves ran away, while the bravest of Lancaster's

African-Americans stayed and fought. And, indeed, in numerous cases, those who chose flight while enslaved were the very same individuals who stood their ground under different circumstances; this was true for Parker and for at least two of the fugitives tracked by Gorsuch.[16]

The members of Lancaster's black self-protection society were no more attentive than the Gap Gang to distinctions between legal and illegal "kidnappings." "Whether the kidnappers were clothed with legal authority or not," Parker explained, "I did not care to inquire, as I never had faith in nor respect for the Fugitive-Slave Law." In part, such an attitude was reflexive. Since the Gap Gang did not abide by the law and since the white community suffered such lawlessness against the African-American residents of the county, the blacks did not enjoy the luxury of protection by sheriffs and judges. According to Parker, "the whites of that region were generally such negro-haters that it was a matter of no moment to them where fugitives were carried—whether to Lancaster, Harrisburg, or elsewhere." In light of such hostility, the blacks had to protect themselves as best they could—with guns and clubs rather than lawyers and writs.[17]

And defend themselves they did, in a series of ferocious battles, which resulted in bloodshed and death on both sides. In a riot outside the Lancaster jail, bricks, clubs, pistols, and fists were the weapons of choice in an unsuccessful attempt to free William Dorsey from the clutches of the law. On another occasion, the alarm was sounded that kidnappers were attempting to take a black girl back to Maryland. "The news soon reached me," Parker reported,

> and with six or seven others, I followed them. We proceeded with all speed to a place called the Gap-Hill, where we overtook them, and took the girl away. Then we beat the kidnappers, and let them go. We learned afterwards that they were all wounded badly, and that two of them died in Lancaster, and the other did not get home for some time. Only one of our men was hurt, and he had only a slight injury in the hand.[18]

The deaths of the two "kidnappers" were at least partly the consequence of the white community's attitudes toward such violence in the name of the law. As the slave-catching party retreated, they had a difficult time finding a local physician who would minister to the wounds of their injured members. "There are plenty of doctors South," across the Maryland line, they were told. "Men coming after such property ought to be killed," another unsympathetic white man lectured the posse. Ultimately, the slave catchers found sympathy and assistance at McKenzie's Tavern in Lancaster city. So incensed was the innkeeper to see the condition of the posse and to hear of their treatment by his fellow citizens, that he declared he would never hire another "nigger" and fired a black woman servant on the spot. For his efforts in the kidnappers' behalf and his public declamations of eagerness to extend hospitality to any slave owner passing through the town, McKenzie became the victim of arsonists, who burned his barn to the ground. The community was divided over the issue of fugitive slaves—bitterly, violently riven by issues of law and justice and race. This was a war, and it was not at all clear who was winning.[19]

The friends of the fugitives lost many battles; they frequently arrived on the scene too late to influence the outcome. Members of the self-protection society were not in time to save Henry Williams from being taken back to Maryland as a slave. They were also too late to help John Williams, who was so badly hurt resisting the Gap Gang that his master refused to pay the kidnappers when they arrived at his Maryland farm with their captive. Williams later died from head injuries suffered in the affray. Parker himself was shot in the ankle during one rescue attempt.[20]

Spies had a role to play in these battles. As in other wars, espionage was dangerous work and required anonymity to succeed. White men such as Padgett recognized that they had to be careful lest Parker's gang discover their betrayal. Parker saw the moral ambiguity, and the irony, of African-Americans resorting to lynch law in the name of justice, but the ends seemed to make the means "excusable, if not altogether justifiable," in handling spies. When they learned that Allen Williams had been betrayed by the black man in whose home the fugitive lived, the self-protection society stalked the Judas and gave him a merciless beating. When they heard that another African-American regularly assisted slave catchers in their bloody work, Parker's gang burned his house to the ground.[21]

Much of this violence occurred before the Fugitive Slave Law became the law of the land. If anything, though, the violence escalated in Lancaster County during the year following adoption of the Compromise of 1850. The new Fugitive Slave Law tipped the balance of power in the battle for freedom toward the slave catchers, as it brought federal law-enforcement officials into the fray on the side of the masters. It was definitely going to be easier to retake fugitive slaves legally. No longer could Pennsylvania's officials openly resist efforts to recover fugitives. No longer would masters be denied protection of the courts when they ventured north to recover their property. Despite several notorious examples of resistance, the law was being tolerated, even tacitly welcomed, in Pennsylvania, as in most other Northern states. According to Stanley W. Campbell, "for the most part . . . the law was enforced quietly and without fanfare." "By midsummer 1851," Campbell contends, "public acquiescence toward the Fugitive Slave Law was in fact becoming general." Some places in the North this was true, but not in Lancaster; Parker's self-protection association continued its work through the summer and into the fall of 1851.[22]

This, then, was the setting of suspicion, tension, hatred, and violence into which the Gorsuch party blundered. Lancaster County was not a vacuum, where all parties could be expected to engage in a reasoned dialogue that recognized the humanity of both sides. The fugitives and their sympathizers had learned to disdain the law that jeopardized their freedom. They had practiced the arts of guerrilla warfare and had gained confidence in their ability to fight. They had honed their hatred of slavery and slave owners, not just on their memories of life in Maryland but also on experiences defending their liberty in the North—against Northern white racists, against fellow African-Americans who regularly betrayed their racial brethren for the antebellum equivalent of Judas' thirty pieces of silver, and against the slave catchers who came from the South. A law, a piece of paper signed by a judge, and the bravado of a Southern gentleman would prove flimsy armor against the weapons of war.

In partial ignorance and in entire disdain for the realities of the slave-catching business—with or without the authority of a federal law—Edward Gorsuch; his son Dickinson; Captain Joshua, the aging innkeeper and a cousin of Edward's; Dr. Thomas Pearce, a nephew; and two neighbors, Nicholas Hutchins and Nathan Nelson, gathered their horses and rode away from the tavern.[23] Dickinson had tried to talk his father out of the enterprise, obviously to no avail. The old man was "determined to have his property" and would listen to no contrary advice. The stubbornness of the slave owner was again remarked on by his son—the unwillingness to listen to logic, to reason, or to measure his loss by any calculation other than his wounded pride. And so, Edward Gorsuch began the ride north to his death.

On September 8, 1851, Gorsuch took an express train to Philadelphia, arriving ahead of his party. On September 9, he secured four warrants authorizing capture of his slaves under the federal government's Fugitive Slave Law adopted the previous year. The fugitive-slave commissioner, Edward Ingraham, also instructed Henry H. Kline, the "notorious, lying, slave-catching Deputy Marshal Kline" as he was known in the anti-slavery press, to head the Gorsuch posse. Two other Philadelphia policemen joined up as deputies and were paid in advance by Gorsuch. Initially, the slave-catching expedition traveled in four separate groups for the purpose of making their arrival less conspicuous than it might otherwise be. Edward Gorsuch rode alone from Philadelphia; Marshall Kline made his way west first by train and then the rest of the way by rented wagon; the two police officers, John Agan and Thompson Tully, journeyed together on a later train; and the rest of the Gorsuch party came up from Baltimore, intending to join the posse at a tavern in Lancaster County.

Right from the start there were problems, which boded ill for the enterprise. Kline's wagon broke down, and he was forced to walk his horses back and hire another.[24] The delay caused Kline to miss the prearranged rendezvous, and he was left wandering about the Lancaster countryside conspicuously looking for the Gorsuches. Kline's cover story, that he was chasing horse thieves, was a transparent ruse.

Even worse, a black man named Samuel Williams followed him all day. Williams, who ran a Philadelphia tavern called the Bolivar House, was known by Kline to be active in the network of agents popularly known as the "Underground Railroad." Kline rightly suspected that Williams had knowledge of the warrants secured by Edward Gorsuch and was sent by the "Special Secret Committee" to warn Lancaster's black community what the marshal and his posse were up to. According to William Parker, Gorsuch had been noticed "in close converse with a certain member of the Philadelphia bar, who had lost the little reputation he ever had by continual dabbling in negro-catching, as well as by association with and support of the notorious Henry H. Kline, a professional kidnapper of the basest stamp."[25]

Having uncovered the slave-catching plot, it remained for Williams to discover what exactly the plans of the kidnappers from Maryland were and then to deliver a warning to those who were threatened. The Secret Committee knew that "one false step would jeopardize their own liberty, and very likely their lives. . . . They knew, too, that they were matched against the most desperate, daring, and brutal men in the kidnappers' ranks." This was not, according to Parker, just another slave-catching expedition like the hundreds of others that had gone before; this was one of the new federal "kidnapping" posses. The Secret Committee knew "that this was the deepest, the most thoroughly organized and best-planned project for man-catching that had been concocted since the infamous Fugitive Slave Law had gone into operation." Perhaps Parker romanticized the encounter for dramatic effect, but there can be no exaggeration of the danger into which Williams, the Philadelphia innkeeper, walked. Kline, who was by no means a brave man and who knew the dangers of the slave-catching business, was also scared. The Gorsuches had lost the element of surprise and thus their advantage, if the fugitives were found.[26]

At 2 a.m., Kline entered a Penningtonville tavern and inquired about the horse thieves. Williams, who had followed him through the door, responded to the inquiry with a clear threat: "I know the kind of horse thieves you are after. They are all gone; and you had better not go after them." When Kline left the bar, Williams was not far behind. The marshal stopped several times at taverns along the road to ask about the "thieves" he was tracking. He reached the Gap Tavern at about three in the morning, saw to his horses, and then went to bed. He got up at about 4:30 and rode to Parkesburg, where he found Agan and Tully asleep in a barroom. The two policemen told Kline where to find Gorsuch and after hearing how things were going informed the marshal that they were returning to Philadelphia. They, too, had seen Williams on the train that morning (before he got off and began following Kline) and suspected that he was following them. Williams had also seen the policemen and knew from the bulk under their jackets that they were heavily armed and up to no good. In light of the foul-ups and the abolitionist spy, the risks now outweighed their salaries in the judgment of the two mercenary cops.[27]

Kline proceeded without his deputies and found the Gorsuches at Sadsbury around 9 a.m. on September 10. Edward Gorsuch was angry with Kline for not making the rendezvous. True to his character, the embarrassed marshal lied and said that his wagon had broken because he had been driving fast to elude the abolitionist spy. In fact, Kline had not met up with Williams until after he had arrived at the tavern in Penningtonville on his second wagon. Gorsuch was also distraught to hear that the policemen intended to return to Philadelphia. Gorsuch and Kline headed off separately to intercept Agan and Tully before they left the area. The rest of the party was to wait at an agreed-upon place. When Kline found his deputies, they told him that they had already spoken to Gorsuch; now they refused to go with Kline. Agan told Kline that he had promised Gorsuch that he would return from Philadelphia on the evening train. The marshal and the Gorsuch party met the train that night, but neither Agan nor Tully got off any of the cars.

At about 1 a.m. on Thursday, September 11, the slave catchers left the Gap on foot and walked towards Christiana, where three of the escaped slaves were reputedly living. On their way, they were joined by a guide hired by Gorsuch for the purpose of conducting them to the fugitives. The guide disguised himself with a straw hat and bandanna to prevent his identification by those he intended to betray. Perhaps this was Padgett, the original informant; in any event, it was a white man who showed the posse the way.[28] First, the guide took them to a house where he said one of the fugitives lived. Gorsuch wanted to split up the posse, with a few of them staying to capture this fugitive while the others moved on to take the other two. Kline protested the foolishness of this proposed plan, pointing out that it would "take all the force" they had to capture the two other slaves. Finally, Gorsuch relented, deciding that since the escaped slave supposedly living in this first house had left a wife back in Maryland, he would probably be the easiest to take. They would leave the married slave alone for the moment and instead try to capture the other two. According to Marshal Kline, Gorsuch reasoned that "if he could see this colored man, the married one, [he] would come home of his own accord—he had been persuaded away; he [Gorsuch] then thought we should go after the other two." The master still persisted in believing, in the face of all evidence to the contrary, that his slaves would return with him to Maryland without any show of resistance, that the question would be settled by persuasion rather than force.[29]

The guide led the Gorsuch party another six or eight miles by a circuitous route, and then they halted briefly to eat some crackers and cheese, prime their weapons, and discuss a general plan of attack. A short time later, after having resumed their journey, Dr. Pearce stopped and was about to get himself a drink from the creek they were passing. "It won't do to stop, for it is daylight," cautioned the nervous Marshal Kline. No time to waste now, the new day was dawning, the fog that covered the valley was beginning to lift, and the slave catchers were about to lose the darkness and mist that shrouded their movements.

A short distance farther, the guide stopped and pointed to a short lane leading up to a stone house where he said the other two fugitives could be found (Figure 3.1). It was a small two-story stone structure with a shingle roof and a chimney at one end. There was also a rickety overhang above the front door. In the front, there were two windows upstairs and two more on either side of the entrance. To the left of the house, as a visitor faced it, was an orchard and then the creek that the posse had passed on their way from the Valley Road. To the right was a cornfield; the stalks were head high and parched from the heat and lack of moisture. There was a fence running from the creek around the orchard, parallel to the Long Lane in front of the house, and around the cornfield to the corner where the Long Lane intersected with Noble Road. Farther down the Long Lane to the northwest, past the orchard and the creek about a mile and a half away, was the residence of Levi Pownall, a Quaker farmer who rented the stone house to its occupants. A half mile in the other direction, around the corner to the southwest on the Noble Road, was the home of Castner Hanway, a white miller and the closest neighbor to the residents of the stone house.

F I G U R E 3.1. The old riot house—William Parker's home *(with permission of the Lancaster County Historical Society)*

The setting was later described in some detail by a local resident with an eye for the strategic significance of the scene:

> This spot must have been an ideal one for seclusion, situated as it is near a fourth of a mile from any public highway, and standing well up on the northern slope of a hill, surrounded by trees, being almost invisible to the outside world, yet in such a position that the ever-alert resident could clearly scan the surrounding country for a long distance, and note the approach of suspicious characters in time to avert any impending danger to the inmates.[30]

The guide's job was now completed, and he walked away, leaving the posse standing in the Long Lane. It is at least possible that he had knowingly led the slave catchers into a trap. Whatever his intentions, circumstances were not exactly as they were represented to the Maryland "kidnapping" party. Whatever his goals, the guide delivered his employers as if on a platter to the very seat of Lancaster's anti-slavery resistance. Nowhere in the county would the posse have been more in danger for their very lives than on the doorstep of the stone house that was William Parker's home.

Inside the house there was at least as much nervousness about the impending encounter as there was out in the lane. The seven people who spent the previous night in the house anticipated the kidnappers' arrival. The warning brought by Samuel Williams had "spread through the vicinity like a fire in the prairies." Messengers crossed the countryside carrying the word, arming themselves and advising those of a like mind to be on the alert. According to Parker, when he returned home from work on Wednesday evening, September 10, Samuel Thompson and Joshua Kite were waiting for him. Also there that evening were Parker's wife, Eliza; Eliza's sister Hannah and her husband, Alexander Pinckney; and Abraham Johnson, a fugitive from Cecil County, Maryland, all of whom lived in the house. Thompson, Kite, and the rest of the household were in an uproar about the "rumor" concerning kidnappers. "I laughed at them," Parker recalled, "and said it was all talk. . . . They stopped for the night with us, and we went to bed as usual."[31]

Perhaps things were not so lighthearted as Parker remembered. Another account of that evening, based on Frederick Douglass's interviews with those in the house shortly after the riot, noted that the seven people "sat up late in apprehension of an attack, but finally went to bed, but sleep—they could not." Under the circumstances, with their lives and liberty at stake and without knowing when the kidnappers would pounce, Douglass's version seems more likely than Parker's. Sarah Pownall, Parker's neighbor from down the lane and the wife of his landlord, also stopped by that night. She wanted to share her concern about the possibility of violence and tried to convince Parker that,

> if the slave-holders should come, not to lead the colored people to resist the Fugitive Slave Law by force of arms, but to escape to Canada. He replied that if the laws protected colored men as they did white men, he too would be non-resistant and not fight, but would appeal to the laws. "But," said he, "the laws for personal protection are not made for us, and we are not bound to obey them. If a fight occurs I want the whites to keep away. They have a country and may obey the laws. But we have no country."[32]

Pacifism makes sense for whites, Parker responded to his Quaker neighbor; the law and the courts do not work for black people, and a man can run only so far. He was polite and appreciated her concern, but it was not her battle and certainly was his. Nothing more could be said between these two people who lived so close together but in such dissimilar worlds. They understood and respected each other but inhabited different spots on the long lane between slavery and freedom, injustice and justice, the law of nature and the rule of law. Parker and his African-American compatriots did not seek, did not need, and did not expect whites to come to their aid. Stay away, Parker advised Sarah Pownall, and try to see that other whites do the same.

One reason that the men whom Parker called Joshua Kite and Samuel Thompson were particularly worried that evening, and were even less likely to sleep than other occupants of the stone house, is because they were two of the fugitives from Gorsuch's farm. The moment they had been dreading, probably ever since they ran away from their northern Maryland enslavement, was now at hand—a confrontation with the "Master" in what could be a battle for their lives. At least they were armed, on their own turf, and in the company of friends who were brave and effective fighters for freedom.

Fear was certainly felt by the fugitives, but perhaps also exhilaration at the possibility of actually fighting for their liberty, of asserting their manhood against the very patriarch who had once ruled their lives. There were risks, to be sure, but this time they were not running away. They must have thought that they had a chance to win, an opportunity to strike a blow for freedom, an occasion to prove themselves equals of men who demeaned them and their race.

As the sun was rising outside, the posse, entering the short lane leading up to the house, startled a black man who was coming the other way. Imagine the emotions, the pounding hearts, the shock of recognition after almost two years, the adrenalin coursing through the bodies of them all. The black man was apparently Nelson Ford, one of the fugitives for whom Gorsuch had come. He had left Parker's house after that long, perhaps sleepless, night and was either on his way home (as Parker claimed) or serving as a lookout. According to an African-American resident of Christiana, who was interviewed many years later, Ford lived at the time in the house of Joseph Pownall and was known by the name of John Beard. The 1850 census lists Beard as a twenty-three-year-old black laborer, so the age and the occupation are just what we would expect. Gorsuch had used Ford as a teamster because he was small and incapable of the physical labors generally expected of field slaves. Beard—or Ford, or Kite (as Parker called him)—was also quick, eluded the slave catchers' grasp, and ran back into the house. "O William! kidnappers! kidnappers!" the young man cried as he burst through Parker's door.[33]

[4]

The Riot

WHAT HAPPENED UP TO THIS POINT in the story of the Christiana Riot is, if not obvious, at least pretty clear. It is possible with some sense of assurance to piece together the sequence of events. But from the moment that Joshua Kite ran back into William Parker's house, the narrative becomes significantly more difficult to reconstruct. The record is a contradictory jumble of individual perspectives, attempted self-vindications, faulty and incomplete recollections, bragging, and lies. Sorting out one version from another and recognizing each for what it is requires some tolerance for imprecision. In the end, the reader deserves a candid admission that even with the voluminous documentation surrounding this extraordinary event, we cannot be entirely certain of the sequence of actions, the precise dialogue, or the roles played by the major actors in the riot.

This is not surprising. Riots are by their very nature wild, confusing, and frightening experiences. Seldom does anyone have a clear perspective of all that goes on or the calm state of mind that contributes to rational perception and objective reporting. This riot was no exception. Chapter 7 will detail the specific testimonies given by some of the survivors; for now, my task is to provide a coherent narrative, which silently makes judgments about what happened during those first two hours after dawn on September 11, 1851, at William Parker's home.

When Joshua Kite burst through the door and delivered his breathless message, the first response of the inhabitants was to gather up weapons and climb the stairs to the top floor of the house. The second-story perspective gained the seven people—five men and two women—a clear advantage over the six men outside. In order to capture their quarry, the posse would have to ascend a narrow staircase one man at a time. The slave catchers could get no clear line of fire from the ground into the second-floor windows, while the Parkers, their relatives, and friends had the "kidnappers" within their sights.[1]

According to plan, four members of the posse staked out the corners of the house, so that none of the inhabitants could sneak through a back window or door. That left Marshal Kline and Edward Gorsuch to confront the blacks directly, to present the four warrants, explain the law, and take custody of the two fugitives whom they believed to be cowering upstairs. The front door was still open; the stairs were immediately inside.[2] The situation called for some courage, creativity, and good judgment. Gorsuch had the courage. Kline was creative, if nothing else.

The marshal called for the owner of the house. The imposing figure of William Parker appeared on the landing: "Who are you?"

"I am the United States Marshal," Kline replied.

"If you take another step," Parker warned, "I'll break your neck." Kline explained that he was there to arrest Gorsuch's slaves Nelson and Josh, that he had proper warrants and the authority of the United States government behind him. "I told him that I did not care for him nor the United States," Parker later recalled. Parker's brother-in-law was losing his nerve. "Where is the use of fighting," Alexander Pinckney asked his companions. "They will take us anyway." Kline heard the resignation in his voice and sought to encourage Pinckney's sense of hopelessness. "Yes, give up," the marshal responded, "for we can take you in any event." Parker tried to inspire his companions to fight to the death. "Yes," scoffed Kline, "I have heard many a negro talk as big as you, and then have taken him; and I'll take you."

"You have not taken me yet," Parker retorted.[3]

Eliza Parker grabbed a corn cutter, which she knew how to wield, and proclaimed that she would chop off the head of the first member of their band who tried to give up. She, too, was a fugitive from Maryland and had married her husband in Pennsylvania about five years before. Now at the age of twenty-one, she was the mother of three young children. Her mother, brothers, and sister were also fugitives, who lived in the Lancaster area. Indeed, Eliza's mother, Cassandra Harris, was helping to care for her two daughters' children, whom she had spirited away from the house temporarily to a safer locale. Eliza Parker and Hannah Pinckney were fighting not just for the fugitives from Gorsuch's farm but also for themselves, their families, and others who shared their fate. In this war against slavery, there were no black noncombatants. Women, children, and elder members of the African-American community were fair game; and anyone who could use a corn knife or corn cutter—implements known as well to women as to men—was a welcome addition to the line of defense.[4]

Gorsuch favored ascending the stairs to confront his slaves. The marshal told him to stop until after the warrants were announced. Kline proclaimed the contents of the official documents three times; from upstairs came the sound of bullets being loaded into guns. The marshal finished reading the warrants with a flourish of bravado—"Now, you see, we are commanded to take you, dead or alive; so you may as well give up at once." Then the two men began again to climb the stairs.[5]

On the way up, Gorsuch shouted to "Nelson" that he had seen him outside, had watched him run into the house, and knew that he was still there. He promised the fugitive that if he would come down peaceably and return to Maryland, he would be treated just as well as he was before the four slaves had run away. There was no point to resistance, the master explained, since he had the proper authority and the force to back it up. He would not leave the premises without his property.[6]

Someone threw a sharp metal object—apparently a five-pronged fish "gig"—at the two slave catchers, who were sufficiently startled to descend the stairs and go back outside. There was an exchange of views, perhaps a debate of sorts, between the occupants of the first and second stories on the meaning of law, the nature of property, the equality of races, and biblical justifications for the respective actions of the two sides. "Do you call a nigger my brother?" shouted the incredulous slave owner.

"Yes," came the chorus of replies from upstairs. A hymn resounded from the second floor:

> Leader, what do you say about the judgment day? I will die on the field of battle, die on the field of battle, with glory in my soul.[7]

Parker presented himself at the window and asked if he was one of the fugitives sought by the posse. Gorsuch, who was now directly below him, answered no. Parker asked his brother-in-law to stand before the window. "Is this one of your men?" Parker asked. No was the reply again. "Abraham Johnson I called next," Parker remembered, "but Gorsuch said he was not his man."

> The only plan left was to call both Pinckney and Johnson again, for had I called the others, he would have recognized them, for they were his slaves. Abraham Johnson said, "Does such a shrivelled up old slaveholder as you own such a nice, genteel young man as I am?" At this Gorsuch took offence.[8]

The ruse did not fool the posse. Kline threatened to burn down the house, pretended to send a message to Lancaster for another hundred men, and continued to assert his authority under the government and the law. Gorsuch again encouraged the fugitives to surrender, promising what seemed to him an irresistible deal, a return to the "mild" form of slavery they had experienced on his farm before running away. When there was no response from upstairs, Gorsuch lost his temper and threatened "Josh" and "Nelson" with harsh retribution. Dickinson Gorsuch was getting more nervous as time passed and his father's temper flared, and eventually pleaded with Edward to back away from the house. The son later recalled the exchange: "I told my father we had better go, for they intended to murder the whole of us. He said it would not do to give it up that way." Parker saw fear etched in their faces. The tension was clearly draining the old man, whose countenance had cooled from fiery red to ashen white.[9]

Upstairs, Parker's wife asked if she should blow the horn to bring friends to assist them. "It was a custom with us," Parker later explained, "when a horn was blown at an unusual hour, to proceed to the spot promptly to see what was the matter." Eliza Parker first went up to the garret and sounded the horn. The posse became visibly nervous about what it might mean and, according to Parker, began to fire on his wife as she trumpeted the alarm. She came back from the attic, knelt below the window where the shots could not reach her, rested the horn on the sill, and "blew blast after blast, while the shots poured thick and fast around her." According to her husband, the posse fired ten or twelve times.[10]

Shots were definitely exchanged. It is not clear exactly how the shooting started. Each side, not surprisingly, blamed the other for firing the first shot. Parker insisted that the posse fired first, when his wife began blowing the horn. According to one of Gorsuch's sons, who got the story secondhand from members of the posse, the inhabitants of the house started the shooting:

> While they [Edward Gorsuch and Kline] were on the steps and intending to proceed, one of the negroes struck at them with a staff, shod with sharp iron. My father then turned and went out the door. Just as he got out a gun was fired at his head from one of the windows, but the aim was too high. The marshal coming out right behind him, fired his pistol in the window.[11]

According to one account, the shot from the upstairs window passed within inches of Edward Gorsuch's head. The skirmishing continued. A metal projectile flew out of an upstairs window and caught Dr. Pearce above the right eye. Pearce shot back, but the pistol misfired. A piece of wood also thrown from the second-floor window struck Joshua Gorsuch on the shoulder, but nothing decisive was happening. The battle between the posse and the occupants of the house was a stand-off as the sun rose over the horizon.[12]

At this point, the slave catchers might have withdrawn in safety, perhaps to seek reinforcements or to fight another day under more favorable conditions. Dickinson Gorsuch, the slaveholder's son, clearly favored this option; Kline apparently agreed. "Don't ask them to give up," Dickinson pleaded with his father and the marshal, "make them do it. We have money, and can call men to take them. What is it that money won't buy?" The value of the slaves was not the issue either to young Gorsuch or to his father. They agreed that money was no object, but at this point the father's sense of honor would not permit him to leave the field of battle, even in a strategic withdrawal. "I will have my property or die in the attempt," the stubborn slave owner insisted. "My property I will have, or I'll breakfast in hell."[13]

Those inside the house wanted time to consider the posse's terms of surrender—"Josh" and "Nelson" turned over, the others to go free. They asked for ten or fifteen minutes to deliberate their fate. When the time was up, they asked for and were granted another five minutes. The posse believed that the fugitives were about to give up. Perhaps the carrot extended by Gorsuch was working—his promise to the two fugitives of no retribution and a return to the former conditions of their enslavement on his farm; or, maybe the posse's collection of sticks had struck fear into the blacks—the authority of the law, the threat to burn down the house, the fabricated note beckoning reinforcements from Lancaster. In retrospect, it looks as if the slave catchers were wrong, that they held out false hopes and misjudged the people upstairs. Those in the house were just stalling for time until friends could respond to the summons of the horn.[14]

Before the five minutes elapsed, people began arriving from every direction. Those inside the house saw Noah Buley, another of Gorsuch's escaped slaves, ride up on a gray horse, and more African-Americans were coming across the fields singly and in small groups. Almost all were armed, some with pistols, shot guns, or hunting rifles; others carried corn cutters, scythes, or other farm tools that would serve nicely as swords in hand-to-hand combat. At least one had a rock that he picked up en route. Zeke Thompson, called the "Indian negro," had a scythe in one hand and a revolver in the other.[15]

Not all the arrivals were black, and not all came on foot.[16] Castner Hanway, the white miller who lived right down the road, was among the first to arrive on his sturdy work horse. In retrospect, there seems nothing suspicious about Hanway's early arrival. He was the Parkers' closest neighbor, and he rode, while most of the others came from longer distances on foot. Not much information survives about the miller's life up to this point, because he led an ordinary existence and was not in the habit of recording his actions or thoughts.

We do know that Hanway had lived in the Christiana area for only a few months. A native of Delaware, his family had moved to Chester County, Pennsylvania, when he was five years old and then to Maryland for a while, before leaving for an unspecified western state. About three years prior to the riot, as a man in his early thirties, Hanway had returned to Chester County. There he married and then moved across the Lancaster County line to practice his trade as a miller. He was a man of no obvious distinction in life, who devoted most of his time to making a living and who was often covered with the white dust of his trade. If he went to church, we do not know which one. There is no record of how, or even whether, he voted; and if he had strong political views to this point in his life, either no one took note or Hanway kept them to himself. He had dark hair, which tended to curl on the sides and the top of his head, a receding hairline, and a beard (Figure 4.1). Nothing was extraordinary about Hanway, either physically or in the way that he lived his life. He was a quiet, unobtrusive man, who apparently got along well with his new neighbors, white and black. He seems to have been a good person, who had no ambitions to be great in the eyes of anybody else.[17]

That morning, Hanway was just sitting down to his breakfast, when his hired man informed him that Elijah Lewis was outside in the road. When Hanway came out and asked what was the matter, Lewis, who was a white storekeeper and the local postmaster, told him that "William Parker's house was surrounded by kidnappers, who were going to take him." Hanway went back inside, gulped down some food, and grabbed his straw hat. He was not feeling too well, so he decided to ride a horse rather than walk with Lewis the half mile to Parker's. Hanway was dressed that morning in the work clothes that marked his profession even to those who never saw the man before. "He looked like a miller," Marshal Kline would testify later.[18]

We do not know what was going through Hanway's mind as he rode down the lane that fronted Parker's house. It was not his fight, and he carried no weapons. Perhaps he hoped to mediate the dispute, to convince the blacks to desist from violence and the posse to withdraw before blood was shed. Possibly he was curious, wanted to check the slave catch-

F I G U R E 4.1. Castner Hanway (*with permission of the Lancaster County Historical Society*)

ers' authority, or merely hoped to witness events as a check on the posse's behavior or in case any of the blacks got themselves in trouble.

In any event, Hanway arrived on the scene even before Lewis, who was making his way across the fields on foot. Lewis, just as Hanway, had started his day with nothing more in mind than plying his trade. Neither the shopkeeper nor the miller had plotted a confrontation at Parker's or had any advance warning of what was to come, although either or both may have heard the news about slave catchers delivered the previous day. Lewis himself was just opening the door of his shop, in ignorance of the unfolding drama, when an African-American farmer named Isaiah Clarkson came up and told him about the "kidnappers." The message was that they were trying to take Parker away, a misunderstanding of the actual circumstances. Clarkson insisted that Lewis must go with him "to see that justice was done." Lewis followed Clarkson, stopping first at Hanway's, which was on the way, then passing a black man named Jacob Woods. "Mr. Lewis came to me where I was working at," Woods later recalled; "I was just putting the chain to harrow; he said William Parker's house was surrounded by kidnappers, and it was no time to take up potatoes." So Lewis was recruiting supporters for the fugitives on his way to the scene.[19]

At the time, the appearance of the white men, first Hanway on his horse and then Lewis shortly behind, seemed to the posse more than a coincidence of timing. After all, on the heels of Hanway's arrival armed blacks were coming from every direction, emerging from the woods and the fields and walking down the lane. In the space of half an hour, there would be somewhere between seventy-five and a hundred and fifty black men and women on the scene, at least fifty of them with guns.[20] To the Gorsuches, who had a low opinion of African-Americans' intelligence and capacity for organizing themselves, Hanway was obviously the "leader" of Lancaster's resistance to the Fugitive Slave Law. "His presence inspired the blacks," J. S. Gorsuch reported a few days later; when Hanway arrived, "they immediately raised a shout, and became confirmed in their opposition."[21]

To the marshal, Hanway and Lewis initially seemed potential allies; after all, they were white like the posse, and the miscreants were black. When Kline saw the miller, he walked over to Hanway's horse and began to discuss the situation. The marshal's testimony on the contents of this conversation varied with each retelling and seems questionable in every version. Since Hanway never gave his account of the discussion, we have only the bits and pieces of what other people thought that they saw and heard in the midst of an increasingly riotous scene.[22]

All sources agree that Kline identified himself as a United States marshal and began to discuss the situation with Hanway when Lewis walked up. "This is the marshal," Hanway explained by way of introduction. Lewis asked if the lawman had shown him papers documenting the posse's authority. Hanway answered no. When Lewis asked, Kline produced the warrants, which Hanway read before passing them on. Lewis had left his eyeglasses at home, so he had trouble reading anything but the signature, which was larger than the type. "I saw the name of Edward D. Ingraham," the federal commissioner, Lewis later testified, "and took it for granted by that, that he had authority." According to Lewis,

> We had some conversation; he wanted us to assist in arresting somebody, I don't know who, and as near as I can recollect the reply of

Castner Hanway, he said he would have nothing to do with it, or something to that effect.[23]

Dr. Pearce, a member of the Gorsuch party, heard Hanway say to the marshal, "You had better go home; you need not come here to make arrests; you cannot do it." Pearce then heard the miller say something that he could not entirely make out. "I could not hear that distinctly," Edward Gorsuch's nephew later testified, "except the word blood; the marshal then told him he would hold him responsible."[24]

By this time a number of black men were milling around the three whites. Lewis later remembered that the blacks had guns and threatened to shoot the marshal and his men:

> Castner Hanway was sitting on his horse, and he beckoned with his arm (hand), "Don't shoot! Don't shoot! For God's sake, don't shoot!"

Hanway and Lewis certainly advised the marshal to leave with his posse or blood would be shed; whether in the exact words remembered by Pearce we cannot know for sure, any more than we can recover the tone in which the advice was given. Pearce and the marshal remembered an aggressive edge to the advice. Lewis recalled the circumstances and considered the warning an act of goodwill delivered by a very nervous miller, who probably feared for his own life. According to Nathan Nelson, another member of the posse, "I said to him [Hanway] or he said to me rather, that he didn't think we could do anything. I said I didn't think we could. Those were the words as well as I can recollect."[25]

Kline was angry with the unarmed miller and shopkeeper for not helping to arrest the fugitives and told them they were committing a federal crime by refusing to assist him. "I told him [Hanway], what the act of Congress was as near as I could tell him," the marshal later testified in court. "That any person aiding or abetting a fugitive slave, and resisting an officer, the punishment was $1,000 damages for the slave, and I think to the best of my knowledge imprisonment for five years." All the while the white men were talking, African-Americans continued to arrive and were nervously pacing up and down the lane, priming their weapons, brandishing them in mock battle, actually pointing them at members of the posse, and waiting for something to occur. After talking to the marshal, Hanway and Lewis explained the situation to several of the black men standing in the lane, informing them that the warrants appeared to be legal and that they would be making a mistake to resist the posse, and advised them to disperse without shedding blood. "Don't shoot! Don't shoot!" another witness heard Hanway say again.[26]

Kline shouted to the rest of the posse that it was time to withdraw, explaining briefly that he would hold Hanway responsible for Gorsuch's "property." It is not clear exactly why the miller alone was fixed with blame rather than both Hanway and Lewis. Probably it was because Hanway got to Parker's first and arrived on a horse, evoking the sort of military image associated with being in charge. Kline called out to the Gorsuches, "come on now, your property is secured to you, provided this man is worth it." In other words, Edward Gorsuch could recoup the value of his fugitive slaves in a federal court, since the marshal would testify that the posse's inability to capture Nelson and Josh was a consequence of Hanway's refusal to help enforce the law. The miller would be liable to the limit of his financial worth for the value of the two slaves. Again, Kline misunderstood Edward Gorsuch's temperament, his reason for being at Parker's that day, and his refusal to leave the grounds even though the posse was now outnumbered by as much as ten or twenty to one. It was not money; it was honor, which could only be recovered by return of the slaves to his farm.[27]

Two of the Marylanders—apparently Nathan Nelson and Nicholas Hutchins—joined the marshal immediately. Dr. Pearce recognized that Edward Gorsuch had not heard, or at least not responded to, Kline's instructions: "I then went to my uncle and told him of the necessity of retiring, from the party outside not allowing us to make arrests." Pearce turned from the house and started toward the Long Lane with, he thought, his uncle right behind him. When he looked around a moment later, Pearce saw that Gorsuch had changed his mind and was headed back to Parker's house.[28]

People were running this way and that, shouting, gesticulating, but the crowd had no focus for its energy, which was still that of individuals rather than of a mob. The trigger that would unleash the anger at a distinct target was yet to be pulled. The rage was as palpable as the mist rising from the ground. Kline was mad at Hanway and Lewis; Gorsuch was furious with his fugitive slaves. Other members of the posse were angry at all of them—at Kline for his incompetence; at Lewis and Hanway, whom they assumed were abolitionist agitators, for refusing to help; and probably even at Edward Gorsuch, their kinsman and friend, for stubbornly refusing to acknowledge the danger faced by them all. The anger of Parker and the other blacks on the field had grown from a multitude of seeds—some of them planted in slavery and nurtured with whips and harsh words, many of them transplanted in the racist soil of the North by people who hoped for better than they got and received less than they deserved, and even a few seedlings of hatred fertilized on that very day by the slave catchers.

The catalyst for violence, the lightning bolt that started the riotous blaze, was a confrontation between Gorsuch and the man known in freedom as Samuel Thompson, one of the fugitives from his farm. Both men were angry by the time that Parker overheard part of their verbal exchange: "Old man, you had better go home to Maryland," said Samuel. "You had better give up, and come home with me," said Gorsuch. Thompson then knocked his former master on the side of the head with a pistol, which felled him to his knees. When the slave owner tried to rise from the ground, he was clubbed again, perhaps a couple of times. Thompson shot him once, then several others poured more bullets into the body, and in what by this time was probably a purely symbolic gesture, an unspecified number of participants whacked him across the top of the head with corn cutters, emulating the scalping of a fallen enemy from another cultural tradition of American violence.[29]

When Dickinson Gorsuch rushed to the aid of his father, someone struck the pistol from his hand with a club. Parker's brother-in-law then unloaded his shotgun at short range into the slave owner's son. Doctors later removed over seventy shot from young Gorsuch's right side and arm. According to the slave catchers' chronicler, by this time

> the negroes were whooping and yelling with savage glee over their victims, and the son, nephew and cousin started [running], to save their lives. . . . Dickinson, staggering under the stunning effects of his wounds, blood gushing from his mouth and streaming from his arm and side, took the southern end of the lane, and, in a distance of a hundred yards, reached the end of the wood, falling down by a large stump, exhausted.

Dickinson lay there for a considerable time, clinging to life by a thread. When he looked up, there was a white man standing over him, whom he asked to hold up his head. Although he made the request a number of times, the man did not touch him or make any move. Then Dickinson told the man he was thirsty and wanted a drink. "After asking him several times, he went and got me some water." At the time, young Gorsuch did not know the name of the man who silently helped him. Later, he identified Joseph Scarlett as the man. Parker said it was his landlord, Levi Pownall.[30]

In the heat of a riot, names, faces, facts, and sequences of events become a jumble. The actions of some are lost in the rush; others, who were surely not even there, are remembered clearly for their valor or cowardice in battle. Perhaps it was Pownall or Scarlett or somebody else who helped the wounded Marylander. In any event, it is fortunate that Dickinson Gorsuch got the water, because he was very badly hurt. By another account, some of the rioters followed young Gorsuch to his resting place, "but an old negro, who had been in the affray, threw himself over the body, and called upon them for God's sake to assist him, for he would die soon anyhow." So perhaps there were two samaritans—one white and one black.[31]

None who saw him in the hours immediately following the battle believed that Dickinson could possibly survive, with blood "gushing from his mouth and streaming from his side." Some "gentlemen" came and gently removed him to the Pownalls' house, where it was the opinion of an attending physician that the heir to Retreat Farm and Edward Gorsuch's slaves would not live through the night. But Dickinson lay there in a critical condition for a number of days. A week later, his brother would write that because of the charity of the people who owned the house, the good medical care of his physician, and the blessing of God, Dickinson still lived, "and we now have strong hopes of his recovery." It was three weeks and a day before the patient was strong enough to leave his bed (Figure 4.2). Between two and three months after suffering the wounds, Dickinson reported that "I have a pain in my side—it hurts me to take a long breath, and it hurts me very much to cough."[32]

When the shooting began, Elijah Lewis started down the lane toward the creek; Kline, behind him some distance, headed in the same direction. Kline caught up with Nicholas Hutchins and asked him to follow Lewis, to see where he went. All that the shopkeeper and Hutchins could see over the top of the cornfield was smoke from the shooting; all they could hear was the explosion of weapons and the shouts of the mob.[33]

Hanway was headed in the other direction. Why had Lewis and Hanway left as the shooting began? "Our object being accomplished," Lewis explained, "—to ascertain that there was authority there, we had no further business." Why did they not go back to assist those injured during the riot? "It is a hard question to answer," Lewis replied. Simply put, they were scared.[34]

After Dr. Pearce saw the apparently lifeless body of Edward Gorsuch on the ground, and after he witnessed the slave owner's son Dickinson being struck with a club and riddled with squirrel shot, Pearce elbowed his way through the crowd, jumped the fence, and ran down the lane toward Joshua Gorsuch, who was standing beside Hanway's horse. In the course of his escape from the mob, Pearce was shot at any number of

FIGURE 4.2. Dickinson Gorsuch (*with permission of the Lancaster County Historical Society*)

times. Later, he estimated that there were between twenty and thirty holes in his clothes; how many of these were from bullets and how many from scattershot he did not say. A pistol bullet had passed through his hat, luckily leaving only a scalp burn where it grazed his skull. Another bullet hit him squarely in the wrist, two more lodged in his spine, and a fifth in his shoulder blade.[35]

Joshua Gorsuch had also run for his life after seeing what the mob did to his cousin Edward. While he was watching the murder of his kinsman, someone beat Joshua over the head with a club. He fired his pistol in return, to what effect he could not tell. "All this time a thought flashed over my mind that I should run. I didn't have any idea of getting farther from where I stood, for I found they were determined to kill me. I ran, and they made after me," Joshua explained, in a still-muddled way, after the event. He ran even before Dickinson arrived to try to assist his father, passing him on the way without uttering a word:

> I jumped over into the lane then, threw my eyes both ways immediately and discovered on the right, a number of colored persons, and on the other side, some whites, but didn't notice who. I ran down, then, through the long lane, they hollering from behind me, "kill him," "kill him," and every one apparently that could get a lick at me, struck me. There was a man come riding by and I asked him to let me get up behind him. I said for God's sake don't let them kill me.[36]

Pearce, Joshua Gorsuch, and Hanway were all there together in the lane. Joshua was addled from so many blows to the head; Pearce was bleeding; and the three men were frightened by the bedlam around them. Pearce was trotting alongside the horse, trying to keep it between himself and a group of armed blacks on the other side of the lane; Joshua was running behind, trying to grab the tail or Hanway's leg to pull himself up behind the rider. And Hanway was just trying to get away without getting killed. The posse members were putting him in the line of fire.[37]

Hanway was a miller, not a warrior, not a hero, but an average man who was beside himself with fear. Pearce told people after the riot that Hanway used his horse to shield him from a group of rioters who pursued him down the lane. Hanway may have saved his life, Pearce told someone later that day. Parker remembered it the same way: Hanway "rode between the fugitive and the Doctor, to shield him. . . . if it had not been for Hanway, he would have been killed." Then one of the rioters chasing Pearce told Hanway to "get out of the way or he would forfeit his life." Hanway took the warning seriously and panicked, as many men would. Maybe he reasoned coldly that these slave catchers were not worth the risk. Whatever his thinking, if rational calculation was even involved, Hanway seized the reins of his horse, gave the animal a good kick in the ribs, and rode off at a gallop, leaving Pearce and Joshua Gorsuch in the lane to face their enemies alone.[38]

The two men continued to run down the lane, hotly pursued by a number of the rioters. As Pearce recounted the scene, "I ran with Joshua for a time, but finding that they were overtaking us rapidly, I ran off as quick as possible, and left Joshua behind." When he looked back, Pearce saw that the rioters had caught up with Joshua, and one of them was beating him over the head with a gun. Pearce made it safely to the field and continued on his way. Somehow Joshua also got away. Perhaps the rioters who caught him had run out of ammunition; possibly they had vented their anger and, mercifully, let the slave catcher get away. Parker's explanation for why the rioters did not kill more white men may be sufficient to explain Joshua's escape: "Our guns got bent and out of order. So damaged did they become, that we could shoot with but two or three of them. Samuel Thompson bent his gun on old Mr. Gorsuch so badly, that it was of no use to us." [39]

As Joshua, the retired sea captain and now innkeeper, wandered away from the scene, he had the good fortune to meet up with Kline. "I was knocked out of my mind," he later recalled. "He was as crazy as a bed bug," according to the marshal. Joshua thought he was within a few miles of home but could not find a familiar lane. Kline took the confused man by the arm and led him to within a mile of Penningtonville, where he got them both some water. This refreshed Joshua and helped restore his memory of where he was and what had just happened. [40]

The two slave catchers could find no one willing to help them. A man who initially agreed to take them into Penningtonville returned the dollar that he had accepted as payment and said that he had changed his mind. We cannot know whether his neighbors convinced the man that he had made a mistake trafficking with "kidnappers," or whether he realized that on his own. No one would help them find a doctor, rent them a horse, or give them a ride. So the two men walked to the next village, where the marshal put Joshua on a train. Relatives in York would take the man in and assist in the recovery of his health. It was fortunate for Joshua that he was wearing a heavy fur hat lined with handkerchiefs when the rioters beat him over the head. As it was, he would suffer headaches and other symptoms of brain damage long after the riot. [41]

Kline could find no doctor in Penningtonville willing to assist wounded members of the posse. He offered five dollars apiece to anyone who would fetch Edward Gorsuch from the riot scene. Finally, two men with a wagon agreed to run the errand, provided that Kline stayed behind. They feared for their safety if caught in the company of the slave-catching marshal. Kline hung out in the tavern for about an hour and a half until word got back to him that Gorsuch was dead and the body was being transported to Christiana for a coroner's inquest. The marshal attended the inquest, which he thought quite irregular because no testimony was taken and no one wanted to hear his account of the murder. Afterwards, Kline arranged for a coffin and shroud and had the body sent back to Maryland on the evening train.[42]

Some sources suggest that Edward Gorsuch was still alive a few minutes after the shooting ended. According to Parker, "the women put an end to him."[43] As the story was told in a number of versions, a sizable sum of money—in excess of three hundred dollars—was taken from the corpse and divided among the women who gathered in a circle around the slain "kidnapper." Several Northern papers reported that, after the riot, blacks had mutilated the corpse. According to Southern sources, the African-American women ceremoniously hacked the body to a bloody pulp with corn cutters before they were through. By at least one retelling, they even unbuttoned Gorsuch's trousers and chopped off his penis. This last detail was not reported in the papers, nor were the effects of mutilation described in official documents associated with the investigation and trial. The original source is not identifiable, but it was widely believed in the South. The governor of Maryland, for example, referred to the mutilation of Gorsuch's body in his annual address to the state legislature the following year. Although we cannot know whether the rumor is literally accurate, it is certain that the retelling rang true to those who clamored for judicial revenge.[44]

There is no questioning the larger truth, however, that black people organized and fought for their freedom at Eliza and William Parker's house that day. The warning of the slave catchers' arrival was delivered by a black man at the behest of a committee of black Philadelphians.[45] Other African-Americans spread the message throughout the countryside. It was the seven black people inside the Parkers' home who held off the posse, trumpeted the alarm, and refused to surrender. African-Americans, perhaps as many as a hundred or more, responded to the call, engaged the "kidnappers" in pitched battle, and won.

The African-Americans of Lancaster County were victims, to be sure—most were victims of poverty, ignorance, and lack of professional skills. Many were still victims of the slavery that they had escaped and of the law that supported claims against their freedom. All of them were victims of racism, which severely restricted their ability to rise above the social status that they endured.

None of the blacks at the Parkers' that morning were merely victims, though. They were not simply resigned to their fate—passive, depressed, incapable of challenging the injustice they suffered. Victimage was not their only status or their sole way of viewing their relationship with the wider world. They were capable people, courageous, and blessed with faith that the world could change for them and their children. They had vivid imaginations, which enabled them to envision a world different from the one they knew, unlike one that had ever existed in this country or, indeed, on the face of this earth. Not only could they picture a better world, but they were prepared to risk their lives, die if need be, to bring it about.

The character of African-Americans who lived in Lancaster County was not limited to the stereotypes portrayed in local newspapers. There were courageous fugitives who had the capacity for independent planning and action. There were free black men and women who rose above the squalor of poverty with honor, intelligence, and skill. These were the people who set the stage for challenges to the slave system. They were the ones who knew how to defend themselves when danger arose. To be sure, Lancaster's African-American community also had its share of cowards, drunks, and Judases. But what race or class of humans does not suffer the same misfortune? The story of the Christiana Riot and of the antebellum experience of Lancaster's black community is not solely, or even primarily, a story of cowardice, incapacitating depression, and betrayal. The African-Americans of Lancaster County were not merely victims of the injustices they endured. Sympathetic whites provided crucial, perhaps on occasion even indispensable, aid. But the blacks of the region were no more the tools of the white people who helped them than Joshua Hammond, Nelson Ford, and Noah Buley were the slaves of the corpse that was riding the rails back to Baltimore as the sun set on what had been a very bloody day.[46]

Aftermath

THE DAY AFTER THE CHRISTIANA RIOT was the hottest one in a very hot month. Thermometers in Philadelphia registered ninety-four degrees at 2 p.m. It was not only hot but also still incredibly dry; and September would be the driest month of the drought-plagued summer of 1851. The soil was parched; springs were unusually low; and the navigation of major rivers was, as one newspaper reported, "considerably impeded." Mills, such as Castner Hanway's, were forced to close part of the time for lack of water to propel the wheels. Farmers postponed sowing winter wheat and rye because of the lack of necessary moisture to germinate the seed, which would undoubtedly affect the size of next spring's crop. Pastures, too, the newspapers reported, "have ceased to be green; wells that have not before been known to fail are dry, and cattle are driven several miles for water."[1]

Leaves were falling prematurely; by the end of the month many trees were already bare. Worse yet, the heat of July and August was now replaced by conditions that were, for farmers, worse yet. September was a month of extremes, with records set for both high and low temperatures. Within the two-week period immediately following the riot, there was a swing of almost fifty degrees. Ice actually formed in some low-lying areas of the countryside.

Edward Gorsuch missed the record-setting heat of September 12 and the cold snap that followed on its heels. The last view he got of this world was of a parched landscape that looked, sounded, and smelled strikingly similar to home. The fugitives from his farm, along with the Parkers and Pinckneys, ran north as the leaves were falling from the trees. The last sensory perceptions of Lancaster County they had were of dry cornstalks rasping in the breeze, shorter by a full foot than they should have been at that time of year; of dust where there might have been mud; of brown instead of green vegetation. No, they would not harvest the crops that they had tended this year. They would not plant next spring's wheat and rye. They would not sleep another night in the stone house or walk again down the Long Lane to the creek. Their lives as fugitives would continue, on the run to another, safer, haven. Like Gorsuch, one of the last things they saw in Lancaster County was blood—the blood that literally ran from the "kidnapper's" body and that made small puddles, where in other Septembers rain might have gathered to soak the parched earth. At least figuratively, the blood was also on their hands.

The blood that was spilled on that hot September day in 1851 was the blood of white men. Several of the rioters were injured, but none very badly. Only two of the African-Americans required medical attention, which was furnished by Dr. Augustus Cain, a local physician sympathetic to their cause. "Of our party, only two were wounded," according to William Parker.

> One received a ball in his hand, near the wrist; but it only entered the skin, and he pushed it out with his thumb. Another received a ball in the fleshy part of his thigh, which had to be extracted; but neither of them were sick or crippled by the wounds.[2]

After consulting with family and friends, the fugitives from slavery and justice determined to split up into small groups. To his great sadness, William Parker decided that it was best to leave Eliza and their children behind for a while, at least until things quieted down. The children would slow the pace of escape, call unwanted attention to the group, and compromise the ability of the adults to defend themselves if confronted by bounty hunters on the road. Initially, a thousand dollars was offered for the capture of Parker; later he heard there was a two thousand dollar reward on the fugitives' heads.

So William struck out for Canada in the company of Alexander Pinckney and Abraham Johnson. The fugitives from Gorsuch's farm traveled separately, successfully eluding detection and making it safely to freedom. Parker's trio hid at a friend's house until 9 p.m. on the night of the riot.[3] They had a couple close brushes with posses at the beginning of their journey but then traveled the five hundred miles to Rochester, New York, without incident, part of the way on foot and the rest by a variety of public and private conveyances, including train and a horse-drawn coach.

The three men reached Rochester two days after leaving Lancaster

County and arrived simultaneously with the publication of stories about the riot and their escape in the New York newspapers. At Rochester, they landed on the doorstep of Frederick Douglass, Parker's acquaintance from their days as Maryland slaves. The fugitives were exhausted and dirty from their travels. After exchanging greetings with their host, they retired to wash the dust from themselves and their clothes. Before they were even done brushing out their hair, Parker and his traveling companions began receiving admirers who wanted to hear details about the riot and their escape. At last, mercifully, they were permitted to withdraw for some much-needed sleep. Then the host went to work in his guests' behalf. As Douglass recounted the scene in his autobiography, the three fugitives burdened him with a dangerous responsibility:

> The work of getting these men safely into Canada was a delicate one. They were not only fugitives from slavery but charged with murder, and officers were in pursuit of them. . . . The hours they spent at my house were therefore hours of anxiety as well as activity.[4]

Douglass asked a friend to travel the three miles to the Genesee River and inquire when the next steamer would depart for any destination in Canada. She returned with the good news that a ship would be leaving for Toronto that very day. "This fact, however, did not end my anxiety," Douglass recalled:

> There was danger that between my house and the landing or at the landing itself we might meet with trouble. Indeed the landing was the place where trouble was likely to occur if at all. As patiently as I could, I waited for the shades of night to come on, and then put the men in my "Democrat carriage," and started for the landing on the Genesee. It was an exciting ride, and somewhat speedy withal. We reached the boat at least fifteen minutes before the time of its departure, and that without remark or molestation. But those fifteen minutes seemed much longer than usual.[5]

Douglass remained on board until the last possible moment and then shook hands with the three men. As a token of appreciation, Parker presented his friend with the pistol that had fallen from the hand of a dying Edward Gorsuch. It was a "momento of the battle for liberty at Christiana," which Douglass greatly appreciated. In his eyes, the fugitives who were sailing off to new lives in Canada that night had, along with the rescuers of Jerry at Syracuse, inflicted fatal wounds on the fugitive slave bill. It became thereafter almost a dead letter, for slave-holders found that not only did it fail to put them in possession of their slaves, but that the attempt to enforce it brought odium upon themselves and weakened the slave system.[6]

According to this famous black abolitionist, "the thing which more than all else destroyed the fugitive law was the resistance made to it by the fugitives themselves." These three African-Americans and those who fought along with them had engaged in a battle for freedom comparable in significance to the Minute Men's engagement of British troops at Lexington and Concord over seventy-five years before. Like their predecessors in the War for Independence, Parker and the heroic black men and women who had fought at his side had won a signal victory in the war for the liberty of their race. These people were heroes in the eyes of many African-Americans and those sympathetic to their battle for freedom, not villains who should be jailed or executed for their violent deeds.[7]

Once the ship cast off from shore, the glow of the hero's welcome that they had received in Rochester quickly faded for the three fugitives, and the reality of their situation began to sink in. They had little money, no real plan for what to do next, no one to greet and guide them on their way. After reaching the Canadian shore and walking around Kingston hoping to see a friendly black face, Parker saw a man he had known back in Maryland as a slave. First, the man claimed not to recognize him, then succumbed to a sense of guilt, bought the three fugitives a meal, but did not invite them to his home. "How different the treatment received from this man," Parker recalled, "—himself an exile for the sake of liberty, and in its full enjoyment on free soil—and the self-sacrificing spirit of our Rochester colored brother, who made haste to welcome us to his ample home."[8]

It could have been lack of trust, lack of charity, or a failure of nerve that led Parker's acquaintance to leave the three men to fend for themselves. To be fair to the man, economic conditions were even worse for blacks in Canada than they were back in Lancaster County. The burden of three more people in need of help may just have been more than the man could bear. Perhaps Parker and his companions also reminded the man of a past that he was trying to forget; or maybe he was embarrassed by his less than "ample" house. It is possible, of course, that he was afraid to welcome the fugitives into his home—scared of lawmen; frightened by Parker, Pinckney, and Johnson themselves; or just plain reluctant to risk the little he had for yet three more among the thousands of African-Americans who were crossing the border to freedom. There was, after all, an attempt in progress to locate the murderers of Edward Gorsuch and extradite them back to the United States to be tried for their crime, so anyone who harbored the fugitives would be taking a risk.

In any event, it took the fugitives three weeks after they arrived in Toronto to find work that produced a meaningful income. "Sometimes we would secure a small job, worth two or three shillings, and sometimes a smaller one, worth not more than one shilling; and these not oftener than once or twice in a week." To add to his misery, Parker missed his family and had good reason to worry about their fate. For a month he received no answer to his letters but heard rumors about the capture of his wife.[9]

Back in Lancaster County, Eliza Parker, her mother, and other black residents also felt like anything but heroes. Eliza planned to make her way north with the children, to travel the back roads by night and hide her brood in haystacks and barns during the day, as her husband and his companions had done so successfully before her. According to her husband, she "had a very bad time. Twice they had her in custody; and, a third time, her young master came after her, which obliged her to flee before day, so that the children had to remain behind for the time." Cassandra Harris, Eliza's mother, was again called on to care for her three grandchildren.[10]

The strain was too much for the grandmother, whom everyone knew as Cassy. She was frightened by the violence, afraid for her family, sickened by the bloodshed, and unhappy with the trials that "freedom" brought into her life. By one account, she tried to convince her sons to turn themselves in after the riot, to return with her to the "master" whom they had fled in Maryland, and give up this hideous existence as fugitives in the North. The men tried to explain to their mother that, as bad as it was, they preferred their current condition to even the mildest form of slavery known in the South. They told their mother that as long as they drew breath, they had no intention of returning to Maryland as slaves. The sons then left her to make their escape, as did her sons-in-law Parker and Pinckney. When Cassy's daughters also left her behind to care for the small children, one of whom became extremely ill with the measles, the old woman apparently got very depressed.

According to some sources, the lawmen who swept down on Lancaster in a frantic attempt to capture Cassandra Harris's family tried, successfully it seems, to scare the poor grandmother to distraction. The white men swore in graphic detail that she and her children faced a certain death on the gallows unless the whole group surrendered to the law. The threats were obviously intended to extract information from Cassy about the location of her fugitive family. She very well may have tried to help the lawmen in her emotionally disturbed state of mind, but she knew nothing about her children's places of hiding or the routes they were taking to escape from the country. Her daughters and sons had left her behind without the resources or information she needed to join them in their new life to the north. Perhaps she just needed to wait calmly and with a little patience until things were safe; but they had run away once before, when they left their mother in slavery, without telling her where or how to find them, and without so much as a word to ease her mind.

One newspaper said that federal officers arrested Cassy Harris; another reported that she turned herself in. One report described in vivid detail her experiences in Philadelphia after she was taken to the city by lawmen, was released on her own, and then begged Commissioner Ingraham and a federal marshal to help her return to her master. By a contradictory account, she never left Lancaster until a hearing before Commissioner Ingraham determined her fate. Either way, it is clear that the law had no regard for the welfare of the children in their grandmother's care.

According to the *Philadelphia Bulletin,* this thoroughly frightened and depressed woman was left to wander around the neighborhood of the federal courthouse in Philadelphia, apparently without funds or the means to get back to her grandchildren in Lancaster. If the story is true, it is possible to imagine some of the sources of Cassy's despair. She was a country woman from the South; almost certainly illiterate, she had seldom or never before been to the city and did not even have the price of a ticket had she been able to figure out how to get home. Her children were gone; she was far from home and deeply worried about her sick granddaughter.

As the *Bulletin* reported the story, Cassandra Harris walked up to the federal commissioner for fugitive slaves, whom she saw standing outside the courthouse on the corner of Seventh and Chestnut. She stood politely beside Commissioner Ingraham, who was talking with an acquaintance, and when he did not acknowledge her presence, she tapped him on the arm. Once she got Ingraham's attention, Harris said that she knew who he was and stated plainly that she wished to return to her master *immediately,* as she was "in a hurry." The commissioner was somewhat taken aback; no fugitive had ever asked to be enslaved, that was not a function the law and his authority were intended to accommodate. The idea was that blacks would be captured and brought to his hearing room by force. Once their identity was established to his satisfaction, despite their protests and denials, they would be involuntarily transported south.

If we can credit the *Bulletin's* account, Ingraham must have been thoroughly baffled by this encounter. Harris's request was unprecedented in his experience and ran counter to all his knowledge of fugitive mentality. He probably thought that the old woman was a little bit off mentally, and that may even have been temporarily true. According to this newspaper, and others that reprinted the story, Ingraham explained to the woman that she would first have to find a federal marshal who would present her "case" in the usual way and, he might have added, ensure through proper procedure that the commissioner received his fee as called for in the Fugitive Slave Law. This had to be done formally and correctly, all according to the book. Harris was not to be put off easily and asked directions to the marshal's office, which she found and where she made the same demand.

A hearing was scheduled and held—whether at Cassy's request or by force, in Philadelphia or Lancaster, it is difficult to tell. Members of the Pennsylvania Abolition Society were present at the hearing to ensure the legality of the proceedings, and three attorneys served as counsel for the self-accused fugitive. Harris told her story in specific and credible detail. She was the slave of Mr. Albert Davis of Harford County, Maryland. About five years previously, she explained (it had actually been eight), on Easter day, her sons were given a holiday by their kindly master. Taking advantage of this lenity, the two young men ran north to Pennsylvania, where they were later joined by their sisters in what must have been a carefully planned escape. When the master found out about the betrayal, he blamed Cassy and said that she must have known what was going on and should have talked her children out of it or, failing that, informed him of the planned escape. He was sure that she must know the whereabouts of the fugitives, and when she insisted that she did not, he dismissed her from his farm and ordered her not to return without her children in tow.

Harris then hit the road north, a slave banished from her slavery, no longer wanted by a master who believed that the betrayal by her biological kin justified his anger at the woman who had nursed him and other children of the Davis family as well as her own. Since there is some dispute about her age—reported as either fifty-one or between sixty and seventy at the time of the riot—it is not certain whether young Master Davis dismissed Harris while she was still a productive working slave or after she had passed an age of real usefulness. Evidence from the 1850 census and the age of at least one of her daughters (Eliza was twenty-one) make it most likely that Cassandra Harris was about forty-three at the time she was ordered off the Davis farm, perhaps having just passed her child-bearing years and therefore of less value as a slave.

In the eyes of the master, a contract of trust and mutual interest was broken by the ungrateful young slaves, who did not appreciate his kindness and how good a life they led on his farm. Better to be done with the lot of them, he reasoned, than to keep the one whom he held responsible for the rest. Cassy Harris would find out the meaning of liberty for herself. The children would have to support themselves and their mother, and the whole family make their own way in the harsh winters of Northern freedom. The mother "kotched up" with her fugitive children in Lancaster County after a year of wandering about the countryside, begging for handouts, in search of the offspring who had left her behind. Now again after the riot, she told the white men in the hearing room, her children had deserted her, and she wanted to go back to the land of her birth.

A neighbor of the young master in question interviewed the fugitive and testified before the hearing that he recognized Harris and that he had established her identity beyond a doubt by asking for details about the Davis family and their Harford County farm. According to the master's representative, Davis had softened on the question of taking Harris back after hearing about her story and desire to return. He was now willing to find a place for her—not on his own farm but as a family nurse to another member of the Davis clan.

No other evidence of ownership was presented, no deed or will indicating that Harris's enslavement had passed from father to son. The testimony of the slave herself and of the master's friend from Harford County seemed *prima facie* evidence of her status and more than enough to satisfy the law. Generally, of course, Commissioner Ingraham dismissed the testimony of the alleged fugitives before him out-of-hand as self-interested and therefore totally unreliable. But this was a special case in any number of ways; a fugitive who wanted to give up her freedom was a political coup for friends of the Fugitive Slave Law, for defenders of the slave system, and for all those who hoped that the Compromise of 1850 would work.

Lawyers for the fugitive were also faced with an unfamiliar situation as the *Bulletin* reported the scene. They had to argue, contrary to their usual ineffective defense, that the accused fugitive lacked credibility because she was old, or confused, or a little bit off. They objected that no title had been proved and insisted that the father's will must be presented to the court. There was good reason to believe, according to defense counsel, that Cassandra Harris was manumitted upon the older man's death. Ingraham dismissed both motions as outrageous, declared the testimony conclusive and closed, and ordered the fugitive into the custody of the claimant.

In the abolitionist version—which took place in Lancaster, not Phila-delphia, after the arrest rather than the voluntary submission of a fugitive named Catherine Warner, not Cassandra Harris, who was fifty-one rather than in her sixties—there was yet another tragic twist to the story. A reporter for the *Liberator*, William Lloyd Garrison's radical periodical, wrote that he interviewed the fugitive in question after the hearing had determined her fate:

> She acknowledged that she had told the officers that she wished to go back, but said she was terrified by their violence and threats and feared a worse fate, if she refused to go. . . . "I thought I might as well go back as to live so. But now," said she with a wo-begone look, "I don't want to go back; O, I don't want to go back."

Harris made one last request of the commissioner; she would like the opportunity to visit her grandchildren to reassure herself of their well-being and that the sick one was returning to health. After cursory consid-eration, the white men determined that such a wish was, at best, an im-pertinence from a slave and an unnecessary inconvenience and expense to the man delegated to return her to slavery. This old woman was a pest, full of unreasonable expectations and demands. Never again would she see her grandchildren, daughters, or sons.

The young ones would eventually be reunited with their parents in Canada, where descendants of William and Eliza Parker still reside. As for Cassy the slave, she would live the rest of her life back in Maryland, how much happier or despondent in slavery than she had been in free-dom we simply do not know. We can suspect that she missed her family, but perhaps she was angry with them, as well—for worrying her so and leaving her twice to her own devices in old age. There were no pensions for slaves or for agricultural laborers in the North. Did her children in-clude her in their plans; would they have sent for her in due course if she had just been a little more patient? Was she even fit for the journey or the new life so much farther to the cold north? Cassandra Harris may have thought in one way or another about all of these things, but her feelings are left to our limited abilities to picture ourselves in her place.

Maybe Harris never really comprehended the meaning of freedom, having lost at a younger age the spark that gives liberty its glow. To be black and on their own in the North was both a blessing and a trial for her children; for the old woman the blessing was more difficult to see.

The Christiana Riot was possibly more tragic for this slave than it was for the Gorsuches, who lost one member of their family while she lost them all.[11]

Cassandra Harris was not the only one who was scared in the aftermath of the riot, and she was not alone in her wish for the comparative security of slavery as opposed to a noose or a jail. Abraham Hall made a similar plea when he was arrested several days after the riot. He had always been a particular favorite of his master, Hall told his captors, but he had run away from Maryland in 1847 out of fear of punishment for hurting his master's grandson. After four years he hoped that tempers had cooled; in any event, accepting the whip that might greet him was preferable to facing the "reign of terror" that followed the riot in Lancaster County.[12]

In point of fact, Hall explained, he had tried several times in the past to return to his Maryland enslavement but was prevented by neighbors and friends. He never said what form this "prevention" took but implied that more than gentle persuasion was involved. Hall's testimony provided more copy for newspapers sympathetic to the interests of slave owners. According to the pro-slavery writers who reported this case, there was reason to believe that fugitive slaves were being kept by force in the North, no doubt by unscrupulous capitalist entrepreneurs who held "free" blacks in wage bondage, while hypocritically and self-interestedly agitating for the abolition of the competing slave system, which was actually more humane to its workers, as the experiences of Harris and Hall pointed out. Many slave owners continued to believe, just as had the late Edward Gorsuch, that if the fugitives had a choice, the opportunity, and full information rather than the lies fed them instead of food by Northern abolitionists, the escaped slaves would really want to come home.[13]

With the possible exceptions of Harris and Hall, the fugitives swept up in the wake of the riot were anything but eager to return to the status of slaves. Another of the tragedies resulting from the Christiana Riot was the opportunity it presented for wholesale arrests of fugitive slaves. As one anti-slavery newspaper reported with both sadness and anger:

> When we saw the horde that, in the name of law, were the other day poured upon Lancaster county, and witnessed the ferocity with which they pursued and indiscriminately seized colored men, whether implicated or not in the Gorsuch affray, we felt assured that one prominent motive of that search with many engaged in it, was the capture of fugitive slaves, and the result is already sadly confirming that conviction.

[85]

Under the guise of seeking out and arresting rioters responsible for the murder of Edward Gorsuch, another Philadelphia periodical claimed, authorities were trying to "excite to greater intensity the already existing unjust and cruel prejudice against the colored inhabitants of the State."[14]

During the two weeks after the riot, for example, a free African-American living in the same area was captured by a Maryland slave-hunting gang. The man was released when resistance seemed to threaten the kidnappers' lives. Fugitives from Virginia engaged in a ferocious battle with those who pursued them, resulting in the serious injury of several white men and the death of at least one. Two of the fugitives apparently escaped, while two more were captured and incarcerated in a Virginia jail until they could be tried and executed for insurrection and murder. Closer to Lancaster, four African-Americans were taken and held in jail on the accusation that they were Edward Gorsuch's escaped slaves by slave catchers who knew they were not. The ruse was designed to buy time while the real owners of the fugitives could be notified by telegraph and travel north with their legal claims to ownership of the four men. Despite protests by outraged opponents of the Fugitive Slave Law, the men were returned to their masters, and it was determined that the falsehood had broken no law.[15]

Whether these and other encounters like them were "caused" by the Christiana Riot or were simply products of the slave-catching business as usual is difficult to say. Clearly though, every "kidnapping" episode would now be reported and analyzed in light of the riot. The battle at the Parkers' became a lens through which the expectations of all sides in the slave-catching controversy would be seen. It was even more difficult after the riot for Southern masters to suppress the reality of their slaves' attitudes toward enslavement and their willingness to engage in violence under circumstances favorable to their triumph. It was also less likely that fugitive slaves and free blacks would believe they were "safe" in the North, that the law and the white population protected them from those who threatened their liberties and their lives. In these senses, the riot did contribute to the atmosphere of violence that surrounded race relations during the 1850s; but before the prosecution of any Christiana rioters, the consequences of violence for those who survived the immediate battle were not entirely clear.

In Lancaster itself, a posse of about fifty locals was assembled by 10 p.m. on the night following the riot and was supplemented over the course of the evening by "gangs of armed ruffians" from Maryland, who were even more eager to vent their anger over Gorsuch's death on the black and white citizens of Lancaster County. "Wo to them who resist!" was the motto of this outraged assemblage of white men from Baltimore and Lancaster County and an accurate reflection of the thirst for revenge that would inspire their actions over the next couple of days. Working-class whites, who had no fondness for the African-American laborers who competed with them for jobs, were amply represented in this group. Almost all of the forty Irish railroad workers employed in the county were deputized, and one of them, when he was handed a horse pistol for the job, declared enthusiastically that he would shoot "the first black thing" he saw, even if it was a cow. According to David R. Forbes, a local chronicler of the riot:

> there never went unhung a gang of more depraved wretches and desperate scoundrels than some of the men employed as "officers of the law" to ravage this country and ransack private houses in the man-hunt which followed the affray.

Indeed, among the new deputies were two men who had done time in the penitentiary for breaking and entering the mayor's office, one of whom had since been indicted on several occasions for stealing chickens. These were the "lawmen" sent out to capture African-American criminals who had fought for their freedom.[16]

Independently of local authorities, federal officials made their own plans to capture those responsible for violent resistance to the Fugitive Slave Law. A contingent of about forty-five marines and a detachment of about forty Philadelphia policemen swept down on this rural community in pursuit of the same men sought by local officials. When a bystander asked what they were up to, one of the marines responded that "We are going to arrest every nigger and damned abolitionist" in the county. True to their word, the troops scoured the countryside in a mad attempt to arrest every black person they could find. A controversy arose about who had primary jurisdiction over the prisoners and whether they would be held and tried locally for murder or taken to Philadelphia to face federal treason charges. The parties reached an agreement that each would make its own arrests.[17]

Both posses hunted fugitives with little regard for the constitutional rights of the citizenry; nor were the deputized laborers, policemen, and marines attentive to which members of the community they captured or how much violence they used to make an arrest. African-Americans were fair game for those who sought to even a score, act out their racial bigotry, or who just enjoyed bashing heads. According to one witness, blacks were "hunted like partridges" by those deputized for the search. A brief "reign of terror" ensued, in which, according to a local historian, "whites and blacks, bond and free, were rather roughly handled; few households in the region searched were safe from rude intrusion; many suffered terrifying scenes and sounds."[18]

Peter Woods, a black man who was seventeen at the time of the riot, later told of his own arrest and that of his white employer, Joseph Scarlett, two days after Edward Gorsuch was killed. "When Scarlet[t] was arrested," Woods recalled,

> they were rough in arresting him. They took him by the throat, and pointed bayonets at him all around him. I said to myself if you arrest a white man like that, I wonder what you will do to a black boy? . . . I was plowing or working the ground, and when I saw the officers come to make the arrests, I quickly got unhitched and went towards Bushong's, and soon there was six of us together and we went to Dr. Dingee's graveyard and hid. . . . Then they got us. . . . The man with the mace, the marshal I guess, said "I got a warrant for Peter Woods." They pointed me out and then he struck me and took me up a flight of stairs, and then they tied me. Then they started away with me and tried to get me over a fence. They had me tied around my legs and around my breast, and they put me in a buggy and took me to Christiana.[19]

Warrants were issued for five white men in addition to dozens of blacks. Elijah Lewis and Castner Hanway rode into Lancaster city when they heard they were wanted and surrendered to the authorities, who were using Frederick Zercher's hotel as their temporary headquarters. The two white men were wise to deliver themselves into the hands of the law before one or both of the posses descended on their homes to drag them both in. Emotions ran high, and the deputies were not in the mood to be gentle or fair.

As Hanway and Lewis stepped onto the porch of the hotel, Marshal Kline approached them in a menacing manner. "You white-livered scoundrels . . . ," Kline addressed the two men with his fists clenched, "when I plead[ed] for my life like a dog and begged you not to let the blacks fire upon us, you turned round and told them to do so." According to witnesses, Lewis responded, "No, I didn't"; but Hanway had nothing to say. Lancaster Alderman J. Franklin Reigart, who would be taking preliminary testimony that day, grabbed Kline by the shoulder to restrain him and insisted that the marshal's behavior was out of place. "I hope you will say nothing to produce a disturbance," Reigart declared, "we wish to do our business legally and in order." Kline apologized and expressed his intention to obey the directive but explained that it was impossible for him to suppress his feelings after the events of the previous day.[20]

There was so much hostility against Lewis and Hanway among those gathered at the hotel that Reigart feared Kline would inspire a serious disturbance. A lynch party composed of the posse was not an unreasonable fear. Much more of the anger over Gorsuch's murder was aimed at the two white men than at the blacks who perpetrated the act. "Against the black persons [brought in by the posse for questioning] nothing was said," Alderman Reigart later remembered; "they seemed much enraged against Hanway and Lewis." On the scene, as elsewhere in the nation, when those unsympathetic to the cause of fugitive slaves learned details of the riot, they saw Hanway and Lewis as the leaders and primarily to blame for the resistance to Kline's posse, Edward Gorsuch's death, and the escape of those fugitive slaves who murdered the Maryland farmer.[21]

Testimony against those captured by the posses continued all day and into the night on the Saturday, Sunday, and Monday following the riot. The hearings at Christiana were brought to a close on Monday at 10 p.m. The local officials had the first crack at the prisoners, but now the federal prosecutors wanted to begin to prepare their treason case. On September 23, 1851, the hearings would resume under federal auspices in Lancaster city at the county courthouse. The principal witnesses against the accused were Marshal Kline and a black drifter named George Washington Harvey Scott. Kline's testimony was clearly aimed at self-vindication and given out of a desire for revenge, in addition to his dedication to enforcing the law. He was being accused of cowardice on the field of battle; rumor had it that the Gorsuch party blamed him for foolishly leading them into a trap and then deserting his posse when the bullets started to fly.

In Kline's first official telling of the riot story that day, Hanway and Lewis were actors, but not "leaders" of the violence per se. They refused to assist the posse and appeared to counsel with the blacks before the violence began. Kline remembered Joseph Scarlett riding up very fast on a sweating horse. "You have been the man giving the negroes information," the marshal recalled saying to Scarlett, who made no reply. So the three whites were certainly blameworthy, guilty of a serious crime, but as yet not the organizers and leaders of violence as they would eventually be portrayed. It was Dr. Pearce, another member of the Gorsuch posse, who first suggested that the blacks in the house were inspired to resist by Hanway's arrival.[22]

Perhaps Pearce's account rang true with the marshal when he first heard it in the courtroom that day. It gave the story a focus and placed blame even more squarely on the shoulders of a man they actually had in custody rather than on Parker and the others who got away. Possibly, the notion of white leadership first suggested by the Southerner accorded with Kline's own views of the role played by white abolitionists in orchestrating resistance to the Fugitive Slave Law. In any event, it was a version that Kline would remember, retell, and embellish in another courtroom on another day.

Counsel for the accused tried to poke holes in the marshal's story, as it was their job to do. Where was he when the murder of Edward Gorsuch occurred? How much of the violence did Kline actually witness, and how much did he just hear and piece together while hiding in a field of dried-out corn? "When I saw the negroes pointing their guns at me I got over the fence into the cornfield," the marshal admitted under cross-examination by Thaddeus Stevens, congressman, abolitionist, and now principal counsel to Hanway and Lewis. Was it not remarkable that Kline was able to see so much and with such clarity from his vantage and on such a foggy morning as he described? How could he identify by name and with such precision black men whom he only glimpsed, at best, and had never seen before? How did he explain the contradictions in his story and the different versions that he had told over the previous couple of days?[23]

The prosecution's other main witness at these hearings claimed to have watched the riot as an unarmed bystander. Harvey Scott provided the names of black men whom he said were actively engaged in the mayhem, and his testimony accorded in every regard with Marshal Kline's. John Morgan, Henry Simms, and William Brown were there, according to Scott. And he also saw the white miller Hanway walking around. Simms shot Edward Gorsuch, and Morgan slashed him on the head with a corn cutter, just as Kline said. Scott said he saw Brown, whom Kline had accused of being among the most violent rioters, at Parker's with a gun. At this, Brown confronted the witness: "Did you see me there George?"

"I saw you there," Scott insisted, "in the yard, pretty soon in the morning."[24]

Neither Dr. Pearce nor Nicholas Hutchins was as useful to the prosecution as Scott and Kline. "I can't say that I recognize those black prisoners," Pearce testified under oath. "I think I saw that large black man Morgan standing near the bars, with a club in his hand," Hutchins tentatively observed after gazing intently at the line-up of black men and women brought into court. The local constable and another of the Parkers' neighbors did not reach the riot scene until after the firing had ceased and thus were unable to link any specific prisoner with any particular crime. The prosecution located several more local people who were able to provide peripheral evidence about which blacks were carrying guns the day preceding the riot and who was spreading the news that kidnappers were on the way, but those were not crimes of interest to the prosecutors. Miller Knott was able to verify that Joseph Scarlett rode up to the Parkers' after the riot on a sweating horse.[25]

Defense witnesses contradicted Scott and Kline on several essential points. Isaac Rogers remembered hearing Hanway say to the rioters, "boys don't shoot," and also saw and heard the miller try to save Dr. Pearce from Abraham Johnson, who was attempting to murder the Marylander with a pistol at short range. Benjamin Elliot, Jesse Morgan, and Hansford Powell all saw the black man John Morgan miles away from the Parkers' at the time of the riot. Powell even implied a plausible explanation for Kline's defective memory about Morgan's actions that day. When Kline and the wounded Joshua Gorsuch reached the tavern on their way to Penningtonville after the riot, the marshal probably saw Morgan out front loading two wagons of coal. A couple days later, in trying to identify African-Americans whom he remembered from the riot scene, Kline apparently recognized Morgan's face but mistook the circumstances under which he had seen the man before.

Even more challenging to the prosecution's attempts to develop a case were the four witnesses who swore that Harvey Scott was nowhere near the Parkers' house on Thursday morning. If John Carr, John Cochran, Benjamin Elliot, and Jesse Morgan were telling the truth—or, in any event, if a jury would believe them—Scott's story was a total fabrication. Scott could not possibly have been locked in his bedroom, come down to breakfast at the break of day, worked in Carr's blacksmith shop all morning, and still identified participants in the riot first-hand. According to Carr:

> I live, I suppose, about three miles from Parker's house near Penningtonville; I know G. W. Harvey Scott: on the 10th and 11th of this month he worked with me in the blacksmith shop; the night before this occurrence, about 9 o'clock, he went up to his room; I fastened the door on the outside by a button. I had two granddaughters in the room he had to pass through; they were not satisfied without I was called up to button the door; I went to the door and found it buttoned; about a quarter of an hour before sunup, I went to the door, and called him by name, and he answered me; he came down and made the fire; he went into the two-acre lot and got the cow; I saw him bring the cow to the smith-shop, about, as I suppose, a quarter of an hour after the time I called him; he came into my shop and was there all day, and blowed and struck for me all day.[26]

The other three witnesses all described in some detail the conditions under which they saw Harvey Scott several miles from the Parkers' at the break of day, the very time that the riot occurred. This was a serious problem for the prosecution; if Scott lacked credibility as a witness, most of the prosecution's case against the rioters would rest on the testimony of Marshal Kline. The black men whom more than one member of the posse could identify with confidence had all gotten away. That left only the two women—Eliza Parker and Hannah Pinckney—and the three white men—Hanway, Lewis, and Scarlett—in custody and readily identifiable by multiple witnesses.[27]

The prosecution released the two women and all other females in custody before proceeding with the plea for indictments. Nowhere in the written records is the logic behind this decision stated or even implied. It would seem that the government's best case for treason—at least for some crime associated with armed resistance to enforcement of the Fugitive Slave Law—could be made against the two women, who were the only occupants of the Parkers' house on the morning of September 11 whom the two posses had managed to capture. There were six surviving witnesses from the slave-catching party who could identify Eliza Parker and testify to her role in summoning the other rioters with a horn.

Why were the women released? Perhaps the prosecutors anticipated difficulty in convincing a jury of twelve men to convict young mothers of a capital crime. Government attorneys themselves may have been horrified by such a prospect or feared the repercussions of such a case. Maybe they imagined the outraged headlines in the Whig and abolitionist press and the political fire storm likely to engulf the North. Possibly they reasoned that Southern honor would not be quenched by the blood of one or two black women. More than likely, they applied the same logic that held white men responsible for the violence of blacks and assumed that the women were only tools of the male rioters rather than willing participants in their own right. Undoubtedly, the line of diminished responsibility for the death of Edward Gorsuch and the amount of political significance that a conviction would carry descended from white men, to black men, to black women, with the last no substitute for the other two.

Gender and race certainly played roles in the decisions made by government officials in the aftermath of the riot, but it is not possible to gauge their significance with precision. The law was enforced with selectivity and vengeance but also sometimes with a lenity that is more difficult to comprehend. Authorities did not even try to return Eliza Parker and Hannah Pinckney with their mother to slavery, even though they had the fugitives in custody and knew the whole story of their escape and the identity of their owner from the story told by Cassandra Harris in her own case. William Parker said that his wife had to run in order to escape from her young master, but there is nothing in any of the records that indicates why she was not detained until he arrived. Why the Fugitive Slave Law challenged by the rioters on September 11 was not used against these two women is not at all clear, especially since the riot provided a sufficient excuse to arrest others who were not even remotely associated with the case.

The prosecution needed to convict white men to avenge Edward Gorsuch's death in the eyes of Southerners. In the legal-political calculus of revenge, several black men or women would simply not do. The government also needed to demonstrate compassion for a Northern constituency of moderates and liberals. Perhaps freeing the two mothers of small children would be a small price to pay for maintaining the goodwill of most white Americans. After all, the women were presumably only following the dictates of their husbands in resisting the posse. Black women seemed even less likely agents of their own actions, to the male white officials, than did black men. Unfortunately, from the perspective of federal authorities, the press did not pick up the story this way.

The success of the Compromise of 1850, and perhaps even the fate of the Union, hinged on such delicate balancing of harshness and humanity. The only capital crime the federal prosecutors had in their arsenal to help establish their commitment to the Fugitive Slave Law was treason. The only white men they had to sacrifice had carried no guns in "levying war" against the government. Witnesses to treason were few and of questionable veracity, but options seemed narrow and the stakes very high. Judicial interpretation of the law of treason was not entirely clear and seemed, on the basis of past court decisions, to leave an opening that gave them a chance for convictions. And immense political pressure was mounting daily for decisive action in defense of the law.

Stratagems

RUMORS CONCERNING THE MUTILATION of Edward Gorsuch's body may, as was suggested in chapter 4, have been the product of fertile Southern imaginations. No witness, no participant—white or black—provided such gruesome details as those uttered in anti-abolitionist circles. Among the firsthand accounts we have only the cryptic observation of William Parker that "the women finished him off." The coroner's report mentions only one bullet wound, a single "incision" on the head, and a "fracture of the left humerus" produced by a blunt instrument. Not even the most virulently racist Democratic newspapers in the North carried the story of corn cutters hacking the corpse to a pulp.[1]

There is no way to tell for certain whether Northern sensibilities led newspaper editors to suppress accounts of the riot's true brutality or whether Southerners simply assumed a savagery that reveals more about the psychology of slave owners, and the politics of interracial violence, than it does about the Christiana rioters. On balance, though, it appears more likely that the mutilation was a figment of white people's fears or an attempt to use the riot for political ends. The story represented the most shocking form of role reversal imaginable to a Southern white man: members of the weaker gender of a subservient race mutilating the body of a male exemplar of the master class. In light of the sexual abuse that female slaves sometimes suffered at the hands of white men, the alleged genital mutilation manifests a symbolic retribution that is appropriate to this historical setting. Still, the symbolic significance of the act could reflect either the plausibility of the story or help to explain the nature of the guilt among white men that would lead to such a horrible fantasy. In other words, hypothesizing on the psychological origins of the story does not really help to resolve the question of its literal truth.

White Northern men, on the other hand, tended to see African-American women as more aggressive than their male counterparts. Such gender characterization was no doubt based on a germ of observable truth, which ignored such contradictory evidence as the actions of Lancaster's black self-protection association and the successes of such local African-American businessmen as Stephen Smith and William Whipper. As a cultural generalization, however, it is possible that black men, who represented the more obvious physical and economic threat to the white community, had continued to act out roles learned under slavery. Foolishness, incompetence, slowness, and foot-shuffling deference were also functional personas in the presence of *Northern* whites. Repression of assertive qualities in public was probably even more necessary for black men than women, if only because it was easier for the men to threaten whites unintentionally. As for the African-American women who may have dealt Edward Gorsuch his last blow and relieved him of the cash in his pocket, cross-gender and cross-racial rage may have combined with the comparative racial and cultural freedom for women to express emotions in a way that makes the mutilation story at least a possibility, however remote.

Whatever the reality, the communal hacking and literal removal of Gorsuch's manhood by black women became part of the riot's lore. It was a fitting symbolic consequence of the fugitives' quest for their freedom, a testament to the clear break with the past, which the riot represented not only to the fugitives from Retreat Farm but also to those who shared in the victory that day and the thousands more who rejoiced in the courage of the black people of Lancaster County. Edward Gorsuch had been a master of slaves; now he was a sacrificial victim, perhaps even castrated on the altar of liberty. To some, Gorsuch was a martyr, who died defending the liberties of property owners; to others, he represented all those guilty of trying to deny the inalienable rights of people based on their race.

Since the violence of the rioters was vented with the death of one man, the metaphor of sacrifice seems appropriate to the case. There was no all-out pursuit of the wounded as they limped away. No one pounced on Dickinson Gorsuch, who lay for at least half an hour in the weeds by a stump. Parker knew where the slave owner's son was and even gave his landlord some water to quench the injured man's thirst. No, the death of one master, one slave catcher, one white man would do, at least on this day. Edward Gorsuch, alone, symbolically represented the others like him who still lived. Let this be a warning; let the violence come to an end. When a sacrifice works, the gods are appeased and bloodshed can stop. Sometimes, though, a sacrifice goes awry and brings on the very sort of bloodletting that it was intended to prevent.

There were numerous signs that this sacrifice had failed. The brutality of indiscriminate arrests discussed in the last chapter was certainly one. The use of the riot for political purposes in the state gubernatorial campaign, which included a possible assassination attempt on the sitting governor, was another. The decision to prosecute white observers of the riot for a capital crime was yet a third piece of evidence that the thirst for blood had grown rather than diminished as a result of Gorsuch's death. The entire nation was caught up in a cycle of revenge that included the Christiana Riot but that neither began nor ended in September 1851—an interracial and interregional vendetta that would grow worse over the course of the next decade and would culminate in this nation's bloodiest war. According to local historian Charles Blockson, the goals of the Confederate Army when it invaded Pennsylvania included the burning of Christiana as retribution for the murder of Edward Gorsuch. The bloody debacle at Gettysburg prevented this defense of Southern honor.[2]

There were as many versions of the riot reported as there were different political and emotional needs to fulfill; and the facts of the case proved a frail restraint on the capacity of Americans to draw lessons from the violence. In the South, the gap between the moral stature of the slain master and the depravity of the white Northern abolitionists who allegedly betrayed him was drawn in stark relief. It was also necessary for Southerners to explain how superior fighting men—white Southern gentlemen—could be outdueled by a ragtag band of escaped slaves. As a consequence, the villains of the moral tale had to be white abolitionists, who directed black pawns for their own devious ends. The African-Americans in the story had to be marginally competent at best, victorious as a consequence of deceit and vastly superior firepower rather than shrewd tactics and bravery in battle. Accordingly, a riot in which one white man and no blacks were killed was transformed into a barely recognizable ambush where as many as four whites and two African-Americans lost their lives after the blacks received strategic advice from white abolitionists.[3]

This transformation of facts began in the North as a consequence of the political ends served by the riot. Abolitionists, pro-Compromise Democrats, and moderate Whigs all had a stake in the way the riot was portrayed. All but the most radical abolitionists hoped to distance themselves from the violence, which they deplored, and to blame one or more of the other political groups for the shedding of blood. Alone among the

Northern press, abolitionist newspapers reported the riot as the enterprise of blacks acting independently of guidance by whites. Abolitionists
did not blame African-American rioters for bloodshed at the Parkers' house.
The *Pennsylvania Freeman* found the riot "deplorable . . . in its character and many of its results." Nonetheless, it was advocates of the Fugitive
Slave Law, pro-Compromise politicians, not the blacks who fired the guns,
who were responsible for Gorsuch's death. According to the *New York
Independent:*

> The recent affray at Christiana is only a new phase of the Hydra that
> was begotten of the spirit of Compromise. The framers of this law counted
> upon the utter degradation of the negro race—their want of manliness
> and heroism—to render feasible its execution. . . . They anticipated no
> resistance from a race cowed down by centuries of oppression, and trained
> to servility. In this, however, they were mistaken. They are beginning
> to discover that men, however abject, who have tasted liberty, soon
> learn to prize it, and are ready to defend it.[4]

Democrats, too, saw the riot as a whip they could use to lacerate their
political foes. Indeed, organs of the Democratic Party provided the exaggerated details reprinted in Southern newspapers, which they neglected
to correct when subsequent information revealed them to be false. To the
Democrats, it was the Whigs and radical abolitionists (who were lumped
together as one) who had Edward Gorsuch's blood on their hands. "It is
absurd to mince matters on such a subject," the *Pennsylvanian* averred;
"and the sense of this whole community traces the cause of these bloody
tumults, not to the poor, deluded, and frenzied blacks, but to those reckless agitators who counsel and applaud opposition to the established laws
of the land."[5]

Among these "reckless agitators," the Democratic papers in Pennsylvania singled out the Whig governor of the state, William F. Johnston, as
particularly responsible for the violence. The Democrats' campaign for
governor had languished during the hot summer months preceding the
riot. They were probing for an issue that would give them a chance to
defeat Johnston in the October election. The state was enjoying an economic upswing, and Johnston was linked in the public mind with the plan
he designed as a state senator four years before to save Pennsylvania from
a short-term debt crisis. Tariffs and taxes were not seizing the popular
imagination this year, so the Democrats tried to exploit the ever-present
racial tensions that existed in the state.[6]

Johnston was "soft" on blacks and abolitionists, according to the Democrats. He had expressed himself in opposition to the Compromise of 1850, including the Fugitive Slave Law, and refused to support repeal of the state's 1847 anti-kidnapping act, which severely limited local efforts to assist in the recapture of fugitive slaves. In his first annual message as governor, before the Fugitive Slave Law was passed, Johnston cautiously expressed his views on the politically sensitive subject:

> While the compromises of the Constitution should be maintained in good faith towards our Southern brethren, it is our duty to see that they are preserved with equal fidelity to ourselves. No encroachments, however sanctioned by use, should be acknowledged as precedents for further wrongs against the interest, prosperity, and happiness of the non-slave-holding States of the Union.[7]

As governor of a "free" state, Johnston's primary concern was for the economic interests of the white citizenry, not for the rights of black fugitives. His fear was that slavery gave other states an unfair competitive advantage in the marketplace and that cheap labor would result in less expensive goods than were possible when African-Americans, immigrants, women, and children were paid, however poorly, to produce crops and manufactured products. This did not stop the Democrats, in the heat of a political campaign that they believed they might lose, from linking Johnston with the "woolly-headed" Whigs and abolitionists whom they held responsible for inciting violence in the African-American community. This was, of course, the antebellum version of red-baiting; if the Democrats could make the label of "abolitionist" stick to Johnston, they had a much better chance of defeating him in the fall.[8]

Since he was playing for the moderate middle ground in Pennsylvania politics, Johnston was vulnerable to the charge. He did tell selected audiences, as the Democrats reported, "that he was in favor of amendment of the Fugitive Slave Law, that it was unjust, that if he had been in Congress at the time of its passage, he would have voted against it, or [have] give[n] the fugitive slave the right of trial by jury in the place of arrest." Governor Johnston did not advocate repeal of the law or resistance to it, as the Democrats claimed. He thought that setting up "inferior tribunals" headed by appointed fugitive slave commissioners, as the federal government had done, opened the process to corruption and threatened the rights of those wrongfully charged under the law. For this reason Johnston supported a change, while advocating obedience until the act was amended by Congress. The Democrats interpreted the governor's position as "vacillation," and chastised him for contributing to an atmosphere supportive of resistance to the law.[9]

Governor Johnston saw the federal law as supplanting the authority of state officials in fugitive cases, thereby relieving them of responsibility for helping to capture escaped slaves. The problem was now one for federal officials, in his opinion, and Johnston intended to do the minimum necessary to bring his state into line with the federal law. He refused to support, or ultimately to sign, a bill repealing the sixth section of Pennsylvania's 1847 anti-kidnapping act. The portion of the law in question forbade usage of the state's jails and cooperation of the state's jailers in the incarceration of fugitive slaves, except in those cases where federal judges had the authority to compel use of state facilities. Repeal was a testament of support for the Compromise measures that the Democrats were eager and the Whigs reluctant to make.[10]

Johnston's refusal to abide this significant gesture helped his political foes portray him as a friend of African-Americans and thus, by implication, an enemy of working-class whites. His reluctance to stand foursquare behind the Constitution and the law of the land made his commitment to the Union appear lukewarm at best. But what drove the point home to the Democrats' advantage was the opportunity provided by the Christiana Riot for dramatizing the consequences of the governor's halfhearted support for the law. Johnston's campaign pledge to veto repeal of the state anti-kidnapping law's enforcement clause seemed to the Democrats like a match held to the torch of black violence. According to the *Pennsylvanian*, Johnston's criticism of the Compromise measures had predictably disastrous consequences:

> This language operates upon the slaves like an appeal to violence. It is the voice of command calling upon those who are at home to cut the throats of their master, and upon those who escape into other states to shoot down in cold blood every officer that comes to arrest and every owner that comes to reclaim them. We do not overrate the influence of Governor Johnston, when we charge him, and upon such as him . . . the dreadful responsibility for the guilty deed.[11]

Not only was Johnston to blame for Gorsuch's death, according to the Democratic press, he was also, along with the state's "notorious abolitionists," responsible for starting a chain of events that could have disastrous consequences for the nation. The Christiana Riot would fuel the fires of secessionism in the South, transform docile slaves into rapists and murderers, and exacerbate interracial tensions in the North. Johnston and his

dated three days after the riot, Johnston contended that local authorities had everything under control and pleaded that things not be blown out of proportion:

> The alleged murderers of Mr. Gorsuch, whose crime is deep enough without exaggerating it, have been arrested, and will be tried, and they and their abettors be made to answer for what they have done in contravention of the law. But in the meantime, let me invite your cooperation, as citizens of Pennsylvania, not only to see that the law is enforced, but to add to the confidence which we all feel in the judicial tribunals of the land, by abstaining from undue violence of language, and letting the law take its course.

Two days later, Governor Johnston would succumb to political pressure, issue the statement of regret, and sign the proclamation offering a thousand dollar reward for the murderers; but by then the political damage was done, and his opponents could plausibly claim that Johnston's inaction was a major contributing factor in the escape of those most responsible for the violence against Gorsuch's posse.[14]

Why did he wait so long to act? "Because," the *Pennsylvanian* charged, "Governor Johnston was afraid to rouse the ire of the abolitionists, his friends," who wanted the murderers to get away. Perhaps, but radical abolionists were not pleased that he had acted at all. Johnston was caught in a political vise. Five days after the event, the governor's response would appear to represent the vacillating course of a man who had neither the courage of his convictions nor the capacity to enforce the laws. He looked less like a statesman than a politician swaying with the political breeze. It was the decisive moment in this political campaign, and his opponents seized it with all the vigor that one might expect.[15]

In a speech delivered to a large audience in front of Independence Hall on the Tuesday following the riot, the governor reaffirmed his affection for the Constitution and his commitment to enforce the Fugitive Slave Law. He denounced violence in the name of a higher law and pledged that the state would do its duty to enforce the recapture of fugitive slaves. At a huge Democratic meeting on the same spot several days later, one of the speakers was John Campbell, the author of *Negro-Mania*, who marshaled the "evidence" of history and science to prove that African-Americans were part of an inferior race and would produce violence in this country until they were excluded from the continent. Using the building in which the Declaration of Independence was signed as a backdrop for their speeches, both political parties pledged to sacrifice the liberty of blacks in return for white votes. For all that divided the Democrats and the Whigs, they could agree that the rights of African-Americans were limited and expendable. The members of these two political parties did not seem concerned that their exclusion of blacks from the nation's founding commitment to the equality of all men made their choice of location for the setting inappropriate. In their eyes, the Declaration of Independence did not apply to fugitive slaves.[16]

Among the twelve resolutions adopted by the Democrats' meeting was one that seemed to endorse bloodshed as an antidote to the violence that had already occurred. The crowd proclaimed enthusiastic support for a wish that "those who teach bloody instruction to others would have the poisoned chalice returned to their own lips." Within a context in which the Democrats were naming few others besides the governor of Pennsylvania as such a "bloody instructor," it takes little imagination to read this resolution as a clarion call for a patriotic assassin. The drafters of the resolution almost certainly did not intend it as a proposal to take the Whig candidate's life, but it was part of a concerted design to fuel the fires of political partisanship, with little thought to consequences other than victory in the coming election.[17]

This is not to say that the alleged attempt on Governor Johnston's life a week later was the direct result of a particular declaration made in the course of a heated campaign, but the political hyperbole certainly contributed to an environment in which such an act seems more than just the random violence of a deluded individual. The shot—if such a shot was even made with the intention of harming the governor—missed but itself became an issue in the campaign. The abolitionist and Whig press, of course, blamed the Democrats for the attempt on Johnston's life. As the *Pennsylvania Freeman* reported the story:

> The inflammatory accusations and malignant violence of such papers as the *Pennsylvanian*, have begun to bear their natural fruit in a mobocratic assault upon Governor Johnston. On Monday night, the 22d ult., he and his friends were assailed twice near Mt. Carbon, by an infuriated mob, with stones, clubs and fire-arms. A pistol was fired within a few feet of him, and several of his escort were wounded. One man had his jaw broken with a stone.

The *Pennsylvanian* retorted that the whole incident was a Whig fabrication designed to gain sympathy for their candidate:

> Somebody in Schuylkill County, had a pistol, it appears, and at a recent public meeting this pistol went off, and, although there were many peo-

ple present, of course it could only have been fired at Governor Johnston. . . . Governor Johnston is a bold, unscrupulous, and desperate
partisan. He feels the ground sliding from his feet. He sees the abyss
yawning before him. He knows he is foredoomed; for there is not even
a straw left to grasp at.—One hope remains; and that is to create the
impression that he is a much injured man. . . . Hence his exceeding
desire to get somebody to shoot at him.[18]

Not only were anonymous "assassins" and black murderers exploited
for their potential contributions to this political campaign, but the family
of the late Edward Gorsuch was also brought into the fray on the Democrats' side. Not surprisingly, the Whigs found the enlistment of Gorsuch's
bereaved son—the Reverend John S. Gorsuch—in shockingly poor taste;
the Democrats, for their part, denied any collusion for political effect.
According to the Democratic newspapers, the letter from John Gorsuch
to Governor Johnston, which laid responsibility for the riot and the escape of his father's murderers at the governor's door, was a spontaneous
act. All they did was circulate copies to newspapers. The source for dozens of facsimiles of this personal letter—which was also printed and posted
around the city of Philadelphia—was not revealed, but we now know that
Gorsuch did provide copies of his letter for the purposes of publication in
the North.[19]

The Whigs cried foul—although it is difficult to tell where, at this
point, they thought the limits of fair campaign practices lay for either
their opponents or themselves. They accused the Democrats of violating
"the sanctity of familiar and domestic sorrow" for political ends. Ruthless
politicians had "persuaded the son of the murdered man—the sod [i]s
hardly smoothed over his father's grave—to enter the arena, and write a
letter of ribald slander for the avowed purpose of defeating Governor
Johnston's election." One Whig paper expressed suspicion that the letter
was a fraud perpetrated by the Democrats.[20]

The issue, of course, was votes, not respect for the dead or sensibilities about appropriate mourning etiquette. The Whigs saw the political
omens and were simply lashing out defensively without a plan for getting
Johnston's campaign back on track. William Bigler, the Democrats' candidate for governor, was an able campaigner in his own right, a back-
woodsman who was reputedly the best shot in Clearfield County. None
of this hurt his popular-man image, especially when juxtaposed against
the alleged aristocratic pretensions of the Whigs. Once a partisan newspaper editor and now a lumber magnate, Bigler was also a two-term vet-
eran of the state senate, where he had gained the respect of those inside

and outside his party. Bigler conducted a respectable but vigorous campaign, leaving the nasty charges and infighting to others.[21]

On October 14, the Whigs' fears were realized, when a slim majority of voters cast their ballots for Bigler. Observers from both parties agreed that the Christiana Riot represented more than the 8,465-vote margin of victory for the Democrats and that it accounted for the election of four of the five Democratic candidates for the state supreme court. The election of Bigler had an impact on national politics as well. He was the candidate of the Buchanan wing of the Democratic Party and was able to wield his influence as governor to help gain control of the party's national convention in 1852. Bigler thus played a major role both in the nomination of James Buchanan over Lewis Cass for President and in Buchanan's successful 1856 campaign. The Christiana Riot was a significant link in this chain of events, making the violence into a triumph for the Democratic Party, as Buchanan, the favorite son of Lancaster County, rose to the highest office in the land as a consequence, in very small part, of the bloodshed so near to his home.[22]

Not surprisingly, emotions ran even higher in Edward Gorsuch's home state, where the Pennsylvania election was watched as a portent of that Northern state's commitment to the Compromise measures and, hence, to the Union. The even bigger test, of course, would come with the arrest and trial of the Christiana "traitors," and the political pressure on Maryland's governor was intense. It was his responsibility to see that the state's honor was redeemed, as Governor E. Louis Lowe's constituents reminded him in private letters, public resolutions, and chance meetings on the street. A "large and highly respectable" group of Baltimore County citizens called for an immediate inquiry by Maryland authorities into the facts of the riot and murder and a communication of the state's outrage to President Millard Fillmore. These same men offered their services "in any form which his excellency may be pleased to point out." A public meeting in Baltimore's Monument Square, reportedly of between 5,000 and 6,000 persons, called for an immediate cessation of commerce with the North and a withdrawal of all Southerners from educational institutions outside of the region:

> the North should be made to feel that she can no longer violate our rights with impunity. She has grown rich from the wealth of the South, poured into her lap by a thousand different channels—it is legal, it is constitutional, that the South should cause these streams to cease to flow; it is legal, it is constitutional, that the South should import for herself, should manufacture for herself, and should no longer send her

sons and daughters to be educated in a community where abolitionists and traitors are permitted to influence public opinion.[23]

Governor Lowe took these expressions of controlled rage seriously, as the thoughtful attempts of responsible men to channel public emotions away from more extreme, and perhaps violent, alternatives. He was more concerned about the hotheads who might start a border war with their vigilante tactics. What most worried him, though, was that federal officials and responsible state leaders in the North would not appreciate just how catastrophic the Christiana "outrage" really was. "I do not know of a single incident that has occurred since the passage of the Compromise measures," Lowe informed President Fillmore, "which tends more to weaken the bonds of Union."[24]

The riot was not just an offense against one citizen and his home state but also a challenge to everyone in the nation who shared Edward Gorsuch's sense of right and wrong. The effects of this "tragedy" could very well "penetrate the soul of the South." Maryland was the Southern state least influenced by the secessionist movement. If the people of Maryland lost faith in the Union, Governor Lowe had no doubt that Virginia and the rest of the slaveholding states would fall into line.[25]

Northerners simply did not take this possibility seriously enough. It really could happen—and soon, unless the federal government took swift and effective action to enforce the Compromise measures. At this point there was only one thing, in Governor Lowe's opinion, that could prevent the nation from crumbling. "It is proper that you should be frankly assured," he told the President, "that nothing can, or will, or ought to satisfy them but the most prompt, thorough, and severe retribution upon the murderous treason recently committed in Pennsylvania." The citizens of Maryland

> would not remain one day in the confederacy if finally assured either that the powers of the federal [government] were inadequate or that the public opinion of the non-slave-holding states was adverse to the protection of the rights, liberties and lives of her citizens. If the Union is to be merely a union of minority slaves to majority tyrants, then indeed our government has failed in the end of its creation, and the sooner it is dissolved the better.[26]

These were not the views of a radical secessionist; on the contrary, they were the forebodings of a man dedicated to preservation of the nation, its Constitution, and its laws. The purpose of the long and emotional letter was to inform the President of the facts and of the sentiments shared by the most sober and responsible residents of the state. These were the opinions being voiced in the General Assembly, from the pulpits of Maryland's churches, and from the benches of its highest courts. The President needed to appreciate the seriousness of the crisis and to act decisively while there was still time.

President Fillmore got the message, but he had to play to a constituency that included more than the South. The administration wanted the federal prosecutor for the eastern district of Pennsylvania to pursue the case of the Christiana rioters with vigor and to the fullest extent of the law; but the President had to tread carefully, lest he get caught in the quagmire of controversy surrounding fugitive slaves. The governor of Maryland was not the only one who offered the President advice on the course that the prosecution should take, and there were other Americans on all sides of the question who blamed Fillmore personally for Gorsuch's death and the failures of the Compromise measures and who believed that the very survival of the Union rested on the outcome of the trials to come. "Who, if not yourself, is the murderer of Gorsuch," one citizen reprimanded the President. "In the name of God," pleaded another, "why don't you put down such injustice, such abominable acts?"[27]

Neither President Fillmore nor Secretary of State Daniel Webster, who was the prosecutor's administrative superior, wanted to be held responsible for the success or failure of the case. Much of the North would be horrified should convictions and executions be the consequence of federal trials. Southerners would be outraged by acquittals. The political stakes were too high, the legal outcomes too unpredictable, the potential repercussions too great for politicians seeking a middle ground on the slavery question. It was not even clear what outcome would be most politically advantageous to administration officials. They had to appear to be putting the full force of the government behind the law. They could spare no expense, nor could they appear to leave any stone unturned in proceeding against those in custody. But they did not want to be associated with a political show trial or to seem overzealous in fulfilling their constitutional responsibilities—to help create abolitionist martyrs, whose executions would fan the flames of anti-Compromise fanaticism in the North. So when federal attorney John W. Ashmead sought advice from his superiors on how he should proceed with the prosecutions, an under secretary replied that "the President declines to advise or direct you. . . . The conduct and management of them are in your hands."[28]

Ashmead had already received instructions "to ascertain whether the facts would make out the crime of treason" and had made the decision to prosecute the Christiana prisoners for that crime. He probably wanted more help than he was getting to interpret the complex web of Anglo-American treason law and how it fit the evidence he had for this case. Perhaps he even sought the opportunity to express a lack of confidence in the course that he suspected his superiors wanted him to pursue.[29]

Despite the refusal to discuss particulars, Ashmead knew the Secretary of State's general opinion on applying the law of treason to fugitive-slave cases. In a speech delivered several months earlier, Webster had outlined his views of the law. "If men get together," Webster had told the audience in Albany, New York,

> and combine, and resolve that they will oppose a law of the government, not in any one case, but in all cases; if they resolve to resist the law, whoever may be attempted to be made the subject of it, and carry that purpose into effect, by resisting the application of the law in any one case, either by force of arms or force of numbers, that, Sir, is treason.[30]

If Webster believed, and so he did, that the rescue of the fugitive slave Shadrach was treason, that the circulation of certain resolutions advocating resistance to the law in Ohio and New York was treason, and that the gathering of an anti-slavery convention in Boston was treasonous in design, then there was little reason to doubt that his opinion of the Christiana Riot case would be the same. And, indeed, Ashmead received indirect expressions of support from his superiors for proceeding with the treason charge. He was on the right course as far as the administration was concerned, and federal officials intended to provide the prosecutor with necessary resources for what might prove to be a series of very expensive trials.[31]

There were limits, of course, both to the financial commitment of the government and to the administration's willingness to leave the prosecution in Ashmead's hands. When the prosecutor asked permission to hire a third attorney to assist him as the trial was about to begin, the request was denied on the grounds that it would create an unnecessary expense. And when Ashmead tried to put conditions on the role to be played by the attorney general of Maryland in handling the case, he received a swift reprimand from Washington that left no doubt who was in charge.[32]

The controversy began when Governor Lowe directed the state's attorney general, Robert J. Brent, to offer his services to the federal prosecutor. It seemed important for Maryland to have a representative at the trial to witness that "full justice" was done and to help "vindicate the insulted dignity of the State." When the governor heard about the formidable array of legal talent that would represent the accused traitors, he also saw fit to employ additional counsel. For reasons of "policy as well as propriety," it seemed best to hire a Pennsylvania lawyer for the purpose, and Senator James Cooper agreed to serve in this capacity. Not only would these two talented attorneys help balance the scales of justice in the courtroom, but the governor wanted a reliable report on the proceedings to help convince the citizens of Maryland, whatever the verdicts, that the federal government had done its best to punish those responsible for the murder of Edward Gorsuch.[33]

Ashmead did not want the help; or, at least, he wanted to make sure that he rather than Brent was running the show. When he received Brent's letter of introduction and request to assist in the prosecution, Ashmead responded defensively, and a bit officiously, that he was willing to tolerate the membership of Brent on the prosecutorial team but that he wanted it "distinctly understood" that he was in charge and that he, not Brent, would make the closing address to the jury. Now Brent was offended and dashed off a note in return in which he explained angrily that the wound Ashmead had inflicted on his honor and on that of the State of Maryland was intolerable. He could not possibly accept preliminary conditions on his participation, however willing he was to acknowledge the authority of the federal prosecutor's official position. Ashmead chose not to respond, probably believing that the issue was settled; Brent had declined his terms, so the prosecutor had succeeded in ridding himself of this unwanted presence in the courtroom.[34]

Perhaps Ashmead underestimated Brent's persistence; he certainly misjudged the possible repercussions of handling the Maryland official in such a cavalier way; and he overestimated his own authority. When the administration told Ashmead that the cases were in his hands, the President and Secretary of State did not intend to let him create a national incident of the very kind they were trying to prevent by prosecuting the Christiana prisoners to the full force of federal law. Brent informed Governor Lowe of Ashmead's unacceptable conditions; Lowe forwarded the correspondence to President Fillmore, accompanied by a very short note in which he abstained from making any comment or request.[35]

The President took the point, and in short order Ashmead received a letter from Secretary of State Webster directing him to accept Brent and Cooper onto the prosecutorial team *and* to offer the two lawyers representing Maryland the opportunity of making a closing address to the jury should they wish to do so. Ashmead followed his orders to the letter, wrote conciliatory notes to Brent and Governor Lowe, and the Maryland officials accepted the new arrangements graciously.[36]

For a brief time it seemed that the problem was smoothed over and the prosecution could get on with its work. Brent's honor was not fully redeemed, however, by total victory over his antagonist. The federal government's capitulation to Brent's terms and the private humiliation of Ashmead were just not enough. So Brent leaked the entire correspondence, which was published in newspapers with additional details that, in Governor Lowe's opinion, could only have been supplied by Brent himself. The only purpose served by the leak was the public embarrassment of the federal prosecutor. The consequences, though, were more far-reaching. In Governor Lowe's opinion, at least, publication of the letters would diminish whatever sympathy existed for the prosecution in the North, increase the antagonism of Pennsylvanians to Maryland, and make cooperation among the prosecutorial team all the more difficult, to the possible detriment of their case. The governor was correct in every regard; the leak was not a very shrewd move *if* the primary goal was conviction of the Christiana "traitors" rather than scoring ephemeral points in a battle of honor against one Yankee lawyer.[37]

The prosecution was off to a rocky start at best, but it was moving forward in a tense public atmosphere that made the private differences among the government's attorneys of secondary concern. The prosecutors, at least, agreed on the course they were taking, however much they might squabble about tactics or each other's skills and moral worth. While the lawyers argued and the grand jury deliberated—a process that took between three and four months—the accused and some of the witnesses languished in Philadelphia's Moyamensing Prison under conditions that varied dramatically depending on the prisoner's race. Eventually, the prosecutors convinced the grand jury to indict thirty-eight men, some of whom were never in custody, on 117 separate counts of treason. The multiple counts were a consequence of charging some with a separate capital crime for resisting the capture of each of Edward Gorsuch's fugitive slaves.[38]

Never before—and, indeed, never since—were so many Americans charged in court with a treasonous crime. At no point in this nation's history until the 1950s was the federal government so eager to prosecute so many Americans to make a political point. Never before had the leaders of this nation felt so vulnerable to a perceived threat by so few. All sides to the fugitive-slave question, in every region of the country, appreciated how much was at stake. The credibility of the federal government, the confidence in and perhaps even the commitment of Southern moderates to the Union, and the lives of dozens of men were all on the line.

If the rhetoric of politicians and newspapers can be believed, the very fate of the nation—its moral fiber and perhaps even its survival—were now to be put in the hands of judges, lawyers, and the twelve citizens who would decide whether Castner Hanway, who would be tried first, would go to the gallows or leave Philadelphia a free man. The story had all the ingredients of classic theater—heroes, villains, and a huge cast of minor characters, some of them even good for comic relief; but no one was laughing or applauding yet. This was a very serious business and would be reported in the minutest detail, down to the clothes worn by women in the gallery, which jurors had colds, and what the prisoners ate for their Thanksgiving meal. At great expense, court reporters were hired to keep a literal transcription of the trial record, which in turn was carried at length in newspapers across the nation.

John Greenleaf Whittier even wrote a poem in honor of the *white* prisoners in Moyamensing Prison, which was as much an indictment of the age and of those who imprisoned Hanway, Lewis, and Scarlett for crimes of conscience as it was an ode to the three men's contribution to the historical quest for freedom. Just as pro-slavery and pro-Compromise advocates focused the blame for Edward Gorsuch's death on the white "leaders" of the riot, so the abolitionist community lionized the three white men with less regard for the role played by African-Americans in the battle for their own liberty. Whittier's poem, like most of the literature about fugitive slaves, commemorated a white battle for black freedom. The poem thus gives us more of an insight into the prejudices of white abolitionists, into the perceptions of one part of the community, than into the facts of what really occurred. By altering, or at least filtering, reality through their racial expectations, the abolitionists no less than the advocates of slavery contributed to the legend of race relations in antebellum America. The myth, in turn, created its own reality, which affected the direction that confrontation would take. The perceptions, in a certain sense, became the reality and helped determine the course of events.

The poem, entitled "For Righteousness' Sake," was "inscribed to Friends under arrest for treason against the slave power," thereby revealing—in its mistaken assumption that these three men were all Quakers and dedicated abolitionists—the way in which heroes and myths are born.

> The age is dull and mean. Men creep,
> Not walk; with blood too pale and tame

To pay the debt they owe to shame;
Buy cheap, sell dear; eat, drink, and sleep
  Down-pillowed, deaf to moaning want;
Pay tithes for soul-insurance; keep
  Six days to Mammon, one to Cant.

In such a time, give thanks to God,
  That somewhat of the holy rage
  With which the prophets in their age
On all its decent seemings trod,
  Has set your feet upon the lie,
That man and ox and soul and clod
  Are market stock to sell and buy!

The hot words from your lips, my own,
  To caution trained, might not repeat;
  But if some tares among the wheat
Of generous thought and deed were sown,
  No common wrong provoked your zeal;
The silken gauntlet that is thrown
  In such a quarrel rings like steel.

The brave old strife the fathers saw
  For freedom calls for men again
  Like those who battled not in vain
For England's Charter, Alfred's law;
  And right of speech and trial just
Wage in your name their ancient war
  With venal courts and perjured trust.

God's ways seem dark, but soon or late,
  They touch the shining hills of day;
  The evil cannot brook delay,
The good can well afford to wait.
  Give ermined knaves their hour of crime;
Ye have the future grand and great,
  The safe appeal of Truth to Time! [39]

The Trial

CHARGING THE CHRISTIANA PRISONERS with treason was a political act of real significance for American jurisprudence, but the long-term consequences for constitutional law were of secondary concern to most people at the time. In the heat of the moment, it was difficult for anyone to see beyond the exigencies of interregional strife, to get past conflicting senses of what justice, honor, and law demanded as retribution for the death of Edward Gorsuch. To those Americans who valued the Compromise measures, Castner Hanway and his "accomplices" had gone beyond the bounds of normal crime. What they did was more than a riot and worse than a murder, so their act needed another name.

"Treason" carried such a burden in the popular mind. Perhaps this was partly because of its association with England's famous state trials and the penalty of drawing and quartering during the not-so-distant past of Anglo-American law. The name Benedict Arnold remained synonymous with "traitor," and school children still read the story of Major John André's execution for treason during the Revolution. Americans also collectively remembered their political trials of the Whiskey rebels, John Fries, and Aaron Burr in the first quarter-century after the War for Independence. For these reasons, among others, treason had a symbolic significance as "the king of crimes," which transcended judicial definitions of its meaning.

As a consequence of this symbolic weight, treason seemed the obvious charge to Southerners most horrified by the Christiana Riot. "It will not be enough," proclaimed one Maryland newspaper, "that these men be convicted and punished for murder and outrage. . . . It is treason—and as traitors these bloody men must die—or we have no interest in their death—no advantage from their execution." The punishment for any capital crime was the same—a man hanged for murder was surely as dead as one hanged for treason—but nothing short of judicially branding the prisoners as traitors could salve the wounded honor of Southerners and restore their faith in the Union.[1]

Others, in the North as well as the South, agreed that the crimes committed at the Parkers' house transcended mere riot, resistance to enforcement of a law, and homicide. "There is something more than even a murderous riot in all this," a Northern Whig newspaper agreed: "It is an act of insurrection—if not also one of treason." And yet, there was also fear among friends of the Compromise measures that a too ambitious prosecution—one that went beyond the available evidence in the case— might produce results just the opposite of those intended. If the reach of the government exceeded its grasp, there was the real possibility that the defendants would get off scot-free. On the other hand, if the government managed to secure a conviction that went beyond the common sense of the law, in a politically charged atmosphere supportive of judicial revenge, the moral stature of the nation and the civil liberties of its citizens would just as surely be losers in the case.[2]

The potential certainly existed for making the prisoners appear the wounded parties rather than the guilty traitors that friends of the Fugitive Slave Law thought them to be. Indeed, it appalled at least one Northern newspaper that the Christiana rioters might become linked in the popular mind with such martyrs for liberty as the seventeenth-century Englishman Algernon Sydney. The *New York Times*, at least, did "not wish to see the half dozen negroes and their white abettors, who were concerned in this Christiana affair, identified with such men, even in the character of their offense. They have committed murder: try and punish them for it, but do not call it treason."[3]

The nation's newspapers printed numerous conjectures on the possible outcome of the case, and second-guesses of the prosecutor's decision to press for treason indictments. The permutations of logic were numerous and complex, which means that a writer's position for or against the treason charge was not necessarily a clue to which side he hoped would win. Perhaps, reasoned some, the government really wanted the prisoners acquitted, which is why the prosecutor decided to charge the defendants with a crime for which no Northern jury would convict. Maybe the President and Secretary of State made a shrewd political calculation and were counting on legal precedents, evidence, and popular sympathy being decisively in favor of the prisoners. That way the government could appear to be doing its utmost to enforce the law without creating abolitionist martyrs.[4]

But what if the government really did have the law, the judges, and the jury on its side? What exactly would the President do if Castner Hanway, and perhaps dozens of others, were convicted and sentenced to death? Would Millard Fillmore permit executions as a sacrificial offering to the South and with the certain knowledge that such an outcome would make it even more difficult—probably impossible—to enforce the Fugitive Slave Law in the North? Would he risk adding fuel to the fires of secessionism by personal intervention in the convicted traitors' behalf?[5]

None of these questions could be answered decisively in the weeks and then months leading up to the trial of Hanway, so the speculation helped newspapers keep interest alive until there was really something new to report. Ultimately, of course, the answer to the most basic question about whether the defendant would be convicted or return home to his quiet life as a miller was a matter of law as well as of politics and popular sympathy. So the same questions were debated in the legal community with equal ferocity and as much disagreement as in the papers, precisely because the American law of treason was unclear.

In retrospect, there is no doubt that the prosecuting attorney responsible for the case hoped to secure convictions for treason, whatever the fears of his superiors, and that all his actions were consistent with that end. This goal was fully compatible with John W. Ashmead's other ambition, which was to satisfy the public that the government was doing everything within its power to enforce the Fugitive Slave Law. There was no disjunction between the demands of politics and law in this case, at least as Ashmead saw it; and all of his knowledge and instincts pointed the same way. His concerns were about tactics, preparation, and the resources he could devote to the case.

Ashmead's correspondence addressed the variety of influences that led him to try Castner Hanway for treason first and alone rather than as part of a joint indictment against some or all of the thirty-eight defendants. Ashmead informed officials at the Department of State on September 26 that he hoped through multiple indictments against each of the prisoners for treason, resisting the posse, and abetting the escape of fugitive slaves to "satisfy the country that every possible means of reaching the offenders has been resorted to, and that the officers of the law have left nothing undone to secure their punishment." The reason he decided to proceed against the defendants serially rather than in a joint indictment was because a jury would be terrified at the idea of returning a verdict of guilty which would involve so great a sacrifice of human life and also because the evidence would be uncertain and indistinct as to some, and in this way might so involve the whole transaction in doubt as to lead to the acquittal of all. Separate indictments would enable us to select the strongest cases for trial first, and present the causes to the jury in our own way.[6]

In most respects the 117 separate treason indictments were classic expressions of the crime, steeped in centuries-long traditions of Anglo-American law. The defendants had, according to the prosecution, assembled "to the number of one hundred persons and upwards, armed and arrayed in a war-like manner" with traitorous designs and "wickedly and traitorously did levy war against the United States." Ashmead also injected a novelty into the indictments, however, drawing on his understanding of English treason law and his desire to score political points for his superiors in the executive branch of the federal government. The government charged that each of the defendants

> traitorously did prepare and compose, and did then and there maliciously and traitorously cause and procure to be prepared and composed, divers books, pamphlets, letters, declarations, resolutions, addresses, papers and writings, and did then and there maliciously and traitorously publish and disperse and cause to be published and dispersed divers other . . . writings . . . containing . . . incitements . . . to resist, oppose, and prevent, by violence and intimidation, the execution, of the said laws.[7]

No matter that the government had not a shred of evidence connecting any of the defendants with such publications or with the circulation of abolitionist tracts; no matter that illiterate African-American defendants were also indicted for writing such "treasonous" literature. So what if the charge of treason by words alone was a remnant of English treason law that was absent from Article III, section 3, of the U.S. Constitution and that such an outrageous charge had never come before a federal court. There was no attempt to document the allegation and no intention to present a jury with evidence of treason by written words. This was a blatantly political accusation made for the purposes of frightening abolitionists, pleasing friends of the Compromise measures, and currying favor with senior administration officials. "If you will examine the last overt act in the Indictment, that which respects speeches and pamphlets," Ashmead informed the Secretary of the Interior, "you will perceive it may alarm some of the persons who are travelling through the country preaching treason." Castner Hanway's trial would be as much about politics as law, and the indictments were intended to help set the stage for a political as well as a legal confrontation in the court.[8]

From Ashmead's perspective, the government needed every advantage—political, legal, and tactical—that he could manufacture, because the prosecution was the decided underdog in the case. All the resources of the abolitionist network were arrayed against him; no expense was being spared to assemble the best legal talent available in Hanway's behalf. Defense lawyers had the resources to investigate the background and views of prospective jurors from the rural countryside surrounding Philadelphia; and what is more, U.S. Marshal Anthony E. Roberts, who was responsible for assembling the jury list, was a close political ally of that "Woolly-Headed Whig" Congressman Thaddeus Stevens. Stevens's patronage had gotten Roberts his job, and now Stevens headed the defense team. That was a suspiciously cozy relationship between politics and law from the prosecution's point of view, and the behavior of Roberts would feed rumors of corruption over the course of the trial.[9]

Senior officials in Washington continued to deny Ashmead specific advice and would not provide what he considered sufficient help in preparing the case. When the prosecutor traveled to Washington looking for guidance, his superiors were either conveniently out of town or otherwise unavailable for consultation. Clearly, they wanted to avoid any personal links with Hanway's trial, which had the potential to ruin political careers. Ashmead also had to contend with bureaucratic rules that inhibited his ability to make financial commitments and to pay those already incurred. The prosecutor complained time and again about how much of his preparation time was squandered justifying accounts and petitioning for funds. "I beg leave to say," Ashmead pleaded at one point, "that the time which has elapsed since my application and the near approach of the day of trial would render a favorable decision on it now, a matter of subordinate importance." He needed to hire an artist, who would visit the scene of the riot and execute drawings for the benefit of the jury. "As to the minute knowledge which I asked the means of obtaining respecting the jurors," Ashmead explained in the same letter in response to a request for further justification of the expense, "this was asked after the fact had become known to me, that similar measures were taken on the part of the defense."[10]

Ashmead needed to pay two attorneys (one of them his cousin), who had assisted in taking testimony and drawing up indictments, and to secure their help with further preparations before trial. He had a bill from

Francis Wharton, the well-known legal scholar, who charged a $150 consultation fee for his opinions on the law of treason; and Ashmead wanted authorization to hire two court reporters to ensure that newspapers got accurate accounts of trial testimony. More controversial, and more pressing, were bills for services rendered by local officials in Lancaster County. Prompt payment seemed necessary to guarantee their further cooperation, which was essential to the case. The federal government refused to pay local lawmen for helping to arrest felons. Sure, as it turned out, the prisoners were given over to federal officials, but they had allegedly also committed crimes that fell under state jurisdiction—murder and riot; and it was expected that if they were not executed for treason, the "traitors" would then be tried locally for those crimes. In the federal government's opinion, county officials were only doing their regular jobs under extraordinary circumstances, nothing more; therefore, they should be reimbursed for their time by the county or state.

The Department of the Interior also refused to reimburse a local hostler for damages inflicted on his property by the marines and federal posses charged with sweeping up suspects in the wake of the riot and for unauthorized food consumed on his premises. Fiscal responsibility was one thing—it did look as if the hotel owner was trying to gouge the government for everything he could get, and lawmen really were already paid to arrest criminals—but alienating local people could have real repercussions for the prosecution. As a consequence, Ashmead spent much ink and energy trying to resolve problems that were only tangentially related to preparing his case against Castner Hanway. He asked for blanket authorization for all "reasonable" expenditures, which request was denied; and he lacked the confidence to make financial commitments without official guarantees.[11]

So Ashmead felt that he had time, money, the federal bureaucracy, and his Maryland "colleagues" working against him, in addition to the lawyers on the other side. Then things got worse. Two of his witnesses disappeared from the prison where they were being held in protective custody. As the *New York Times* reported the story datelined November 10:

> Yesterday morning, about 4 o'clock, two of the most important witnesses in the Christiana treason case, escaped from the debtor's apartment of the Moyamensing Prison. . . . They were evidently assisted from the outside of the building. Not the least singular part of the business, is a fact of which I have but this afternoon been informed. It is that, though the United States Marshal has repeatedly visited the prison

since the occurrence, he was not informed of it until 12 o'clock today. This is a mystery which needs explanation.

It is a mystery that has never been explained. No lock was broken, but the two black men were gone. The other African-American witnesses and defendants housed in the same part of the prison claimed total ignorance of the escape. We will never know who paid whom to release the witnesses or who among the prison guards was sympathetic to Hanway's defense or if the two men just got tired of being in jail and found their own way out. Whether Marshal Roberts himself was involved, was kept ignorant to cover the escape or to cover himself, is not clear. The prosecution had its suspicions; and Southerners were not too surprised that "justice" in the North was anything but fair—that marshals, guards, witnesses, and probably jurors and judges as well were either closet abolitionists or corrupted by abolitionist money.[12]

The two escapees, Josephus Washington and John Clark, were so-called "voluntary" witnesses in the pay of the prosecution for a dollar and a quarter per day. Their anticipated testimony related to the preexisting conspiracy against the posse rather than directly to events at the scene of the riot itself. On the day before Edward Gorsuch's death, the two men had possession of a written notice proclaiming the posse's imminent arrival, listing the names of the fugitives the lawmen were after, and alerting the local African-American populace to arm for battle. Had they testified, Clark and Washington might have helped prosecutors establish the intentions of rioters and perhaps the role of Samuel Williams, the black informant who followed Marshal Kline from Philadelphia; but as far as we know, they had no specific information bearing on Castner Hanway's intentions, words, or actions during the riot.[13]

The escape was not the only "evidence" available to suspicious minds of a snug relationship between the prisoners and officials responsible for bringing them to justice. It was the abolitionist press that reported on "Thanksgiving among the 'Traitors,'" several days after the trial began, but it was Southerners who took the obvious lessons about Northern "justice" from the story. According to the *Pennsylvania Freeman*:

> Thomas L. Kane, Esq. (son of the judge) sent to the prison for their use six superior turkeys, two of them extra size, together with a pound cake, weighing 16 pounds. The turkeys were cooked, with appropriate fixings, by order of Mr. Freed, the Superintendent, in the prison kitchen, by a female prisoner detached for the purpose. The dinner for the white prisoners, Messrs. Hanaway [sic], Lewis and Scarlet[t], was served in ap-

propriate style in the room of Mr. Morrison, one of the keepers. The U.S. Marshal, A. E. Roberts, Esq., several of the keepers, and Mr. Hawes, one of the prison officers, dined with the prisoners as their guests. Mayor Gilpin coming in, accepted an invitation to test the quality of the pound cake.

When prisoners and friends had eaten their fill, Mrs. Hanway, who served as hostess, made up plates of food for each of the black prisoners incarcerated on charges of treason. And there was still enough left after that to serve the rest of the prisoners in the corridor a fine holiday meal.[14]

Perhaps Brent and the other Southerners associated with the trial were jealous. No Northerners extended hospitality to these Southern gentlemen; no one invited the men into his home. Dickinson Gorsuch's diary suggests that they spent some time in the prosecuting attorney's office, attending to the business of the case, but it must have been depressing, and probably seemed grossly unfair, that everyone around them was celebrating—even the "traitors"—while they, literally the wounded parties in the affair, were treated as social pariahs, more repulsive in some ways to Northern whites than the African-American "murderers" in jail. If they needed any additional proof of the cultural distance between Maryland and Pennsylvania, this was it; if they lacked sufficient evidence of the difficulty they would have in getting a sympathetic hearing from a Northern jury, they could read it in the faces and unspoken gestures of the people around them in court the next day.[15]

The proliferation of sympathetic stories in the newspapers about the Christiana prisoners, their health, and their daily activities testifies to the celebrity status accorded them throughout the Northeast, to the significance attached to the trial on both sides of the Mason-Dixon Line, and to the number of reporters on the scene whose jobs were to find, or if necessary to manufacture, news. Even such a small event as a bird flying into the courtroom during preliminary proceedings did not pass without comment. The resulting satire reflects the slow pace of events, which demanded creativity from the reporters, and the growing sophistication of readers, who were becoming well versed on the intricacies of treason law even before the trial began:

The very room of the United States District Court, has been the scene of "resistance to the officers of the law," by a woodpecker, which flew into the window on Saturday. Marshal Roberts, District Attorney Ashmead, and others, talk of bringing in a bill against the fugitive, as if it had not bill enough already, because the bird, assuming the principles abolitionist cohorts were, as the Democrats portrayed them, "the pledged assassins of the Constitution. In their insane zeal for the slave, they forget the white. In their hypocritical hostility to slavery, they would plunge into ruin the whole fabric of rational freedom."[12]

Little wonder, the *Pennsylvanian* observed, that radical secessionist newspapers in the South refrained from denouncing Johnston, while pro-Union Southern newspapers had harsh words for the governor. Johnston played into the hands of secessionists, who were trying to convince their readers that the Compromise measures would never work. His "abolition-ist" sympathies made the efforts of Southern moderates all the more dif-ficult. Johnston represented the epitome of Northern irresponsibility, and this image helped convert Southerners to the secessionist cause.[13]

Perhaps such inflammatory charges against Johnston would have been less effective had he been able to avoid direct association with the riot. Unfortunately for the governor, however, the train taking him on a cam-paign swing to Philadelphia not only passed through Lancaster County on the very day of the bloodshed but stopped close enough for passengers to visit the riot scene, which some of them did. Johnston decided not even to get off the train—unusual behavior for a politician in the midst of a campaign—but there could be no doubt that the governor knew of the riot a few hours after it occurred and that he could have known more had he made it his business to do so.

Johnston might have interviewed witnesses himself, issued a state-ment of regret as the chief executive of the state, authorized a reward for the capture of Gorsuch's murderers, and called out the militia to comb the countryside for William Parker and his accomplices. Instead, he chose to let local and federal officials handle the matter. On the one hand, the case seemed to fall under the Fugitive Slave Law, which meant—as John-ston interpreted the law—that the governor of Pennsylvania lacked juris-diction; on the other hand, local officials seemed to be doing just fine.

Governor Johnston was either grossly misinformed for several days after the riot or was playing dumb in an attempt to avoid becoming em-broiled in this potentially volatile affair. He should have known from his own cursory inquiry on the day of the riot that Parker and his accomplices were at large, and yet he claimed throughout the weekend following the incident that Gorsuch's murderers were in the Lancaster jail. In truth, on the day of the riot—when Johnston's train stopped in Christiana—no one was incarcerated for involvement in the riot, and no attempts were un-derway to arrest anyone. Local law-enforcement officials were in utter disarray. "All was confusion," one man observed. There was no one in charge. And yet, in a letter responding to concerned Philadelphia citizens of the "higher law," would not suffer itself to be captured, without an effort to preserve its freedom. The offense not being general among the woodpeckers, the crime cannot be charged as treason.[16]

By the time that Castner Hanway's trial actually began at 11 a.m. on Monday, November 24, 1851, the nation was ready, indeed impatient; everyone, on all sides of the issue, believed that "justice" was long over-due. The courtroom was cleaned and shined; new gas fixtures and state-of-the-art ventilating devices had been installed specially for the event:

> Additional officers were selected by the U.S. marshall to preserve or-der. The crowd was very orderly. Benches were placed on either side of the court room, capable of seating seventy or eighty persons; and these benches completely filled up the vacant space when occupied. They were totally inadequate to the wants of the public, but equal to the capacity of the room.

Reporters had reserved seats. The papers reported that no women, save the defendant's wife, sought admittance, and no seats were occupied by black men on the trial's first day. Spectators assembled earlier every morning of the trial thereafter, and the size of the crowd seeking admission to the proceedings grew ever larger in size. The mix of the onlookers also changed. Marshals tried to segregate seating by gender and race but eventually lost control even of that minimal order, to the horror of Southerners and some Northerners. The number of women, many of them recognizable by their dress as members of the Society of Friends, grew each succeeding morning until by the end of the week they constituted more than half the observers seated in court. The *North American* reported on Saturday, December 6, that "the crowd increases with every day's proceedings, and the ladies bid fair to monopolize two-thirds of the seats in the room." By the following Tuesday, spectators had to arrive no later than 7 a.m., three hours before the session began, in order to gain entry. By Thursday, the newspapers reported that all of the chairs not reserved for reporters, trial principals, and court personnel were taken by women, all of them clearly sympathetic to Hanway's acquittal. The papers reported that Lucretia Mott, the famous Quaker preacher and anti-slavery advocate, had begun to attend. She sat quietly next to the African-American prisoners, with her head down, attending to the knitting on her lap, seemingly impervious to what went on around her in the room. Hundreds more women and men, of both races, frustrated by the limited seating, filled the stairway and entry to Independence Hall and over-flowed onto the sidewalk and street. Opponents of slavery and of the Fugitive Slave Law were making silent witness to the proceedings on the second floor of Independence Hall.[17]

On the first day, Castner Hanway entered the courtroom with his wife at his side, embracing his arm. For most people attending the trial, including the reporters, this was a first glimpse of the alleged traitor, and they were intrigued by his looks. The defendant was a tall man, in his mid-thirties, "but spare in form, and inclining to stoop a little." More surprising was the way that he dressed.

> The impression has gone abroad, that the prisoner is a member of the Society of Friends, and many suppose that he appears in court arrayed in the peculiar dress of that sect. This is a great mistake. . . . He is dressed in a full suit of fashionable black clothes, with black silk neck handkerchief, and standing collar.

Hanway's stature and countenance and, even more, the way that he dressed were the first clues detected by reporters for their reading public that this unremarkable miller might be something other than he seemed. Perhaps he really was not a Quaker; he certainly did not look like the sort of wild-eyed radical cum military strategist for African-American mobs that Southerners and many Northerners believed him to be. Hanway's character, what went on in his mind and his heart, was also of interest to the reporters, who searched his eyes and his manner for the key to his soul. Hanway had a "firm and singular look," one reporter concluded after watching his reactions to prospective jurors; he appeared to be "respectful and reserved." Since Hanway never spoke in his own defense or made any public statement about his actions and beliefs, this was the closest that strangers ever got to what the man thought.[18]

The first task before the court was selection of jurors from the list provided by Marshal Roberts. Seventy-eight of the 116 prospective jurors initially responded to their names; three more showed up late, to bring the total pool to eighty-one men. The court released nineteen for one reason or another; the excuses for wanting to be spared this public duty read like a textbook on the ills and infirmities that plague modern man. "I am subject to violent attacks of sick headache," explained Mr. Brodhead, "as often as once in eight or ten days, which cuts me down for a day or two." Mr. Toland suffered from rheumatic gout; Mr. Culbertson had vertigo; Mr. Brown was deaf and had a defective memory; Mr. Taylor pled impaired hearing exacerbated by a very bad cold. "Your disease has become epidemic today," Judge Grier cynically responded, no doubt at an enhanced volume, before excusing Taylor from the court. Mr. Massey endured *angina pectoris;* Mr. Cope was in general ill-health. Attorney D. P. Brown, who represented other defendants in the Christiana case, sarcastically remarked to the court on the "number of deaf men, or those getting deaf. I think they are all getting deaf, but I thank Heaven they are not dumb." The court was somewhat less sympathetic to a banker and a company president, who believed their businesses would collapse if they left them in the hands of others for even two weeks; but the judges tried to accommodate all reasonable needs as best they could.[19]

Here again, in selecting a jury the prosecution believed itself at a distinct disadvantage and even suspected an abolitionist conspiracy to put in a fix. Ashmead had neither the time nor the resources to investigate as thoroughly as he would have liked the personal backgrounds of those on Marshal Roberts's list. The defense lawyers, on the other hand, seemed to know enough about jurors without asking many questions and found surprisingly few who did not suit them just fine. According to Maryland's Attorney General Brent:

> In striking the jury, we had great difficulty, because from the most satisfactory information in our power, we believed that a large majority of the appearing jurors were unfavorable to a conviction, and which belief was strengthened by the fact, that out of eighty-three [sic] jurors, appearing for challenge, the prisoner accepted fifty-nine, of whom fifty-one were set aside by the United States under their qualified right of challenge, until the whole panel was exhausted.

In light of Marshal Roberts's other behavior—eating dinner with the prisoners during the trial and his suspected complicity in the escape of two prosecution witnesses—it seemed obvious to Southerners that the abolitionist lawman had conspired with defense attorneys to ensure selection of a jury favorable to Hanway's cause. What is more, Brent contended,

> it is also a fact within my personal knowledge, that free negroes were admitted through the Marshal's office into the court-room, when crowds of white citizens were kept outside of the door; and complaint was made to me, by a respectable gentleman, one of the witnesses from Maryland, that after the recision of the order of the court to exclude witnesses, he was refused admission by a deputy of the Marshal, when a colored man was passed at once into the court-room, upon the written permit either of the Marshal, or somebody else.

All of this information, whether based in fact or on unwarranted suspicions, would have its effect on a Southern audience already skeptical about what Northern "justice" might mean. After two full days of interviews, the lawyers on the prosecution team were most concerned about the last two jurors they had to accept. Their allotted preemptory challenges had run out, and they could find no substantive cause to dismiss the two men who seemed likely to favor the defendant's case. The jury sworn in by the clerk included a carpenter, two "gentlemen," a surveyor, a blacksmith, two merchants, and five farmers. Their average age was fifty-three years, and, not surprisingly for this trial in which information was recorded in minute detail, we even know that their average weight was 178 pounds. Corpulence corresponded with success among the jurors; by every account they were men of standing in their communities—one was a Whig member of the state legislature, another had been an unsuccessful candidate for Congress the previous year (running against Stevens), and a third was later a judge. So this was a jury of twelve weighty men, in both senses of the term, and undoubtedly not nearly so prejudiced against the government as Brent suspected and Ashmead feared.[20]

Associate justice of the Supreme Court Robert C. Grier, who presided in this circuit and was also "a man of large proportions," sat in judgment with district judge John K. Kane. Both men had expressed their dedication to enforcing the Fugitive Slave Law, as Justice Grier put it, "till the last hour it remains on the books." Judge Kane had instructed the grand jury on the law of treason in a fashion that also concerned the defense. When Justice Grier expressed his "extreme desire" to complete Hanway's case within two weeks, so he could keep an appointment in Washington, Thaddeus Stevens responded with biting sarcasm for the defense that he hoped it would not take that long. "In our country," Stevens observed, "we hang a man in three days, and I hope these gentlemen [that is, the prosecution] will not take so long a time."[21]

Wisely, it seems in retrospect, the defense decided not to attack slavery or the Fugitive Slave Law as part of its case. An acquittal was preferable, for their client at least, to conviction and martyrdom in the name of a higher law. So, after Stevens's cynical outburst, he played a somewhat more restrained role and did not deliver a summation at the end. The defense apparently balanced the potential gain from his fiery eloquence against the possible harm he might do by alienating more conservative jurors and rested content with a substantive challenge to the government's evidence. Hanway had the benefit of Stevens's quick mind and razor-sharp wit, but it was unclear how the lawyer's reputation would play to the politically mixed jury of a somewhat conservative bent.[22]

The prosecution was less prone to histrionics than the defense and less talented in the dramatic arts of trial law; indeed, Senator Cooper thought that Ashmead's opening address was extremely, perhaps damagingly, dull. The prosecutor read word for word from a written text on the law of treason as it applied to this case. "The speech was well enough in itself," Cooper wrote to Maryland's Governor Lowe, "but none but extempore addresses are ever effective when addressed to courts and juries." Still and all, by the end of the first week and the close of the prosecution's case, Cooper was hopeful that they had enough to convict. "I think we have established the material overt act, by *more* than two witnesses," Cooper concluded. "It is to be feared however, that the character of the principal witness, Kline, will be successfully assailed by the prisoner, and especially inasmuch as there are some discrepancies between him and our other witnesses and some contradictions of his former statements made at various times."[23]

As Ashmead presented the law, "any combination or conspiracy by force and intimidation to prevent the execution of an act of Congress, so as to render it inoperative and ineffective, is in legal estimation high treason." The convictions of the Whiskey rebels and John Fries during the 1790s had set that clear precedent. And the facts in this case proved, according to the prosecution, that Hanway was on the ground at the time of the riot, that he refused to assist Marshal Kline when asked to do so, and that he then advised the blacks to resist the posse by force. Hanway's presence in advance of most of the rioters and the circumstances of their arrival suggested to the prosecution a preexisting conspiracy, which ultimately resulted in violent resistance to the posse, serious injury to several of its members, and the death of Edward Gorsuch, who

> had no weapon of any kind in his hands, and was therefore cruelly, wantonly and unnecessarily wounded by the defendant and his associates, while carrying out their combination and conspiracy to resist, oppose and render inoperative and void the acts of Congress referred to in the indictment.[24]

Even with Hanway's presence and role proved, however, it was necessary for the prosecution to establish the broader intentions of the defendant in order to secure a conviction for treason rather than for some lesser crime. According to Ashmead's presentation of the law,

> the intent with which the act was committed, is the essential ingredient in the offense. If it was not levelled at the statute, but simply designed

to prevent the arrest of the slaves belonging to the late Mr. Gorsuch, it amounted, as far as the United States is concerned, to nothing more than a high misdemeanor.

Even under the best of circumstances—credible witnesses, sympathetic judges and jury, and direct oral and documentary evidence of the defendant's intent—treason was a devilishly difficult charge for the prosecution to prove. One gap in the line of evidence from conception, through plot, to execution of a treasonous overt act and the case could come tumbling down. Everything had to go right for the prosecution, and in this case everything seemed to go wrong.[25]

Under cross-examination, Kline had to admit that he spent much of the riot hiding in a cornfield, which limited his vision of the violence somewhat, but denied that he was cowering in the woods when the first shots were fired, visually blocked from events that he claimed to describe. The deputy marshal not only insisted that he was there but also that he could identify a number of the rioters—some by name, as in the case of Harvey Scott, and others he recognized when he saw them, even though he did not know what they were called. Kline acknowledged that he did not hear what Hanway said to the small band of black men with whom he spoke before the riot began and that he did not actually witness the murder of Gorsuch or even see the corpse until after the violence had ceased.[26]

Thomas Pearce also had to concede that he later told people that Hanway had probably saved his life: "I said he might have turned a part of them back, and saved my life in consequence of that being the fact." Pearce granted that he did not hear what Hanway said to "inspire the Negroes," but he was certain that the miller's presence alone gave heart to the dispirited band of African-Americans holed up in William Parker's house. Pearce denied that he called Kline a coward after the riot or that he had laid blame for the violence squarely on the deputy marshal's incompetence.[27]

Nathan Nelson likewise disavowed, under cross-examination, that he had ever said Kline hid out in the woods rather than helping the rest of the posse. Even when the defense attorney read back to him the transcript of his deposition under oath, Nelson repudiated the testimony recorded as his own. All of the prosecution's witnesses agreed that Hanway "inspired" the rioters; and all of them used the same language to characterize his inspirational role. None of them heard Hanway's words to the African-Americans, but they agreed that he must have served as the master strategist and commander of those who "levied war" against the government and its laws.[28]

Surviving members of the Gorsuch party agreed that the rioters responded to trumpet calls from inside *and* outside the house, which the posse interpreted as evidence of a preconcerted plot to wage war against law enforcement. The prosecution also introduced evidence of a written call to arms circulating among members of Lancaster's African-American community the day preceding the riot; and, of course, Kline testified that the abolitionist "spy" Samuel Williams doggedly tracked him from Philadelphia to Lancaster County. Taken as a whole, according to the prosecution, this evidence proved a conspiracy and demonstrated the treasonous intent of those who engaged in the riot.

Perhaps all this was true, countered lawyers for the defense, and yet where is the connecting link between the conspirators and Castner Hanway? What if Williams circulated information of the posse's arrival; what if black people armed in response to the news; what if horns called them to arms on the morning of the riot, and they arrived at Parker's with the intention of levying war against the government's enforcement of the Fugitive Slave Law? The prosecution offered no testimony connecting Hanway to Williams or to the spy's information and none coupling Hanway with the larger plot to levy war. Hanway was on the scene at the time the riot occurred; the defense readily acknowledged that fact. His lawyers denied that Hanway "inspired" or in any sense led the rioters, and the prosecution had no witness to his intentions or to his knowledge of any conspiracy.[29]

Judge Kane decided against the defense on this important question of law and ruled that even where testimony did not specifically tie the defendant to the conspiracy, evidence of the plot could be relevant to his conviction for treason. The precedent here was the Whiskey Rebellion cases, which were still good law for the judges in Hanway's trial. "If a man is found armed," reasoned Judge Kane,

> or in the company with one hundred other men opposing an officer, and he is charged with treason, evidence may be admitted that there were meetings held and speeches made inciting to rebellion against the law, even if that person was not present. It becomes a part of the history—of the *res gestae;* and we must have the whole *res gestae* to judge of what was the intention of the parties.

So the prosecution's evidence was potentially relevant to the conviction of Hanway, and its case would not fail in Kane's courtroom for a couple weak links in the chain. The defense would have to challenge the evidence and perhaps contest the judges' interpretation of treason to win Castner Hanway's freedom.[30]

Theodore Cuyler made the opening speech for Hanway's defense. His words bespoke moral outrage; his manner reflected disgust. Cuyler's tone dripped with sarcasm, as when he referred to the "persecution; I beg pardon; prosecution" of his client. "In no period of English law," Cuyler continued in the same vein, "for the last two hundred years, have events such as have been detailed here in evidence been held to be high treason, except when the law was pronounced through the polluted lips of a Scroggs or a Jeffries," those infamous judges from an era renowned for judicial butchery. Why, then, when the weight of law, evidence, and humanity all balanced against such an outrageous charge, was Castner Hanway in this courtroom on trial for his life? Quite simply, Cuyler answered in the opening volley of the miller's defense, because "the state of Maryland does thirst for blood, or else this cause, inadmissible even in Quarter Sessions practice, would not have been tried. Sir—did you hear it?" Cuyler asked the jury in a rhetorical flourish,

> That three harmless, non-resisting Quakers, and eight-and-thirty wretched, miserable, penniless negroes, armed with corn-cutters, clubs, and a few muskets and headed by a miller, in a felt hat, without a coat, without arms, and mounted on a sorrel nag, levied war against the United States.
> Blessed be God that our Union has survived the shock.[31]

The defense proceeded to draw a word picture quite different from the prosecution's blood-red portrait of a treasonous conspiracy against federal law. Instead, the testimony brought before the jury in Hanway's behalf sketched a background of illegal kidnapping over a course of months, indeed years, which led the black community to organize and arm against criminals who trafficked in stolen human goods. As Thaddeus Stevens explained to the court,

> what we propose to show is this: That there were in that immediate neighborhood a gang of professional kidnappers. . . . And that when the prisoner in the morning (for the first time) came out of his own house, not having heard anything of this, he was informed that there were kidnappers trying to kidnap Parker, whom it was supposed was the object of the attack.

So Hanway's intentions were very different, according to his defense, than what the prosecution asserted without any credible evidence connecting him to a treasonous conspiracy. Actions that might appear treasonous under one set of circumstances would amount to at worst a misdemeanor when comprehended in light of the facts. Hanway rode his horse to the scene of the riot when he heard that kidnappers were out to get Parker. Even if there was a conspiracy, and the defense was not admitting that there was, Hanway was ignorant of its existence and misinformed about the nature of the confrontation at his neighbor's house. A series of witnesses would testify to the pattern of race-related violence in Lancaster County, which made Hanway's story seem plausible in light of the facts. The miller "had a legal right," John Read added for the defense,

> to go and see this difficulty. He had a right to go to see that the parties were armed with the proper process of laws. And we shall contend that having gone with this rightful purpose . . . he subsequently left the ground in consequence of ascertaining that they had legal process, and that there was no right to interfere with them in any way.[32]

The other line of the defense lawyers' counterattack, just as Senator Cooper predicted in his letter to Governor Lowe, was aimed at the credibility of the prosecution's principal witness, Henry Kline. "We shall show you by ample proof," Cuyler informed the jury, "the notorious bad name of Kline for truth" and, by contrast, the reputation of Castner Hanway "for every good quality which can do honor to the character of a citizen." If it came down to the word of the defendant against that of his main accuser, Cuyler believed that the jury should discount any testimony from the "lying lips" of Marshal Kline, and witnesses for the defense would explain why.[33]

The bailiff swore in Judge William D. Kelley of Philadelphia. Stevens asked if the witness knew Henry Kline. He did.

"Do you know his general character for truth and veracity?"

"I have heard it much spoken of."

"What is it?"

"Very bad."

Stevens asked Francis Jobson the same questions.

"I have been a good deal with him, and seen him frequently, every week and every day perhaps for ten years," Jobson replied.

"What is that character?"

"I should say notoriously bad."

William Franke testified that he had known Kline for better than four-teen years.

"From that character, could you believe him on oath?" asked Stevens.

"I think not, sir."

Daniel Evans gave his opinion of Kline's reputation: "It is bad." George Simpson had known the deputy marshal for fifteen years.

"What is his general character for truth and veracity?" inquired Stevens.

"It is bad."

"From that character would you believe him on oath?"

"I would not."

Isaiah G. Stratton, William Stroud, and Jacob Walker all answered the same questions in the same way. John Hinkle had "never heard anything good of him in my life." Norman Ackley, Anthony Hoover, Aaron B. Fithian, George K. Wise, John Mackey, Andrew Redheffer, and John McEwen all testified that Kline could not be trusted to tell the truth, even under oath.[34]

The defense put John Carr on the stand to ask if he knew Harvey Scott, one of the black men whom Kline identified from the riot scene. Justice Grier inquired, in response to an objection by the prosecution, as to the purpose of this testimony. "To prove that what the United States gave in evidence by Kline, is utterly and totally false," responded Thaddeus Stevens for the defense. Go ahead, then, agreed Grier. Carr, John S. Cochran, and William McClyman all testified that Scott was miles away from the Parkers' at the time of the riot. Thomas Liston, William Hopkins, James Smith, and William Nutt next swore in succession that Kline had a bad general reputation for telling the truth and that they would not believe what he said, even under oath.[35]

The defense continued this pattern, to apparently devastating effect, first calling a witness to challenge some part of Kline's testimony and then another witness or two who reminded the jury of the deputy marshal's generally bad reputation in the community where he lived. Then they put on the stand a series of witnesses who collectively portrayed Castner Hanway in a starkly contrasting manner. Enoch Harlan described Hanway as a "remarkably quiet man; rather more so than most young men, and of a peaceable disposition." Harlan was a Quaker, and Stevens asked if the defendant was a member of that religious sect. "He is not a member of either branch of the Society of Friends that I know of," Harlan responded, "and he never was to my knowledge." So much for the prosecution theory connecting Hanway to Quakerism, thus to abolitionism, and therefore by implication to general opposition to the Fugitive Slave Law.

Charles H. Roberts testified next that Kline's reputation was very bad; then Joseph M. Thompson told the court that Hanway's reputation in the community was "very good—I never heard it called in question." George Mitchell, Levi Wayne Thompson, Andrew Mitchell, Wharton Pennock, Samuel Pennock, John Bernard, Calvin Russel, Isaac Walton, James Coates, Ellis P. Irvin, and George W. Irwin agreed.[36]

With this volley of testimonials, the defense rested its case, content that the jury had a positive image of Hanway and that Kline's testimony was completely done in. Witnesses for the defense had rebutted prosecution witnesses, exposed inconsistencies in the stories offered by various members of the posse, and explained Hanway's actions on the day of the riot in ways that sounded nothing like treason; or, at least, the defense hoped that the jury heard it that way. Their case challenged both the evidence and the prosecution's understanding of law. Defense lawyers also spiced their presentations with a sometimes cold but usually hot disdain for the "outrageous" charges that brought their client to court. "One man I imagine could not levy war against the United States," Brent acknowledged for the prosecution. "One old woman could," responded Thaddeus Stevens an instant after the words fell from the Marylander's mouth. If the trial was essentially a battle of words, the defense was routing the prosecution, but the case was not over yet.[37]

The prosecution had its rebuttal—one more chance to pull itself together, reestablish the credibility of its witnesses, and redirect the jury's attention from the assassination of Kline's character to the crime that was committed by the rioters with Castner Hanway at their head. "In a city like Philadelphia," George Ashmead explained to the jury,

> it is impossible for a police officer to have continued for several years in his office without raising round him, in all probability, a host of enemies. . . . the more faithful a police officer is, and the more boldly he discharges his duties, the greater is the number of enemies he has clustered around him.

So the prosecution brought into court a series of witnesses, most of them policemen or men associated with the Democratic Party in Philadelphia, to counter the negative image of Kline. The defense brought in twenty-nine character assassins; the prosecution was prepared to respond with seventy or more witnesses who would testify that Kline had a good reputation for veracity and that they would believe what he said under oath. "Are you going to be content with the odd trick, or are you going to have two to one?" Justice Grier asked the prosecutor impatiently after this stream of witnesses seemed to be turning into an endless flood. "We have a number of other witnesses to the same point," George Ashmead responded, "but we will conclude the examination of witnesses as to character for the United States, here."[38]

The prosecution also intended to show that the alleged pattern of kidnapping that the defense claimed to exist was, by and large, the quite legal attempts of Maryland slave owners and persons in their employ to retake fugitives who hid out in Lancaster County. They would also introduce testimony designed to show that Dr. Pearce had never impugned the courage of Marshal Kline or told others that Kline was to blame for Edward Gorsuch's death. What is more, the prosecution would put Harvey Scott himself on the stand:

> We shall produce Harvey Scott himself before you, and he will corroborate the statement of Kline, with whom he has had no interview and no conversation. He will tell you that he was present upon that occasion, and he will describe to you how he got out of Carr's house, and at what time he reached it when he returned.[39]

On Thursday, December 4, Harvey Scott took the stand.

"Were you there on the morning of the 11th of Sept. last?" George Ashmead confidently asked the witness.

"I was proved to be there, but I was not there," Scott responded after some prodding.

"On the morning of the 11th of Sept. last?" the prosecutor pressed him, in total disbelief.

"No, sir—Kline swore I was there, and at the time I was taken up, I told the man I was not there, and they took me to Christiana, and I was frightened, and I didn't know what to say, and I said what they told me."

"I had a conversation with this witness three or four days ago," George Ashmead then told the court, "and he said he was there."

"Yes," Justice Grier responded sympathetically, "others have had a conversation later than you." They had Scott's deposition, in which he admitted to being on the scene at the time of the riot; and George Ashmead had questioned him again several days before the trial testimony to make sure that he still had the story straight. Now, though, there was nothing to be done with the witness, and he had embarrassed the prosecution, undermined its credibility, and thus seriously damaged its case.

"Let him go," Judge Grier advised the prosecution, "and if you owe him any thing, pay him, that he may not be tempted to steal."

"The truth is," Thaddeus Stevens spoke up, throwing salt on the prosecution's wounds, "that he is not right in his mind." Whatever the state of Scott's mental health, he was obviously a frail reed on which to rely. He was a vagabond, who spent the years between 1837 and 1859 wandering around Lancaster and Chester counties looking for temporary work, in and out of almshouses and jails. When he died in a consumptive fit on the streets of West Chester eight years after this trial, Scott was not a man that the community missed. He had appeared in court numerous times before, but always as a defendant charged with vagrancy or petty theft. Once a slave in rural Lancaster County, then a carter in the town, Scott was a homeless man who reflected broader patterns of social change in southeastern Pennsylvania, as life became increasingly difficult for people of African-American descent. But this was not the story about Scott that the newspapers reported. Instead, he served as comic relief; a victim of some pity and more contempt, he was not taken seriously by anyone in this case. He got a new suit of clothes for his trouble—the government wanted Scott to look respectable for the court—and the dollar and a quarter a day that was owed him before the bailiff led him to the door. That was it; he was done; the trial went on.[40]

Scott was not the only black man in court with a new suit of clothes. The defense was also playing a sartorial game with images and identities, but in Castner Hanway's behalf. As a reporter for the *North American* recounted the scene:

> The object that first struck the eye on entering the court room . . . was a row of colored men seated on the north side of the room. . . . These were the colored persons alleged to have been engaged in the treason at Christiana, and numbered twenty-four. They were all similarly attired, wearing around their necks "red, white, and blue" scarfs.

The accused African-Americans were neatly groomed and dressed. Each wore a patriotic neckerchief, where the prosecution wanted to put a traitor's noose. The defense strategy, no doubt in concert with the anti-slavery society that chose and purchased the clothes, was to project an image quite different from the one drawn by the government's lawyers. The black defendants' costumes were also identical, which made identification by members of the posse even more difficult than it already was. Survivors from the Gorsuch party labored under the handicaps of faulty memories, caused by the stress of the riot scene, and a racist myopeia, which made African-Americans whom they did not know, all look a lot alike. Without the testimony of Harvey Scott and his previous willingness to identify rioters, the cases against both Hanway and the others were falling apart.[41]

Maryland's Attorney General Brent was in a rage at the end of the day's proceedings on December 4. Scott had turned on the prosecution that day, which was "the result," according to Brent, "of bribery and tampering in prison and of a piece with the escape of two other of our main witnesses." Ashmead had also botched what Brent believed was the "most important testimony" in the trial. The prosecution had made a serious blunder by saving a series of witnesses who would testify to the existence of illegal black gangs in Lancaster until after the defense presented its case. The defense objected to the introduction of new evidence—"evidence in chief"—at this point rather than just rebutting testimony, and the judge ruled against the prosecution.[42]

Brent no longer believed that they had a reasonable chance of conviction, and his mood was even more glum than usual. "The fact is," he reported to Governor Lowe, "the whole state is tainted and rotten, so much that the good and true men are few and far between—The outside pressure is all with the prisoners and crowds of women and negroes openly applaud the favourable points or the wit of his counsel." The courtroom spectators, whom Brent mistakenly saw as representative of Northern public opinion, favored the defendant; the court was corrupt and the federal prosecutor incompetent in the eyes of Maryland's chief judicial official. The trial was, in his opinion, "now a broad farce." His only ambition was to make a "calm, collected, but severe speech" summing up the prosecution's case; his only hope was for a favorable charge by the judge to the jury, which he did not really expect.[43]

The judge's statement came on December 11, eighteen days after the trial began. "The evidence has clearly shown," proclaimed Justice Grier, "that the participants in this transaction are guilty of riot and murder at least." But Castner Hanway was charged with treason; the other crimes were matters for the state courts. Grier also spoke on the question of treason, and in his opinion, the jury would have to acquit: "Not because the numbers or force was insufficient. But 1st, For want of any proof of previous conspiracy to make a *general and public resistance to any law* of the United States." What is more, according to Grier, the prosecution had offered no evidence that the rioters even knew of the new Fugitive Slave Law or that they "had any other intention than to protect one another from what they termed kidnappers." After the judge finished his charge, the jury retired to consider the case and returned in less than fifteen minutes to deliver a verdict of "not guilty," to the surprise of no one and to the pleasure of all the spectators still seated in the room.

Later, one of the jurors admitted that they had been ready to declare Hanway's innocence even before his lawyers offered a defense. As presented in court, it seemed a very weak case to persons not schooled in the tangled law of treason, as well as to Northern lawyers who saw the trial as a political sham.[44]

Hanway's acquittal did not make him and the other defendants free men. There were still federal misdemeanor charges against the miller, and the others charged with him still had treason indictments hanging over their heads. Eventually, when District Attorney Ashmead calmed down, the two other white men and twenty-three blacks still in prison were released on bail, but the federal charges against them were not dropped. Hanway was also left with huge debts arising from the case, perhaps as much as several thousand dollars; good lawyers cost money, as did investigators, and witnesses' expenses and court fees had to be paid. His lawyers petitioned the court for financial assistance, citing precedents from the Burr case among others, to help with such ruinous costs. At a hearing before Judge Kane the following week, Hanway's lawyers made their best case for reimbursing the prisoner for the costs of his witnesses, but the judge found no suitable precedent or applicable federal law.[45]

So Hanway was financially ruined, despite being found innocent, unless he could get help; the other prisoners, too, had sizable debts. Then the angels showed up. The African-American vigilance committees in Rochester, New York City, and Philadelphia came to the aid of the black prisoners. The Sadsbury Monthly Meeting of the Society of Friends paid the debts of the two white prisoners who were Quakers and also of Castner Hanway, who was not. As usual, each racial group took care of its own. The miller was, of course, extremely grateful and, in one of the many ironies of this case, ended up joining the Progressive Friends of Longwood—an association of abolitionist Quakers, who admitted some non-Quakers to their ranks.[46]

Thus Hanway became after the trial exactly the sort of Quaker abolitionist that the prosecution accused him of being at the time of the riot. Most likely his attitudes toward fugitive slaves and the Compromise measures were not radically changed by his ordeal, but he now became actively committed to the cause in a way that he had not been before. After a few more weeks in the public eye, Castner Hanway returned to his mill and lived out his life in the quiet obscurity that he knew before the day that he rode his horse over to Parker's—because he heard there were kidnappers and because he was too sick to walk. He must have been immensely relieved at the way things turned out, but we will never know any more about what the man thought or what he believed or how it felt for such a quiet, unassuming man to be thrust into the limelight of politics, social conflict, and law.

Back in Lancaster, at the January session of the quarter-sessions court, a grand jury did consider charging those in custody for murder and riot. The problem was that the principals most directly associated with the crimes had all escaped to Canada, and the main witness against the others was the locally notorious scoundrel, Deputy U.S. Marshal Henry Kline. Since the seven people who resisted the posse from inside the Parkers' house—and the man who actually shot Edward Gorsuch—were beyond the reach of the law and since there was no credible witness who identified any of the persons in custody as guilty of any violent act, no one was indicted for any crime associated with the Christiana Riot.

The grand jury heard testimony from Castner Hanway and others, however, that led to the indictment of Kline for perjuring himself under oath to a county official in the riot's immediate aftermath. Hanway claimed that he never uttered the words ascribed to him by Kline and never acted in the ways that Kline said; others testified that several of the black men whom Kline placed at the riot, including Harvey Scott, were not really there. One month later the charges against Kline were dropped. The federal government had decided not to press lesser charges against the Christiana prisoners, so it only seemed fair—and politically shrewd—to let Kline off the hook.[47]

Nonetheless, the outcome of the case outraged Attorney General Brent and his fellow Marylanders: Gorsuch lay dead, others still carried grapeshot in their bodies and nursed serious wounds suffered during the riot, and yet all of the "traitors" got off scot-free. No one was convicted of any crime associated with the riot. Where was justice; who defended the law; what did the Constitution mean up there in the North? According to Governor Lowe, after he read Brent's report, "the trial of Castner Hanway was a farce, which only added new insult to old injury." A citizen of Maryland was murdered while exercising his legal rights, and "his dead body was brutally insulted." So it was a question of honor as well as of politics and law. "If Hanway's offence was not treason," Lowe explained to the Maryland General Assembly, "then, no resistance to the fugitive slave act, henceforth, can be brought within the law of treason. Any one must see, at a single glance, that, if this decision stands, the fugitive slave act is a mockery and a delusion."[48]

Senator Cooper, Maryland's other senior counsel along with Brent at the trial, was significantly more upbeat than his colleague and Governor Lowe after Hanway's acquittal. Justice Grier had instructed the jury on the law just as the prosecution would want, with only one significant exception. As Cooper interpreted the judge's opinion, "there was not sufficient evidence, especially of combination on the part of the prisoner with others, to obstruct and overthrow the law, as would justify them in finding him guilty." Cooper's reading was that the government lost the case for lack of evidence rather than unfavorable rulings on law. This cheered him because of the message he thought the trial would send to other abolitionists: "it will teach them that there is danger in their interference," which would make them less likely to resist the law.[49]

Cooper was wrong about how Hanway's acquittal would be read. Opponents of the Compromise measures were elated by the prosecution's failure. Leaders of the Pennsylvania Anti-Slavery Society thought the uproar over Hanway's trial reinvigorated their cause and created an environment ideal for bringing the abolitionist speaker Joshua Giddings to Philadelphia for a speech. "The treason trials are making a great deal of talk here now," they wrote to Giddings, "and thousands are ready to listen who have long been indifferent." This invitation was a real provocation to mainstream opinion because, a month earlier, Giddings had publicly rejoiced in the murder of Gorsuch and praised the rioters for their actions. Giddings accepted, and as predicted, a large crowd turned out on December 18 to hear him speak. The *white* heroes of the Christiana Riot—Castner Hanway and Elijah Lewis—were first introduced to the crowd, which greeted the two men with thunderous applause. Then the orator, whom the assembly had paid to hear, delivered his message indicting the slaveocracy and the Compromise measures and advocating resistance to such evils in the name of a higher moral law. Hanway's acquittal strengthened, not weakened, the abolitionist resolve; its adherents were emboldened, not cowed, by the miller's ordeal. Their fervor knew even fewer limits; their message was even more strident than before. "Let the slave hunters understand," wrote Stephen Foster in praise of the Christiana rioters, "that they can only pursue their prey at the peril of their lives and they will soon find a more honorable calling." Neither Foster nor Giddings specifically advocated additional violence, but neither of them renounced it or urged caution or expressed any regret for the death of Edward Gorsuch and others who shared his fate. These white abolitionists had not lit the match, but they were playing with fire and fanning the flames.[50]

Moderate Southerners, especially in Maryland, were as distraught as the abolitionists were thrilled. For them, just as much as for the abolitionists in the North, the battle at Christiana and Hanway's trial had moral—not just legal or financial—implications. "The cost of capturing a fugitive slave," explained the legislative committee in Maryland charged to investigate the Christiana affair,

> even where the master may chance to be successful, is greater than his value, and yet masters have attempted to enforce their rights, even at a pecuniary loss and the risk of life, because they felt it their solemn duty to assert, at any cost and all hazard, their chartered rights, which had been ruthlessly invaded.[51]

Moderate pro-slavery Southerners feared, quite rightly it seems, that among the consequences of Hanway's acquittal was the potential for greater violence on the border between slavery and freedom than had existed before. Let Pennsylvanians know, insisted Governor Lowe, "that, henceforth, words will give place to acts. You owe it to your honor," he told Maryland's legislature. "Beware that your State does not become a mockery!" Just as their political leaders, other Marylanders believed that the law had failed to avenge Gorsuch's death and the humiliation done to his body, which meant that they would have to take "justice" into their own hands.

That is exactly what happened some months after the trial, when an anonymous band of Marylanders killed a white man named Joseph Miller and then hung his body from a tree. Word had it, informally of course, that the vigilante action was revenge for the murder of Edward Gorsuch. The sacrifice of one white Lancaster County man seemed fair retribution for Gorsuch's death. Miller was in Baltimore County seeking by legal means to gain the release of a free black woman who had been kidnapped from his farm. So the locales and the quests of Gorsuch and Miller were precisely reversed, which made the revenge an exact equivalent of Maryland's loss. But where, others at the time surely asked, would more bloodshed lead, and when would it end?[52]

Slave catchers certainly felt less safe plying their trade, as the abolitionists predicted; law enforcement officials were more reluctant than ever to get involved in the war over fugitive slaves, as Maryland's political leaders foresaw. African-Americans were even more frightened—and were just as brutalized and poor as before the riot—which led many more to move on, farther north, over the rest of the decade. But those who remained were still determined to fight, as were the marginal whites who enjoyed bashing black heads and getting paid for it when they delivered their victims to slave masters or unscrupulous traffickers in the South.[53]

The Christiana Riot is important both because it is unique *and* because it is part of a larger historical pattern of rioting defined as rebellion by national leaders for political ends. The uproar occasioned by the event created a documentary record of the violence that is extraordinary for this time and place. We have to remember, however, that it is the reaction rather than the violence itself that is singular. The trial record opens a window on patterns of violent interaction across racial, class, and interregional lines that have a much longer history, were more common than most of us know or would like to believe, and which were then, and still are, mostly hidden from view. As we plunge into the dark past of interpersonal violence and rioting in antebellum Lancaster County, it is well to keep the Christiana Riot in mind as a guide—a small lantern, if you will—to both our collective capacity for violence and our individual tolerance for harm done to others, especially those who are different because of race, class, gender, or some combination of characteristics that help us to look the other way.

[8]

Race, Violence, and Law

THERE WAS A COMPLICATED INTERPLAY among race, class, gender, politics, and law in nineteenth-century Lancaster, as there was in
the previous century and as there still is today. African-Americans are
certainly more visible in the antebellum records than in those from the
colonial period. Nonetheless, race is still an elusive variable in the local
equation of justice, and verdicts defy any categorical statements about
discrimination in law based on a defendant's race. Surely the more frequent appearance of blacks in the courtroom reflected their increased
presence in the county, their changing social circumstances, and white
fears about the growing numbers of free blacks in their midst. And yet,
the Christiana rioters were released without even a trial for their role in
Edward Gorsuch's death.

Of course, the grand jurors who considered charges against the Christiana rioters did not have before them the black men literally responsible
for dealing death blows to the fallen slave master; or, at least, they did
not have in custody anyone who could be placed at the scene with a gun,
stick, sword, knife, or stone in his hand by a credible witness. But such
legal niceties were not always a bar to judicial revenge against racial mi-
norities during that period, in either the North or the South. So it is
essential to explore this one act of violence within the context of others
committed by individuals and groups.

The stories told in the courtroom rather than aggregate quantifiable
data are of greatest interest here. The richest information about what people believed, or what they tried to convince others was true, comes from
the testimony of historical actors on this legal stage. The "truths" embodied in their stories are often to be read between the lines jotted down—

no doubt imperfectly—by officers of the court and newspaper men. Often lost to my reading, and hence inevitably to yours, are the tears, the language of faces and bodies, the inflections that accompanied the words—all of the physical mannerisms that help us to measure and weigh the meanings of everyday speech that we witness and hear. So we are laboring with multiple layers of interpretation—those of the testifier, the chronicler, the historian, and the reader—in addition to damaged and incomplete records.

Despite the impenetrable problems of interpreting these texts, they help us to get closer than we normally are to a small fraction of the population in this one county during a brief moment in time. My focus on violence and crime is only one fragment of experience, selected because it is part of the story told in this book. And for all the limitations that I see and gladly admit, and all of those that I do not even know, these are incredibly rich sources from which each of us can learn something—not necessarily the same thing—about violence and race, gender and class, law and community, and the meanings of the Christiana Riot in its own time and for ours.

Take, for example, an extraordinary case from the April 1839 docket of Lancaster's quarter-sessions court. An Irish weaver named Michael Morrison was dead, the victim of severe blows to the head that, in turn, caused blood to coagulate on his brain. According to Dr. Adam Sheller, who performed an autopsy, "the body bore the appearance of strong robust health. The face [was] very much swollen; caused, I suppose, by the blows. From the appearance of the blow on the right temple I should suppose it was inflicted with a stick; it appeared to me as if it must have been rough on the surface."[1]

Thomas McCarron and his son John, in whose home the Irishman died, brought two black men—Samuel Caldwell and Richard Weye—before a local justice of the peace. The justice asked Caldwell whether he had struck the dead man. "He said he did," testified Jacob Dysert; "I called up Richard Weye and asked him whether he had struck the man with the stick? He said he did; it was a small switch and went to represent the size of it with one of his fingers; of course they said they had no intention to kill." All parties agreed that the stick was smooth-surfaced oak, about two feet in length.

The court heard testimony on the premeditated intentions of the accused. Joseph Gibble, who ran a tavern from his house in Springville, told the court that on the day of the murder—Sunday, January 20, 1839—the defendants and another black man named Lewis Getz showed up looking to purchase some liquor. According to the taverner, Caldwell announced that

> he wanted to go somewhere and whip a man. He mentioned a name
> but I do not recollect what name, and Richard [Weye, the other defendant] said he'd go along and help him. Sam said he'd be God damned
> he could do it himself. Then Rich said let us go and kill the dam [sic]
> Irish bugger. Then Rich said we'll both get hung before spring.

According to Gibble, Caldwell plunked down a half-dollar on the counter
and asked to buy liquor for his friends. Gibble claimed under cross-examination that he "gave Sam liquor, and not Lewis and Rich . . . [because] they would get drunk and cut up, and have to do as Sam told
them; if they did not do as he told them, he would lick them." Caldwell
laughed at the white man's concern and "said he could get liquor in any
grog shop in that place and did not care. Then Sam screwed up his mouth
and said 'Damn the Irish, Rich let us go.' "

The story told in the courtroom continued at the residence of Thomas
and Catherine McCarron, a small log house on the outskirts of Richland,
not far from Mountjoy. The husband was an unsuccessful tailor, and the
wife sold liquor (apparently illegally) out of the home. According to one
of their neighbors, the McCarrons' was not a peaceful place; the family
split their firewood indoors, for one thing, which told the whole story of
their degradation as far as the neighbor was concerned; and there was a
lot of yelling and screaming that went on. William Shields, who lived
across the alley from the McCarrons, testified that there were

> generally noises there in the evening, and that when other people are
> in the bed too; quarreling is not an unusual thing there; I have seen
> drunkards go in and out there, I have seen Sam Caldwell go in and out
> there before now. . . . I have heard a noise frequently between McCarron and his wife quarreling and fighting.

So it was a disreputable place, a house frequented by blacks, where God-knows-what went on until all hours of the night; where the husband beat
his wife on a regular basis, and the children were often victims of both
parents' wrath. Under cross-examination Catherine McCarron told the court
that she was afraid of her husband, who was often drunk before breakfast.
Other witnesses verified the obvious—that this was a poor, degraded family that suffered from the common run of problems endured by their class.

The murdered man, Michael Morrison, was economically worse off than the McCarrons even before he met up with Caldwell and Weye. From time to time, he was on the public dole, but not at the moment. Now he lived with the tailor's family and slept on the floor where he died. On the evening of Morrison's death, as "Kitty" McCarron told the story, she and her boarder went out to fetch some water,

> because I had none in the house, and I knew if my husband would get awake, he'd make me and the children get up in the clouds of the night and go and get some. I don't know whether my husband wanted water or not that night. The reason we left the door open was that no noise should be made that my husband would get awake—he is so cross to me and the children.

When they returned from the well, the door was wide open, and a light was on. Even before McCarron and Morrison entered the house, they could tell "by their voices" that black men were there. "We knowed by their tongues that it was niggers," swore Kitty's thirteen-year-old son, who also told the court that the family did not own a clock and revealed inadvertently that he did not know his right hand from his left. One of the first things Catherine McCarron noticed on entering the front room was that the meat and bread were missing from her table. She asked bluntly who stole them and who was in the back. Caldwell emerged with some apples, for which he turned over a nickel to the mistress of the house; but he denied taking the food. Meanwhile, Weye—who had eaten the meat and pilfered the bread—slipped the loaf from under his jacket and put it back on the table. Lewis Getz, who was still with Caldwell and Weye, apparently sat quietly by the fire throughout the dispute.[2]

McCarron then exchanged words with Weye and Caldwell. Morrison's mistake was butting in. None of the witnesses heard, or at least was willing to repeat, exactly what Morrison said in taking his landlady's side in the dispute over the food. There was some suggestion, thirdhand, that Morrison called Caldwell a "nigger" and recalled aloud a time not too long ago when a black man "would not speak to a white woman the way he did." It was also suggested that the Irishman may have challenged the blacks with a claim that he could "whip any nigger" around. Whatever he said, Morrison clearly enraged Caldwell and Weye, who may, according to Joseph Gibble, already have been looking to bash in the head of this, another, or any-old Irishman for reasons not spelled out in the records.[3]

Over the next half hour or more, Morrison suffered a beating at the hands of the two men charged in his death. Caldwell struck him in the face with his fist; Weye hefted his stick and beat the Irishman over the top of his skull. When Mrs. McCarron interceded in Morrison's behalf, the two men stopped pounding on him, and he sat down in a chair. "Then they began plaguing him," McCarron told the court,

> calling him red face; and bloated face; and things to that purpose. Then they began making fun of him—of the way he came into this country because he was an Irishman—the way that Irishmen came into this country was by tying a string to a potato, catching hold of it and pulling themselves into the country by it. He said nothing to them either good or bad, but just sat on the chair and listened to them.

Eventually, Morrison told the men to stop or he would file a complaint with a justice of the peace the next day. "I don't care a God damn for you or the squire," Caldwell responded, or at least McCarron and her son claimed that he answered this way. When the two black men were ready to leave, Caldwell approached Morrison and put out his hand. The Irishman then made another mistake, according to the witnesses; instead of just shaking hands and letting it go, he could not help adding, "Good night, we will meet again."

"In what manner will we meet again?" asked Caldwell, who detected a threat in those words.

"We will meet in good friendship," responded Morrison, belatedly trying to cover himself against further abuse.

"That is not what you said," Caldwell shot back.

This was, as the witnesses told the story, the beginning of Morrison's end. Caldwell beat the Irishman about the head with his fists, taunting him all the while. When Morrison yelled out, "Murder!" Caldwell responded, "if you hallo murder I'll give you something to hallo murder for," began kicking the prostrate body of Morrison, and then picked him up over his head and slammed the smaller man ferociously into the floor. When Morrison dragged himself to the back room and laid down on the bed, Weye sought him out, beat him again on the head with his stick, and then hauled him out front and slammed him one more time into the floor. When they were satisfied that Morrison had paid the price for his insults, Weye, Caldwell, and Getz left and went home.[4]

McCarron said that she and her son retired for the night, after attending to Morrison, who needed a rag to catch the blood running from his nose and a pot in case he got sick. Thomas McCarron, the master of the house, was reportedly in a drunken stupor through almost the entire affair; one witness did remember him waking up at some point, wandering to the scene of the noise, asking what was going on, and then returning to bed and passing out again. Morrison was still alive when the family woke up the next morning but expired soon after as the blood finally coagulated on his brain. Had Mrs. McCarron gotten him medical attention, Morrison might very well have lived, according to two physicians who testified to the court; but she said she did not realize how seriously injured the man was. In any event, the parents sent their son John to fetch a physician when they discovered that Morrison was dead, but three turned him down. Only when the father went out himself did Dr. Sheller return to the house. "McCarron's family are poor; they have no means to pay," the doctor explained when asked why he and the others did not respond to the initial call for their help.

What baffled and outraged the editor of the *Lancaster Intelligencer*, who reprinted the trial testimony from the prosecutor's notes, was how in light of the story told by the three witnesses—Kitty McCarron, her son John, and the black man Lewis Getz—the jury could return an acquittal. Even if jurors found Joseph Gibble's testimony inconclusive on the question of premeditation, they still had the confessions reported by Justice Dysert and three witnesses to the act. So they had ample grounds to find the defendants guilty of second-degree murder, at the least. The account given by Getz in no sense contradicted the more detailed story provided by the other two witnesses; and he was the defendants' companion and friend. By what process of logic could the jury have found Caldwell and Weye not guilty of first-degree murder or any conceivable lesser charge? The *Intelligencer* had an explanation:

> The answer is plain. ABOLITION HAS BEEN THE AGENT! We know that there were on that jury men who would have starved before submitting to anything less than an Acquittal! We know too that these individuals were Abolitionists—open-mouthed, brawling disciples of Garrison! And knowing this, and the extremes to which modern Abolition has gone and will go, the conclusion is literally forced upon us that these two Negro Murderers owe their escape—their triumphant acquittal—to this cause.

Public opinion was outraged, according to the *Intelligencer;* any fair-minded person who read the trial notes printed in the paper would see that a shocking travesty of justice was committed in this case. The blame must fall squarely on the shoulders of radical abolitionists, whose sympathy for African-Americans knew no reasonable bounds. James Buchanan, the

Democratic senator from Lancaster and future President of the United States, reportedly declared in a public rage that if it had been white men on trial for this crime they would have gone to the gallows. The moral was clear, abolitionism was running amok and threatening to destroy that noble institution of trial by jury, at least when the defendants were black.[5]

That is one story of what happened in this case; a version based on evidence published for all to read. There are corroborating accounts given freely under oath; a semiofficial text provided by a judicial official; a printed transcript of the document in a responsible newspaper; and a logical explanation for the outcome of the trial based on these "facts." As we know, however, "truth" is often a matter of perspective, and stories are sometimes not even true in that way. A close reading of the text as supplemented by additional information tells quite a different story, which may in certain respects be significantly more "true" than that of the witnesses and the newspaper.

First, there is an inconsistency in the testimony. The witnesses agreed that Morrison was struck on the top of the head with a smooth stick made of oak. And yet, the physician who performed the autopsy concluded that the deathblow hit Morrison on the temple—the side of the head—and that the wound was consistent with a rough—not a smooth—stick. Why was the murder weapon burned before it could be examined by lawmen? Perhaps it was just a mistake made by the children, as their mother claimed; or, maybe there was something that the family wanted to hide. Then there is the problem of collaboration among the witnesses, which may account for the similarities in their stories. John McCarron admitted that he went over his story twice with his mother; a source external to the trial record—another newspaper—also claimed that Joseph Gibble, the taverner who testified to the premeditation of the accused murderers, was living with Catherine McCarron's daughter. So this was a family story about violence committed by racial outsiders. One witness for the defense contradicted Mrs. McCarron's claim that Morrison was not drunk; and several others testified that she was prone to lie and that they would not believe her even when she spoke under oath.

So here is an alternative story; one no more provable than the witnesses' account but potentially more true. Perhaps Morrison and the two accused murderers were all drunk that night as some sources suggest, and perhaps they did engage in a brawl that bore some resemblance to the one described by Lewis Getz and the McCarrons. Morrison was hit on the head with an oak stick by one of the defendants—Richard Weye confessed to that fact. Let us also assume that the racial taunting exchanged by the black men and the dead Irishman really did occur and may even have been the proximate cause of the affray, or at least a stage in the process by which angry words were supplemented by weapons and fists.

Now take one final huge leap. Throughout the printed testimony—which left out large parts of the case for the defense—there is the hint that Morrison and his landlady were more than good friends. There are also implications that Mrs. McCarron sometimes sold her body for spare change and that she may even have negotiated (apparently unsuccessfully) with Sam Caldwell for her favors that night. Perhaps Morrison was jealous of Caldwell, which contributed to the fight. Possibly the husband awoke from his stupor to find Morrison engaged in a sexual act with his wife, grabbed a log from the pile that we know was in the room, and bashed the Irishman alongside the head. The stories by the white witnesses then were concocted in a way that would take advantage of the interracial fight earlier in the evening and could be verified by Lewis Getz, one of the black men who watched the event. Such a scenario is consistent with what we know about McCarron's violent temper and his relationship with his wife, who had several years earlier testified in the quarter-sessions court that her husband struck her "three strokes with a stick of stove wood on her neck and arms threatened to take her life and has put his chopping axe under the bed as I believe with the intention of taking my life and at sundry times has threatened my life while he was intoxicated." So McCarron had used firewood as a weapon in the past, was drunk on the night of the murder, and was prone to violent rages when under the influence of liquor. Perhaps the family was trying to protect him (and thus themselves) from the law.[6]

This version of the murder story is not mine; well, at least not entirely so.[7] It is pieced together from the trial testimony and other slivers of evidence about the defense case. Less important here is what "really" happened— although, of course, we wish we could "know"—than how the defense attorneys told their version, what the jury believed, and why they believed what they did. To my reading there were more than enough problems with the witnesses' accounts to leave a "reasonable doubt" in the minds of twelve fair-minded men. The jurors were not all abolitionists, and at least two were loyal members of the very wing of the Democratic Party that denounced the verdict. At least one had recently run for public office under the Democrats' banner. No, this trial was not what the *Intelligencer* claimed; by blasting the jury the paper was indicting some of its own men.

According to the *Lancaster Examiner and Herald*, which supported Thaddeus Stevens and other abolitionists for public office, Buchanan and the *Intelligencer* were attempting to politicize this trial for their own partisan ends. "Truth" was not the issue; politics was. Race, violence, and the law could serve political needs, so the very sorts of cases that are entirely lost to the historian of eighteenth-century Lancaster became celebrated causes debated in the newspapers during the antebellum years. There are no simple lessons or clear-cut morals to be drawn from this one fascinating trial, but it does reveal something about the contemporary linkages between violence, race, politics, and perhaps class in this one place and, thereby, helps establish a broader context of meaning for what happened in the Christiana Riot and the community's response to that violent event.

As was the case with the riot, the reaction to Morrison's murder shows that some, probably most, white Pennsylvanians were afraid of being overwhelmed by "outsiders"; increasingly visible violence was one symptom of the fear on both sides. Intraclass tensions across racial lines sparked violence at the McCarrons' house and account for the way the story of that violence was retold. So the courtroom was a place where social problems and politics shared the same stage, where a solitary case could take on a symbolic significance much larger than the crime or the characters otherwise would. Any trial that involved violence and race had the potential to become a political cause.[8]

The stories told in the court, the newspapers, and on the political stump highlight some of the divisions within the white community on questions of race, class, violence, and law. They may even tell us that an African-American charged with violence against a white man could get a fair trial if the wounded party was a poor Irishman and the witnesses against him were a lower-class woman of questionable virtue, her illiterate son, and another black man. But the question of "justice" is not one that we can answer with certitude. We can tell that Caldwell and Weye stood accused of killing an outsider, just as the Christiana rioters would be a decade later. Morrison resided in the county, but he was a poor immigrant—and an Irishman at that—so the part of the community represented in court did not value his life as it would others who really belonged. The pressure to convict someone, anyone, for the crime was not as great as it might otherwise be. *Some* whites thought the acquittal in this case a travesty of justice nonetheless; that is certainly an important part of the story—the ways this community fought over issues of violence and race, politicized them, and handled them in court. The case also alerts us to some of the ways that race, gender, and class are essential parts of the law; it reminds us to ask why stories are told and believed, in addition to wondering which stories are true.

At the time of this trial, violence constituted about half the business of Lancaster's courts, as it had during the eighteenth century. Assault-and-battery cases continued to represent 90 percent or more of the violent crimes presented each year and still ran about even with illegal alcohol sales as the most common charges before the quarter-sessions court. Constables still took their lumps and maintained their collective reputation for brutality throughout the antebellum years. Such continuities also mask change, because the courts—and by implication the larger community—were more sensitive to violence, less tolerant, and more punitive than during the previous century.[9]

As a consequence, the stories told by those who claimed to be victims did not change perceptibly over time, but the court's empathy did; judges and juries were more willing than in the colonial period to credit the accounts of some classes of brutalized persons in a wider range of social interactions. An apprentice was more likely to get a sympathetic hearing when he filed a complaint against his master; a woman now had greater recourse against her wife-beating spouse; and there were even a handful of cases where the courts extended protection to children whose mothers made pleas to the court. The judicial system was also increasingly responsive to victims of socially horizontal violence, thereby extending the ken of the state into the bedroom, the nursery, the workplace, and the laboring-class tavern as never before in Lancaster County. The local, regional, and national cultures were changing, and the community's decreasing tolerance for violence was part of that transformation. A higher sense of order, a greater confidence in reform, and an enhanced paternalistic ideal were innovations, which other historians have explored; this cultural transition undoubtedly influenced what went on in the courts. The community was also more fearful of violence—particularly by groups (see Chapter 9). All of this means that a rough doubling of the volume of cases heard by the court between the 1790s and 1830s reflects an imponderable mix of causes—fear, population increase, and changing values, but not necessarily an objectively *more* violent environment—that we cannot sort out.[10]

William Carter, an apprentice in the cabinetmaking trade, complained in 1834 that his master "cruelly abused and ill treated the said apprentice, and particularly by tying him and beating him with a cow hide & obliging him to do work which his bodily strength was not sufficient to do." The court released him from his apprenticeship agreement and assessed the master court costs. Ann Kent, an African-American servant, charged Zachariah Lovet, also black, with attempting to rape her. According to her story, she was covering the fire for the night after the rest of the family had gone to bed, when Lovet grabbed her by the hand

> and dragged her to the barn, and while he was opening the door of it, she this deponent got away from him, and ran from him, and ran for the house, and just as she this deponent had got to the house, he the said Zakariah Lovet, got upon with her and dragged her into the weeds and threw her down, and put his knees on her and had his trousers unbuttoned, when John McBlarity he heard her cries came to her and relieved her.

The court sentenced Lovet to thirteen months in the state penitentiary in addition to a small fine and court costs. A jury also found Nancy Reaff, an illiterate woman, guilty of striking the son of Adam Sheffer on the head with a rock and fined her $1 plus $25.25 in court costs. Andrew Shute, John Fryer, and William Spurier were also found guilty of an assault on Isaiah Latshem, sentenced to six weeks in jail, and fined $4 each plus court costs.[11]

George Kiehl told the court that he had reason to believe that the schoolmaster Edward Henry was in the habit of buggering his mare. One jury found Henry innocent of the sodomy charge, and then another set of jurors convicted Kiehl of assaulting Henry "on the head with the butt of a loaded whip." A jury also found Robert Hedger guilty of running a bayonet through the arm of James Swords. On the basis of Jacob Ostrander's testimony, John and Michael Keenan were fined and ordered to pay court costs for assaulting Jacob Ostrander by "striking and kicking him in the face and body that the blood ran." Daniel Grove, Jr., was also found guilty of striking Arthur Connelly five times with a fence post.[12]

Such cases reflect the general pattern of conviction and sentencing for assaults and batteries in the antebellum court. Each illustrates the community's increased interest in socially horizontal violence and the greater credibility of witnesses who were more severely handicapped in the eighteenth century by their class, gender, or race. To be sure, the court was still flooded with contradictory assault and battery accusations that it could not resolve. William Janse said that Abraham Green struck him with a canoe pole, which the assailant allegedly broke in the act; but there were no corroborating witnesses, and Green no doubt had a different story, so the case got thrown out. Likewise, the court decided there was no actionable cause for the complaint of Solomon Landis, who said that David Miller snuck up behind him, gave him a punch that was one round in a long-standing feud, and then took off. This apparently seemed a rather frivolous charge. And Joseph Mulholin lost his case against three men whom he accused of stabbing him several times with a knife and then striking him on the head with a club. Clearly the complainant suffered serious injuries in some kind of affray, but his story did not carry the day against the version, now lost to us, that the three defendants told to the court. So problems of evidence and credibility still played decisive roles, but it seems clear that complainants were no longer dismissed out of hand simply because of their gender, race, or class, or because socially horizontal violence among working-class people was of no concern to the court.[13]

The handling of wife-beating complaints is particularly revealing in this regard and illustrates most clearly the changing attitudes toward violence in Lancaster County. Although women constituted approximately the same percentage of victims of violence in the 1830s as they had in the eighteenth century—between 25 percent and 30 percent—the records of the later period suggest that the court was much more likely to believe their stories and to punish working-class men for socially horizontal violence against women, even when the victim had only a woman of her same class as a witness or no corroborating witness at all to the violent act. The court had always been inclined to take a woman's word on the father of her bastard child in the face of vehement denials from the accused man. But now the wife who appeared alone also had a reasonable chance of being believed; indeed, in a total reversal of the eighteenth-century pattern, women who presented their husbands to the court for acts of violence or threats to do them bodily harm virtually always won their cases during the last three decades before the Civil War.[14]

When Magdalena Wagoner complained that her husband beat her up, the court slapped a bond for good behavior of $500 on him and assessed him court costs. Jacob Coble (or Cable) ended up in jail when he could not come up with the $100 bond and $13.11 court costs levied against him for threatening his wife. Barbara Nissly testified that her husband was "often intoxicated and abuses her [al]most daily and says it is impossible to live with him any long as she is in danger." The case ended up in common-pleas court, where a judge declared Jacob Nissly a habitual drunk and appointed a committee to manage his estate. Hester White agreed to an unspecified out-of-court settlement with her husband after filing a complaint that he

> struck her in the face in the side room of the house and very much abused her and throwed his [sic?] medicine out of the window together with glasses that she had only been about two weeks out of child bed

and swore if she said one word more he would put her out of the window as he had done the medicine and bottles and that he ordered her to be gone immediately from the house and that before she was able to be out of bed as aforesaid he much abused her and frequently struck and dragged her down by the hair before this time and that she is afraid to live with him.

In another departure from eighteenth-century practice, mothers occasionally appeared in court to complain about violence against their children. Unfortunately, the details of violence against children by fathers is extremely sketchy—and there is no recorded case of abuse by a mother—but the records do attest that battering children was now sometimes a crime when one parent complained. The case papers also reveal that parents were more likely to press charges against another adult who had done violence to their children than during the eighteenth century, when not a single complaint of this kind came to Lancaster's courts. Just as during the previous century, however, the vast majority of women signed their complaints with a mark.[15]

In addition to cross-gender assaults, there are also significantly more acts of violence across racial lines visible in the antebellum court records. For a number of reasons—the transition out of slavery, immigration of blacks from the South, changing attitudes about race, growing resentment of African-Americans among laboring-class whites, and the elimination of special "Negro courts"—we would expect to find more interracial violence before the quarter-sessions courts and more blacks in the courtroom than during the eighteenth century. African-Americans appear as complainants as well as alleged perpetrators of violent crimes—most often, but not always, as victims of violence by others of their own race. Nonetheless, the percentage of African-American defendants during the 1830s (about 3 percent) was no higher than their presence in the total population; and the frequency of their appearance as complainants was considerably lower than that (under 1 percent).[16]

Two murder trials from the 1830s reflect the violent environment cohabited by laboring-class whites and blacks in Lancaster County. Both were extreme examples of the "normal" fighting that sometimes got out of hand. The first case involved white Henry Ferguson and black Ephraim Tully (or Tally), who worked together at a forge. They agreed to make the joint purchase of a quart of whiskey during their midday break and then got into a dispute over change. When Tully returned from dinner, Ferguson renewed the argument. At one point they had each other by the throat; at another, Ferguson attempted to club his African-American opponent with a shovel, but fellow workers interceded to separate the two men. Then Ferguson ran for the tools, grabbed an axe, and plunged it into Tully's head before anyone could stop him.

The jury convicted the white man for second-degree murder of the black, and the judge sentenced him to twelve years in solitary confinement, which was the maximum sentence permitted by law. How or even whether race played a role in this case is not clear. Except for the last swing of the axe, this looks like a typical working-class fight—a dispute over liquor renewed after the potion was probably consumed, with the combatants grabbing whatever weapons came to hand. The verdict and sentence suggest that the court would not tolerate this degree of violence within the working classes or across racial lines when the facts and the blame were not in dispute.[17]

An attack by William McCork (or McGirk) on Jesse Williams left witnesses baffled about the cause of the attack. The two men were acquaintances, perhaps even friends, and the day before Williams's death others had witnessed McCork inviting him to a bar for a drink. Moments before the fateful assault, McCork came upon Williams sitting quietly under a tree and urged the black man to go with him to Christian Smith's tavern. The *Lancaster Journal* reported, by way of summarizing the witnesses' accounts, that

> as the deceased entered the bar room, the prisoner, who had preceded him, and was still within a few feet of the door, gave him, without either of the parties having uttered a word, a blow upon the head and a kick upon the stomach, the deceased staggered back, out of the room, over the porch, and fell upon the ground evidently much injured; he complained of much pain and great thirst; a physician was sent for, who visited him in the evening, replaced his shoulder, which had been dislocated and bled him; the following day he was placed in a Dearborne wagon, in order to be taken to the poor house, but died on the road. The prisoner made no attempt to escape, but remained with the deceased after his fall and attended upon him with care and kindness.

The jury returned a verdict of manslaughter, and the judge sentenced the defendant to six years in prison. It was suggested that several mitigating factors weighed in McCork's behalf—that he stayed and cared for the wounded man without trying to escape, and that the medical care received by Williams was deficient at best. There was not even really a fight. It is possible that the punch and the kick were "playfully" delivered; or, alternatively, that Williams was set up by the white man as the butt of a racially motivated joke.[18]

The trials, convictions, and sentencing of Ferguson and McCork do suggest, however, that the court was concerned with socially horizontal violence within the working classes and that interracial homicides were but one manifestation of "normal" working-class life. Class, as much or even more than race, defined the parameters of this sort of violence. Fights were apparently no more or less violent across lines of race and no more likely to result in the serious injury or death of one of the combatants. African-Americans were not disproportionately likely to be perpetrators or victims of such assaults, and rates of conviction and sentencing patterns do not suggest a harsher or more lenient justice dispensed according to race. Intraracial assaults were far more common than cross-racial ones. That is not to say that race was an insignificant factor, but it must take its place alongside an array of other catalysts—ethnicity, consumption of alcohol, child-rearing practices, social and economic circumstances, and religious beliefs—in the larger culture of working-class violence.

When violence by blacks traversed race, class, *and* gender, it was a different story. The community did not want to hear about mitigating factors in the trial of the accused perpetrators of the "Manheim Tragedy," which occurred in 1857—a quarter of a century after the violence perpetrated by Ferguson and McCork and during the same decade as the Christiana Riot. The scene of this double murder challenged communal myths about the locale of violence, as did the timing of the horrible act under the full light of day. Lancastrians, just like other Americans at the time, equated random brutality with cities or frontiers, alleys or forests, and the darkness of night. No matter that county court records and newspapers were filled with accounts of local violence; those stories were about lower-class victims, most of them immigrants and descendants of slaves, not about the middle-class populace that lived in white-washed houses surrounded by neat picket fences. The stories were about "them," not about "us." So when two middle-aged farmers' wives were raped and brutally murdered "in one of the most beautiful and fertile sections of the county" at almost high noon by a couple of mendicant blacks, shock accompanied the horror of such an unprecedented act.[19]

The identities of the murderers and their victims embodied the community's worst fears. Violence had crossed lines of gender, race, and class in the most offensive and least tolerable of ways. The rapes and murders challenged fragile interracial accommodations and local dedication to the rule of law, and fulfilled the dire predictions of the community's most virulent advocates of racial separation. The trial of Michael Morrison's alleged murderers tells one story about division within the white community over questions of race; the convictions of Ferguson and McCork tell yet another about the ways white and black Lancastrians interacted. The "Manheim Tragedy" provides a third variation on this theme and, thus, serves as a fitting conclusion to this chapter's story about interpersonal violence in antebellum Lancaster County.

Shortly after the murders, a constable's posse arrested Alexander Anderson and Henry Richards for the crimes. Each pleaded innocent, blaming the other for both murders and rapes. There was no point denying their presence at the murder scene; multiple witnesses saw them arriving and leaving the premises at the appropriate times. Nor could the prisoners easily explain away the blood on their clothes—Anderson's story was that he bloodied himself killing a turkey; Richards claimed that Anderson grabbed him with a bloody hand, dipped one of the dead women's shoes in a pool of her blood, and then made him put on the shoes. A hatchet in Anderson's possession that morning was found near the bodies and had clearly been used to murder one of the women. Richards left his old shoes in the house. The men also had cash and clothing missing from the home—Richards said that Anderson took the money and clothes and then gave him half as a bribe to shut him up. The circumstances left no doubt as far as the newspapers, law-enforcement officials, and the mob that milled around outside the jail were concerned; Alexander Anderson and Henry Richards murdered, raped, and robbed Mrs. Anna Garber, age fifty-five years, and Mrs. Elizabeth Ream, who was fifty-nine years old at the time of her death. The problem was going to be keeping the two men alive until they could be tried and executed according to law.[20]

The funeral of the two women—who were related by the marriage of Garber's daughter to Ream's son—was, according to the newspapers, "the largest which has ever taken place in this county, over four hundred carriages alone being in the line of the procession." At least one of the three Baptist sermons delivered to the throng fed its passion for vengeance rather than preaching forbearance and calling for calm. "A more cold-blooded murder has never been committed in this county," the newspapers screamed, thereby fanning the flames. In the heat of the moment, some remembered that an Irishman named Haggerty had butchered three people—a man, his wife, and their infant child—in Lancaster city not more than a decade before, but even that act of barbarism paled in the community's eyes by comparison with *this* abhorrent crime. Loud cries of "lynch the damned niggers" echoed through the streets of Lancaster and reached the ears of the prisoners inside the jail. The mob tested the strength of the prison gates time and again over a period of days and prevented the sheriff from moving his prisoners down the street to the courthouse for a preliminary hearing. According to the *Lancaster Intelligencer,*

When it was learned that . . . the prisoners would not be brought down [the] street, much indignation was manifested, and the crowd freely expressed themselves in favor of hanging the "wretches." Some of the farmers from the neighborhood of the tragedy declared that "hanging was too good for them," and a very respectable gentleman, and of a peaceable and law abiding reputation, said that they had the wood all ready to burn the murderers, and intended to take them out for that purpose, and thus "save the country the expense of trying them!"

Others proclaimed their lack of faith in the courts and their fears that the prisoners might either escape or be set free by some technicality in the law.[21]

By late January 1858—when the trials commenced—the public fever was down, but not much. Spectators took all available seats long before the event was scheduled to being. Then the halls and stairways of the courthouse filled up as well. The sheriff called in tipstaves to guard the doors, letting just one person in for every one that went out. The system did not work. There were three rushes at the door by those outside, which overpowered the guards. Only a show of force and locking the doors—keeping the spectators virtual prisoners in the room—held back the mob that wanted desperately to get in. The lawmen were worried, and rightly so it would seem, that a lynching was still possible if things got out of hand.[22]

The prosecution called witness after witness, each telling her or his part of the heart-rending story. Neighbors identified the prisoners, swore that they saw them in the vicinity, entering the house, or on the road later that day. Others remembered the activities and appearance of the accused after the fact—the cash they sported and the blood on their clothing and shoes. One daughter tearfully identified items stolen from her parents' home. Another recounted in painful detail how she found the corpses of her mother and mother-in-law; she recalled the blood spattered on the ceiling and walls, the skull smashed in by a hatchet, and the posture of the bodies that revealed the sexual violation of the victims. In testimony orchestrated by the prosecution for maximum emotional effect, Conrad Garber took the stand. The husband of one victim would not be kept long, but he had an important role to play. The prosecuting attorney handed the witness a piece of cloth that the defendant Anderson wore around his neck on the day of his arrest:

When showed a black-barred neckerchief, he [Garber] said it was his, and proceeded to take the one off his own neck, remarking *that* would show it; the two were laid together and proved to have been cut apart, the bars matching; he said his wife had cut them apart and hemmed them for him.

Then Garber broke down and had to be helped back to his seat. Few dry eyes were left in the courtroom; the spectators had their display and were able to vent some of their sorrow. The communal rage at the crimes and the criminals who stood in the dock remained to be sated by the judgment and sentence of the court.[23]

Counsel for the accused now had his turn. Anderson's lawyer said he had no defense to offer. The court appointed him to the case and his client had no money to pay for preparation or witnesses in his behalf. So the attorney would not take up much of the court's and the spectators' time; he would not try their patience with complicated stratagems intended to help Anderson get free. Still and all, he felt obliged to say something to the jury. "He admitted," according to the newspapers, "that the array of circumstantial evidence against the prisoner looked formidable, and he knew the feeling of the community was strongly against his client." Since a "great multitude" of Pennsylvanians opposed capital punishment, however, and since there were examples where the wrong man was hanged, he encouraged the jury to consider convicting his client on a lesser charge.[24]

The lawyer then went on to explain that in Pennsylvania the only crime punishable by death was first-degree murder, which required evidence of premeditation. The prosecutor had offered no witnesses to the intentions of the accused, so at worst a conviction for second-degree murder and a harsh prison term should be the fate of his client according to the laws of the state. The newspapers reported that defense counsel "was here interrupted by a startling volley of hisses and groans from the spectators, which cut his sentence short off." This was precisely the sort of "legal technicality" that the populace most feared.[25]

The judge reprimanded the gallery but also contradicted the defense attorney's understanding of law. There was plenty of evidence to convict for murder in the first degree, Judge Hays instructed jurors; he disagreed with counsel for the defense about public sentiments on capital punishment. The continued existence of the law on the state's statute books reflected the citizens' will, according to the judge; in any event, the law—not popular opinion—was what they were charged to enforce.[26]

It took the jury only a few minutes to return its verdict, which agreed with the judge. The trial of Richards that afternoon took even less time to accomplish the same end. His court-appointed attorney argued that

Richards was weak of mind—"easily led"—which made him less responsible for whatever role he played in the robbery, murders, and rapes. Without putting his client on the stand, the lawyer repeated Richards's story laying full responsibility for the entire crime on Anderson's head. Although witnesses testified for the defense that Richards was a bit "simple," none would agree that his diminished capacity made him less able to tell right from wrong.[27]

On April 9, the two men would be hanged within the walls of the prison according to the Commonwealth's "private" execution law. During the intervening two months the prisoners remained public figures with their own orchestrated roles to play in this drama. Clergymen now took the place alongside them, while judicial officials faded from view. The souls of the killers were now of utmost concern, and the community wanted, needed, demanded to see confessions from the men who claimed their innocence in court.[28]

Clergymen convinced Anderson to make a full confession for the good of his soul. A local editor also explained to the condemned man that a published version of his life accompanied by a description of the crime could produce a financial windfall for his wife and children. Anderson obliged the white men and helped them draft a story of his descent into crime that pandered to the tastes of a potential reading public (Figure 8.1). From the resulting document we can tell something about Anderson and more about the community in which he lived—about the poverty and violence that defined the contours of one black man's life.[29]

Anderson was a native of Lancaster city, born in 1820 and orphaned at the age of four. He then spent a short time in the poorhouse until bound out to Christian Diffenbach, a tanner and distiller who put the young boy to work. Over the next two years Anderson developed a taste for his master's whiskey, according to the account. Perhaps this is true, but we must also notice that it fits neatly the fashionable attribution of crime to the influence of drink. The temperance-promoting clergymen who counseled the prisoner undoubtedly encouraged an interpretation of Anderson's life that emphasized the early influence of alcohol, leading to theft, which in turn spiraled downward to the point that he brutally murdered two women who refused him the cash to purchase a pint. Anderson also explained that at the time of the murders he and Richards were pretty drunk.[30]

When Anderson was six years old, the story goes, Diffenbach returned him to the poorhouse. The master could not control the behavior of the boy who was supposed to be paying through labor for his own keep and would no longer tolerate the theft and consumption of liquor by his young

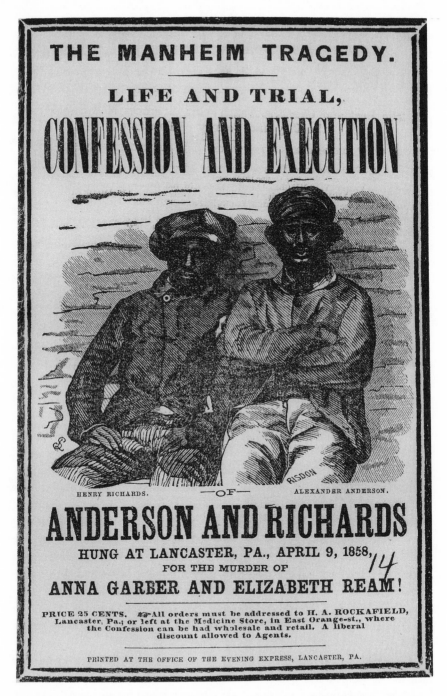

FIGURE 8.1. The Anderson story *(with permission of the Library Company of Philadelphia)*

charge. An African-American chimney sweep named Isaac Gilmore next took young Anderson in and put him to work in the tight spots where a small boy was of indispensable use in this trade. Anderson stayed with the chimney sweep until he was fourteen; he remembered that Gilmore treated him badly and recalled that "I was continually learning to steal."[31]

The condemned man's recollection of his life of crime was that poverty made him want, and dishonest habits coupled with the influence of drink led him to steal. He offered no interpretation of the relationship between the violence inflicted on him as a child and the fits of temper that plagued him throughout his adult life. Anderson's first bout with the law came when he stopped a woman and demanded some change. She refused, and he threw clods of dirt at her carriage as she made her escape. As a result of this white woman's complaint to a constable, Anderson got thrown into jail. Since he could not make bail, the young man spent two months in a cell until the next session of the mayor's court. The judge agreed to let Anderson go if he pledged to leave town, which he did.[32]

Anderson spent another four months in jail for stealing a pair of boots, a total of six years and five months in the Dauphin County prison for theft, and also did time in Eastern State Penitentiary. He worked in the lunatic asylum, a whorehouse, as a traveling salesman, a chimney sweep, and a lock tender on the Conestoga Canal. Each of these trades presented opportunities for crime, which by Anderson's account was his major source of sustenance over the years. He once knifed a man in a fight and whipped a woman with a fishing rod after she called him some names. He also admitted to sexually assaulting a young woman, for which he never got caught.[33]

For all the exceptional qualities of his life, as Anderson told it, his confession gives us a glimpse into the fringes of local society inhabited by immigrants, fugitive slaves, and free blacks. His transience was typical of his class, as was his inability to subsist on odd jobs without supplementing his income by theft. The violence that surrounded him—the roommate who attacked him with a club, the black man in prison who stabbed the warden with a homemade knife, the stranger beaten up and robbed on the road—was not all of his doing. The petty thefts of chickens and turkeys, hats, baskets, and shoes confessed by Anderson were only the tip of a local iceberg of crime, a mere fraction of which we see reported in the court records.[34]

Writing as he was for an audience primarily of whites, Anderson gives us scant insight into his attitudes and perceptions about race. To be sure, his last violent act crossed racial lines; and the two murdered women were not the first white victims of Anderson's violence and theft. The attitude of the two black men to their victims, however, is lost to our view, except to the extent that we interpret the act as a statement of rage that embodied perspectives on gender and race.

It is clear that the condemned man's advisors wanted enough detail to titillate but not so much that it challenged the sensibilities of "gentle" and juvenile readers. After all, from the point of view of the clergymen, the purpose of Anderson's life and confession was to impress the audience with the dissipation of drink, the habituating qualities of dishonesty, the need for repentance, and God's unbounded capacity for forgiveness. Even the grieving husband of one of the deceased women was enticed to play another cameo role in this performance. Conrad Garber presented himself to Anderson in the condemned man's cell, where the latter begged for his forgiveness, and then Garber graciously—according to the published confession—complied.[35]

The community at large was less forgiving and demanded blood vengeance for the crimes. The cries of the mob to "hang the damn niggers" and the newspapers' description of the condemned men as "two worthless negroes" illustrate the linkage of race and violence in the minds of those whites who eagerly anticipated the executions. A heavy rain the night before the hanging apparently kept few away, as the roads were filled with people wending their way through the mud and gloom from all points on the compass. As the sun rose over Lancaster's jail, hundreds had already gathered in the hope of catching "even a glance at the enclosure within which the dreadful tragedy of the law was to be enacted." Chants to open the gates and physical pressure aimed at bringing them down were to no avail.[36]

Authorities were determined to enforce the letter of the law that kept hangings from public view. The newspapers found something barbaric in the public's demand to see justice done. And yet no one commented unfavorably on the presence of state senator Crabb, who arrived with a letter from the governor admitting him as one of the witnesses to this "private" event. According to the papers, Crabb had "a singular mania for witnessing executions, and has attended nearly all in the State for several years past." So the senator joined the twenty-four jurors who convicted Anderson and Richards, the sheriff, two deputies, and two clergymen, who served as official witnesses[37] (Figure 8.2).

Outside the prison walls, however, the public had thoroughly defeated the intentions of legislators who drafted the private-execution law and officials who sought to enforce the spirit of the act. Entrepreneurs had built scaffolds on surrounding hills and sold tickets that gave a full view; others rented space on the roofs of their houses and barns for up to a

FIGURE 8.2. The execution of Anderson and Richards (*with permission of the Library Company of Philadelphia*)

dollar a head. Witnesses to this "private" hanging hung out windows, climbed trees, or found other serviceable spots. Those who arrived late, were less nimble than those in the treetops, or who could not afford a good seat settled for cupping their ears against the jail wall. The collective shudder and gasp—followed by giggles, screams, and a cheer—when the trap door dropped revealed the folly of the law. None who wanted to partake of this communal experience were denied the satisfaction of hearing—if not seeing—the strain of the ropes against the beam of the gallows. No one who needed to participate in this state-sanctioned violence missed out. As some of us know, and as many knew then, public sacrifice as vengeance for the death of innocent victims does not diminish the horror or the frequency of crime. The deaths of Anderson and Richards must have satisfied some primal need of the mob; the "public" witnesses walked away slowly, more quietly, than they came.[38]

There were no private acts of vengeance in Lancaster for the "Manheim Tragedy." The court had reached the only solution acceptable to the wider community. The portion of the populace that newspapers labeled "the mob" did not get exactly what it wanted—a lynching; or, failing that, a public execution outside the walls of the prison. But the public courtroom drama played to the emotions of a full house and helped quench the collective thirst for revenge. The fact that the execution was not hidden from view helped to spend residual passions that might otherwise have been channeled against the prisoners, lawmen, or the local community of blacks. In other words, the law "worked" in a way that it did not for the injured parties in the case of the Christiana Riot.

This de facto accommodation of Lancaster's citizens enabled constables to do their jobs. Indeed, the law functioned just as it is intended to do. Everyone, right down to the penitent criminals, played their roles according to this culture's script. "It was liquor that brought me here, and will soon send me to the gallows," proclaimed Anderson in dying words that were almost certainly coached: "All my crimes have been the fruits of whiskey." The ministers who tended Anderson's last moments were undoubtedly pleased.[39]

The "respectable" black community also had a role to act out. Elders of the African Baptist church denied Anderson's pleas to be buried in their cemetery—thereby showing with their lack of Christian charity that they were the most injured of all. They knew that God—as represented by the white ministers who attended the prisoners and served them last Communion on execution day—and even the husband of one victim forgave the perpetrators of this horrible crime. Still, the African-American Christians could not make their peace. The trustees informed Anderson in response to his request that they would "not have no murderer on [sic] their grave yard, Though God has pardoned him, we cannot have his body." By refusing the corpse of the murderer, perhaps they could symbolically disassociate themselves from his crime. To sanction burial in their cemetery would be an admission that Anderson was one of them. No, they were right; they could not have his corpse on the grounds of the African-American church for any number of reasons that related to violence and race.[40]

The cultural landscape of interpersonal violence was not stable over time, any more than it was fixed across space. There was little, if any, discernible change in the kinds of stories that victims of violence told to Lancaster's courts. In the nineteenth century, just as in the eighteenth and twentieth, husbands beat their wives; taverns and the workplace were frequently the scenes of interpersonal bouts; and random violence against both women and men struck fear into the hearts of the citizenry. But the receptivity of judges and juries to some types of stories did shift in significant ways between 1760 and 1860. Whereas once the judicial system had been unresponsive to complaints about lower-class violence that did not spill over into the lives of property-owning citizens or about brutality aimed at servants and slaves, the courts now reflected the community's lower tolerance for all violent acts. Gender, class, and race defined the parameters of tolerance and change, as they did for cases of collective violence that came into court.

The community's attitude toward collective violence also exhibited elements of both continuity and change (see Chapter 9). Although it makes sense to examine individual and collective violence as distinctive phenomena, there is also good cause to see them as interrelated. The cultures of violence that produced one created an environment in which the other could breed. The Christiana Riot and other similar events are more understandable in the light of violent interpersonal relations of the sort discussed here. And we might also suspect that as a community's tolerance for violence by individuals declined there would be a parallel change in the way that it listened to stories about mobs.

[9]

Race, Riots,
and Law

WATERSHED CHANGES IN THE NUMBER and kind of riots reported to Lancaster's courts began in 1834. The twenty-year period between 1834 and 1853 saw a tripling of the riot complaints over any comparable period up to that time, while the ratio of prosecutions to accusations remained about the same as during the previous century.[1] Even more striking is the fact that only three out of the seventy-four complaints—about 4 percent—during the entire twenty years resulted in convictions, which represents a significant decline from the 25 percent conviction rate of the eighteenth century and the 31 percent of the first thirteen years of the nineteenth century. Something was new, something was different, in the relationship between this community and the collective violence that occurred within its territorial boundaries.[2]

At first glance, the nature, meaning, and possible cause of the changes are elusive, and surviving evidence seems to point in contradictory directions. The court received far more complaints about rioting from individuals and grand juries than it ever had in the past but let the vast majority of the alleged rioters go; the defendants in six of the nine cases that actually went to trial over the course of twenty years were found innocent by petit juries for reasons not revealed in the records. On closer observation, several patterns emerge that help to explain the apparent anomalies in this judicial behavior.[3]

In part, the sudden and dramatic increase in the number of presentments for rioting was a function of growing sensitivity to disorder sparked by brutal riots in Baltimore, Boston, New York, and Philadelphia. Local newspapers reprinted full accounts of "outrageous" and "disgraceful" riots that were infecting the cities and deplored the scourge of disorder that seemed to be sweeping the nation. "The spirit of riot has been rapidly spreading for some time past over the country," reported the *Lancaster Examiner* in 1834, "extending its evil influence far and wide, and alarming, everywhere, the peaceful and well disposed portion of the community." According to the same newspaper, "accounts of the late riotous proceedings in New York will be perused with feelings of regret and mortification by every friend of good order. . . . Mobs—no matter what may be their exciting cause—are *always* wrong, and cannot be justified under any circumstances."[4]

While each of Lancaster's newspapers reported the race riots in urban locales during the summer of 1834, not all took the same strong stand as the *Examiner* against all mobs. It seemed to the *Lancaster Journal* that African-Americans were the proximate cause of race riots—by their presence and behavior where they were not welcome—and that white rioters were not necessarily to blame for reasonable fears, which could be addressed only by wholesale deportation—"colonization"—of the black populace to Africa. Articles about interracial assaults were accompanied in the same editions by blatantly racist characterizations of blacks and warnings against the threats posed by amalgamation and black voters—"De Wigs of Color." The *Journal* agreed with its competitor that the "reign of terror" in the cities was a horror, but it found liberal whites—"certain weak-minded men"—and black victims of mob violence responsible for the wholesale threat to order in the cities.[5]

Lancaster's newspapers were thus a reflection of and contributors to an environment in which Northern communities were increasingly fearful of the destructive power of mobs. The 1830s witnessed the beginning of what contemporaries and historians have described as America's greatest sustained plague of rioting. New York's anti-abolitionist riots of 1834 and Astor Place Riot of 1849—in which thirty-one people died and over a hundred were wounded—were part of this trend. Closer to home for Lancastrians were Baltimore's Nunnery Riot of 1839 and a series of Philadelphia riots, which included the race riot of August 1834, the destruction of Pennsylvania Hall by an anti-abolitionist mob in 1838, and the city's nativist riots of 1844, the last of which brought death to twenty people, injury to over a hundred, and remains to this day the bloodiest riot in Philadelphia's history.[6]

Although, as Michael Feldberg discovered in his study of collective disorder, "it was the exception rather than the rule for pre-Civil War rioting to claim the lives of its victims, or for more than one or two persons to be killed in the course of even the most serious fighting"; urban riots were more than ferocious enough and death was sufficiently frequent to strike fear into the hearts of Lancastrians and to lead them to examine their community for early symptoms of a similar social disease. According to David Grimsted, over a thousand Americans died in riots during the antebellum years, and one function of improved networks of trade and communication was that the people of Lancaster had access in their local newspapers to the goriest details of such bloodshed wherever it occurred. It should not be surprising, then, that rural folks began to see the disorder they had always accepted as a matter of course in a new and more threatening light during the 1830s. They had never felt closer in terms of culture, values, commercial integration, and physical distance to Philadelphia and Baltimore; and never, within their perhaps faulty memories, had the cities been more violent places.[7]

So what we begin to see in 1834 are charges of riot aimed at working-class Lancastrians for a wide variety of acts that would have been judicially ignored during the previous century. These included intraclass brawls that did not even spill outside the taverns where they occurred or result in serious injury to any of the combatants. More striking, the courts began to prosecute riots in which the energy of the mob was aimed more at destruction of property than at injuring persons. It is possible that such riots represented some sort of change in the nature of rioting—more frequent assemblage of mobs but less interpersonal violence perpetrated by rioters. It seems more likely, however, that the courts were noticing disorder that was ignored during the eighteenth century rather than that mobs never destroyed property or rioted so placidly before the antebellum era. Local authorities were certainly more fearful of riots beginning in the 1830s, less tolerant of disorder, held all members of the community to higher standards of behavior, and were more confident of their ability to reform the working-class culture of drunken recreational violence.

Such attitudinal changes among law-enforcement officials manifested themselves in the definition of rioting, which greatly expanded to meet the need for a more ordered community. After 1834, charges of unlawful riot were leveled at everything from domestic violence pitting a woman against her daughter-in-law to a disturbance created by an underage elopement. Thus, individuals who made the accusations, grand juries that considered the complaints, and judges participated in a functional redefinition of "riot." This is true despite the fact that an overwhelming proportion of complaints was never prosecuted by the courts.[8]

The riot charge enabled law-enforcement authorities to demand a substantial bond for good behavior over a period of one or two years; this money would be forfeited in the event of a subsequent disorderly offense.

The court would then usually continue the case from session to session until, with the tacit agreement of the accused, the charges would be dismissed upon payment of court costs. The defendants could, of course, challenge the system and demand a jury trial, which very few did.[9] The accused would then risk a substantial fine, much higher court costs no matter what the outcome (because those found innocent were also generally assessed costs), and the levying of a considerable bond on top of it all.

This was an ingenious method of social control, which operated at very low cost to the community and was apparently quite successful. The court brought in working-class defendants, impressed them—"intimidated" is probably a better word—with the majesty of the law and the possibility of ruining fines or incarceration for substantial periods of time, gave them the option of standing against the array of authority before them, and placed the accused at the mercy of propertied employers who would sign for the bond, thereby putting the defendant in a position of literal dependence on the goodwill of the boss. This was not a new device, born of a revolution in an industrializing capitalist society. Eighteenth-century courts had used the same tools to the same ends. What was different was stretching the definitional limits of "riot" so far and applying the control mechanisms of bonds to so many people. Nineteenth-century courts were not content to ferret out "leaders" of disorder, as was done in the previous century. Antebellum judges, unlike their eighteenth-century counterparts, assumed neither a hierarchical relationship between leaders and followers nor an unreformable disorderliness among the working classes. Reform more than labeling and punishing was the agenda of the court in almost all these cases of "riot," and judicial officials applied long-standing methods to what they saw, in a fit of historical amnesia, as a "new" wave of disorder.[10]

After 1833, just as before, recreational riots—in which working-class folks expressed drunken exuberance in a range of raucous or violent ways—remained by far the most common form of collective action before the courts. For example, Jacob Hoag and six drinking companions were indicted in 1833 for raising a ruckus in the public square of Lancaster and for refusing to disperse as ordered by officers of the law. Three years later, William Lyttle and five friends—including two women—were accused of making "great noises, riot, tumult, and disturbance . . . to the great terror of the citizens." In such cases, defendants were not charged with having injured anyone or destroying property, nor were they prosecuted by the court. In this era of heightened sensitivity to disorder, however, several people making noise in public was enough to produce an accusation of riot and to require a bond for good behavior of fifty or a hundred dollars.[11]

There were also charges against recreational rioters who destroyed property, but did not physically assault anyone. In 1849 nine people, including Francis Stain, were accused of riot for attempting to force the door of William Brewster with clubs. The next year, John S. Shenk and two others allegedly "came together at the public house of . . . Phillip Roger and then and there in a violent and forcible manner did break several tumblers and also threatened to break the stove, bar, and clock." Usually, as in this case, the riot occurred in or outside a tavern and involved breaking furniture, windows, or pottery. In this sort of "riot," where only property was involved, restitution was the first order of the court's business; charges were even dropped on two occasions after the parties reached a settlement. Costs and bonds would still be assessed, in amounts between a hundred and three hundred dollars, apparently depending on the amount of the damage.[12]

Much more common were riots in which violence against persons, and sometimes also property, occurred. The court took this category of collective action more seriously than the others when it involved property damage *and* physical injury and levied bonds ranging from two hundred to a thousand dollars (in one case), in addition to court costs. Sometimes there would be a charge of assault in addition to riot, which could result in a separate conviction and fine even when the accusation of riot was dropped. In 1844, for example, John Shaitzer and several companions "assembled together, by their own authority, with intent mutually to assist one another against any who would oppose them, to the terror of the people." Eventually this small band of rowdies found the fight they were looking for at the boarding house run by Widow Boggs, and physical injuries as well as property damage were the results. Two years later, sixteen men ganged up on Benjamin Slater, "forced him into the street, placed him upon a rail, and carried him through the streets, meanwhile beating him with a rawhide upon the back." This type of rioting also included an occasional case of breaking and entering, individual and collective assaults—sometimes against women—riots during church services, and, most commonly, barroom brawls.[13]

The attitude of the court toward "rescues" of persons or property in the custody of local deputies did not reflect any obvious change after 1833. From time to time, such cases continued to appear on the docket, but even in this period of intensified concern for the maintenance of order, the court treated such episodes as no higher crime than other comparable riots where violence was aimed at working-class citizens. In 1835, for example, a party of four people used force to release John Hart and his possessions, which had been confiscated to settle a debt. In a similar case during the same year, Jackson Johnson and five others "rescued" his goods from the custody of the law. Both charges were dismissed upon return of the prisoner and property to the sheriff, with no restitution for the deputy's wounds. In these two examples it is not even clear that bonds and costs were assessed. So the court did not go out of its way either to protect the deputies responsible for enforcing its edicts or to help make their jobs any easier. On the contrary, the message apparently sent and received was that using force and engaging resistance were expected parts of the job. It seems likely that the class of the deputies accounts for the court's comparative lack of concern; the rough tactics of the lawmen were well known to the court from the assault charges regularly brought against constables.[14]

As during the eighteenth century, who was attacked and the degree of injury were clearly factors in assessing the seriousness of the crime. Those who signed their complaints with a mark—whether they were officers of the law or common citizens—were of less concern than those who could read and write and were property owners of standing in the community. In that sense, class transcended gender as a defining quality considered by the court in riot cases. Six riots involving women as either perpetrators or victims of riots appear in the court records after 1833. It seems from this handful of cases that women victims, just as males, were accorded a hearing in the antebellum courts commensurate with their class. In 1834, an illiterate woman named Barbara Howard complained that a gang of four men assaulted and threatened her. The court slapped a bond of fifty dollars on the one perpetrator identified by the woman and her three witnesses and continued the case indefinitely. On the other hand, when Martha Wilson, a property-owning woman, complained that Joseph Hughes and others broke into her house, destroyed her furniture, and beat her up, the court demanded a thousand dollars—the largest bond of the century on a riot charge. Attacks on middle-class women challenged cultural ideals, aroused the protective instincts of white judges, and apparently defined one limit of tolerance for riots that incorporated the essential qualifiers of class and, almost certainly, race.[15]

It is possible to look more closely at the conjunctures of race and class in the antebellum riots and explore some of the ways that being black or poor played a role in collective violence across racial lines. One way to do this is to examine a set of interracial riots—those in the town of Columbia, Lancaster County, during 1834 and 1835—for which we have comparatively full information about who rioted, against whom, and why. The Columbia Race Riots enable us to put faces on the composite characterizations distilled from the county court records of the era. Just as Lancaster's other great riots of the eighteenth and antebellum nineteenth centuries, the Columbia Riots reveal a community in stress, some of its values, and the limits of its tolerance for disorder at a particular time. They raise questions and provide some answers about the interplay of class and race from the perspectives of rioters, victims, the court, and the community whose interests the court represented. Like the Christiana Riot, the Columbia Riots were exceptional events that help us to comprehend the meanings of "normal" day-to-day violence in the past.

The race riots in Philadelphia and other large cities during the summer of 1834 inspired some residents of Columbia, even as urban violence contributed to an environment of fear that infected the region. The first episodes in Columbia occurred over the course of four nights, beginning on Saturday, August 16. At first the rioters—who were teenage white men from the laboring classes—limited themselves to breaking windows, shouting insults, and making a good bit of noise in the black section of town. On Tuesday night, however, the expressions of bigotry took an uglier turn, as the ranks of the rioters swelled to over fifty and now included a number of older and more socially accomplished participants. Although damage was still confined to property and the nerves of inhabitants—who were kept awake until after 2 a.m. by shouting, shattering glass, and the celebratory firing of guns—the number of dwellings singled out for attack was expanded, and damage was more serious than on the previous evenings.[16]

The community expressed concern about the riots—in resolutions adopted by a town meeting and a proclamation issued by the chief burgess—and some leading citizens diagnosed the causes and prescribed cures for the violence. The town meeting, which gathered on Wednesday, August 20, issued a blanket condemnation of rioting, recommended the establishment of a fifty-member special police force, and reminded citizens of their duty to assist in suppressing riots when called on by "any respectable person." The chief burgess included a similar reminder in the proclamation issued two days later but focused primarily on restricting the activity of the black community as a means of restoring calm. The document commanded "all coloured persons from and after the issuing of this Proclamation and until publicly revoked, to cease from the holding of all public religious meetings whatsoever, of any kind, after the hour of 8 o'clock in the evening, within the borough limits."[17]

The editor of the *Columbia Spy* agreed that the damage to homes of

black residents was "partly on account of their own imprudence." It seemed
to him that "the abolitionists have now placed their coloured protégés,
whom they were feeding up with foolish notions of equality until they had
become unbearably insolent, in a most unhappy condition; watched and
hated by the people and liable on the slightest occasion to be sacrificed
to the bloody demon of unlawful violence." In other words, the blacks,
inspired by their abolitionist friends, were to blame, but the newspaper
was not by any means endorsing the violence that resulted from attempts
to amalgamate black with white society. "A mob is altogether an irrational
animal," the same paper observed, "blinded by the ferocity of its temper,
it rushes madly on to gratify its excited enmity, and voice of argument
and the claims of duty are urged upon its ears in vain." The way to tame
the mob beast seemed to the editor equally clear: "two races never can,
never ought to be amalgamated." The blacks had to go back to Africa
before the violence got worse.[18]

A "meeting of the working men and others favourable to their cause"
took place in Columbia on August 23 and joined this crescendo of blame
leveled at abolitionists and African-Americans themselves for the interracial violence of working-class whites. The resolutions adopted by this
meeting make it clear that the riots had their origin in economic rather
than purely racial causes, as the *Columbia Spy* had recognized from the
start. By acclamation, the white working men denounced "the practice of
others in employing the negroes to do that labour which was formerly
done entirely by whites." "And is it come to this?" the white laborers
rhetorically asked:

> Must the poor honest citizens that so long have maintained their fami-
> lies by their labor, fly from their native place that a band of disorderly
> negroes may revel with the money that ought to support the white man
> and his family. . . . The cause of the late disgraceful riots throughout
> every part of the country may be traced to the efforts of those who
> would wish the poor whites to amalgamate with the blacks. . . . that
> the poor whites may gradually sink into the degraded condition of the
> negroes—that, like them, they may be slaves and tools, and that the
> blacks are to witness their disgusting servility to their employers and
> their unbearable insolence to the working class.[19]

This passage is revealing in at least two ways: it frames the economic
terms of interracial conflict, and it illustrates the connecting link between
riots against racially marginal people in the eighteenth and nineteenth
centuries. The laboring-class whites who endorsed this document and who

rioted against Columbia's black populace during 1834 and 1835 sought to define their identities against racial outsiders and, thereby, to realize their socioeconomic ambitions in reference to middle-class whites. The problem was, as they saw it, that blacks were unfair competition and challenged the white laborers' very identity as "white," with all the cultural freight that identity carried. If blacks were more economically successful than they—owned attractive homes, dressed in more stylish clothes, rode in horse-drawn carriages, or simply ate better meals—then the blacks were more "white" than the white laborers who perceived a class-based "insolence" that they simply could not bear.

So the white working men did not riot against just any black residents of the town—although, to be sure, they wished that all of Columbia's black population would be gone. They aimed their venom at those representatives of the racially marginal group who manifested the characteristics most challenging to their own sense of racial identity with all of its social, economic, and cultural dimensions. The victims of the rioters were members of the black middle class, the most visible embodiments of African-American success in this "white" town.

The impression of those whites hostile to the African-American presence in Columbia was that the town was being overrun by racial outsiders. The best guess of the working men and their supporters was that there were well over a thousand blacks in their small community of fewer than twenty-five hundred, that fugitive slaves were daily swelling the numbers who lived on "Tow Hill," that the competition for jobs had gotten much worse over the previous few years, and that unless something was done to halt black immigration, whites would soon be outnumbered in the borough. They resolved to address the problem by an economic boycott of white merchants who hired black laborers and by voting against any politician associated with such "unfair" labor practices. In its political guise, the meeting of August 23 was an assemblage of constituents and leaders of the Democratic Party, who united around their opposition to abolitionism, their endorsement of the colonization movement, and their celebration of the common *white* man that was a hallmark of the age.

The meeting also expressed its opposition to the recent anti-black riots, described itself as an assemblage of "peaceable men," and vowed "to protect the persons and property of citizens in case of disturbance." For the most part, this was surely an honest expression of hostility to mobs. Most of the men at the meeting that day never threw stones at windows in Tow Hill; most of them never raised a club to beat or a pistol to fire at a black man, woman, or child; most of them never personally assisted in the violence associated with kidnapping fugitive slaves.

Nonetheless, those who rioted before and after the meeting came from the working-class constituency represented at the assembly. The kidnappers who assaulted and spirited away black Lancastrians in the dead of night also came from this group, were inspired by its indictment of the African-American presence in their community, but disagreed with the respectable leaders of the Democratic Party about the tactics and tools of reform. A club, a rock, a pistol, or a fist seemed to them more effective means to an end they all sought. And there was money to be made by banging blacks on the head and carting them back to Maryland for rewards—in the case of genuine fugitive slaves—or to where they could be sold into bondage even when they were legally free in the North. The methods used against blacks certainly split the white community, for the most part along class lines. The goals of the working men and their supporters divided whites as well—those who profited from the black presence from those who did not; those who found the ambitions of both the Democrats and the rioters morally reprehensible from those who endorsed the ends of, even when they deplored the means used by, the laboring men.

On the heels of this meeting came another assembly of the town, which responded concretely to the concerns of the white working men. Those gathered on August 26 resolved to find out exactly how many blacks there were in the community, how many owned property, whether African-American freeholders would be willing to sell their property at a fair market value and move on, and to "advise the colored persons in said borough to refuse receiving any colored persons from other places as residents among them." The town meeting also pledged to cooperate in the identification, capture, and return of any fugitives from slavery who lived in their midst.[20]

As local historian Carl Oblinger discovered, two-thirds of Columbia's anti-black rioters—a total of thirty-four men—were free laborers and mechanics who were only sporadically employed. These were men on the lowest rung of the economic ladder and they resented those blacks holding steadier jobs and enjoying greater economic success. The other one-third of the rioters were professionals who were relative newcomers to the town. These "new-money" whites had political ambitions that united them with working-class sorts, and they felt particularly threatened by the likes of Stephen Smith, the black lumber and real-estate entrepreneur, who challenged their economic standing and leadership in the town. These white Democrats were also concerned about the recent establishment of a black self-protection association. So leaders of the white community were split over tactics, with some working for a peaceful resolution through purchase of property and colonization while others supported the mob.[21]

The committee charged with identifying the scope of Columbia's black "problem" reported back to a town meeting on September 1. They found 649 African-Americans—214 men, 171 women, and 264 children—resident in the borough. Of these, thirty-seven were freeholders, black men of property and standing in the community; and eleven were vagrants. The assembly officially accepted the report and then immediately adjourned so the contents could be digested by various committees. These committees, in turn, were to report back two days later with specific recommendations in response to the information gathered about blacks.[22]

On the next day, before this process could work itself through, another mob aimed its destructive force at the property of two African-Americans. As the *Columbia Spy* reported the incident:

> At the dead hour of midnight—fit time for such deeds of darkness—a band of riotous persons assembled and attacked a house in Front Street occupied by a black man, the porch and a part of the frame of which they tore down, the inmates leaving the building at the first alarm. Thence the mob proceeded to the office of another colored person, who deals in lumber, broke open the window and doors, rifled the desk, and scattered the papers along the pavement. After attempting to upset the building, they marched off, having gained "glory enough for one night."[23]

Although we cannot know for certain why these two victims were chosen by the mob on this particular evening, the timing and consequences of the riot provide a plausible explanation. The two men whose property was assaulted were among the African-American freeholders identified in the previous day's report. The committee had called on members of the black middle class and found "the disposition manifested by most of them decidedly favorable" to the question of whether they would liquidate their holdings for a fair market price. "Some of them are anxious," the committee reported, "many willing to sell at once provided a reasonable price were offered—others would dispose of their property as soon as they could find any other eligible situation." From the language of the report, the timing of the riot, and the focus on just two members of the black middle class, we might surmise that the victims whose property was attacked by the mob were unwilling to meet the hypothetical terms offered by the committee. They were "examples" of what could happen to any or all blacks who declined to sell at a "fair" price and get out of town.[24]

If intimidation was a goal of the rioters, it certainly worked. Stephen

Smith, the lumber merchant whose offices were ransacked and whose property was destroyed, took out an advertisement in the next issue of the *Columbia Spy,* proclaiming his desire to abandon his business:

> I offer my entire stock of lumber, either wholesale or retail, at a re-
> duced price, as I am determined to close my business at Columbia.
> . . . I will also dispose of my real property in the borough, consisting
> of a number of houses and lots, some of them desirable situations for
> business.

As the wealthiest of the African-American freeholders and among the wealthiest citizens of either race, Smith personified the problem that concerned the white working men of the town.[25]

There had been no black property owners in the township during the eighteenth century and no visible collective violence against African-Americans. It was not until 1818 that any blacks appeared on Columbia's tax list, at which point there were only three. Two years later, eight blacks were paying taxes in the borough, and in that year Stephen Smith owned one and a half unfinished town lots worth about three hundred dollars. By 1829 he had title to five houses and five lots valued at twenty-three hundred dollars, and a horse worth another forty. Over the next four years, Smith's fortune continued to soar, and other African-American members of Columbia's middle class prospered as well. The 1833 tax list shows Smith as owner of six houses and lots valued at three thousand dollars, stocks and bonds worth another three thousand, a pleasure carriage, a horse, and a cow. There were now twenty-six other black property owners in the borough, who possessed a total of thirty-two houses and twenty-nine lots valued at approximately $8,460.

So Smith, as owner of 42 percent of the black community's real estate, was by far the most successful member of this group; he was also part of a larger trend visible to white workers. Not only was the total black population rising, albeit more slowly than white laborers feared, but there also was a discernible black presence among the town's middle class, which stood as a symbolic and real challenge to the laborers' sense of themselves and an indictment of their industry, their talents, and skills. Smith personified these unwelcome changes in the eyes of the white working men, and this made him a symbol of the confusion that brought hatred, fear, and violence to this small town.[26]

The attempt to rid Columbia of its black middle class continued on two fronts during October 1834. The town appointed a committee of five "gentlemen" to "form an association for the purpose of purchasing the property of the blacks in this borough." At the same time, working-class whites resorted to violence in pursuit of the same goal. As the *Columbia Spy* reported the riots, which occurred on October 2, the night

> was one of bustle and alarm to all classes of our citizens at one hour or another such as we have not lately experienced; the fury of disorderly men and the ravages of the destructive element of fire, conspired to make it a season of confusion and terror.[27]

Between 11 p.m. and midnight, a mob began stoning four houses belonging to blacks; then, rioters broke into the dwellings, destroyed the interiors and furniture, and scattered the remains on the street. One of these houses belonged to James Smith, who watched as the mob broke his windows and then smashed down his door; he cowered inside with his family as the inside of the house was destroyed and listened in terror to the threats of worse aimed at them. Another of the victims selected for abuse was James Richards, who witnessed in the space of about thirty minutes the breaking of every window in his house, the battering down of exterior doors, and the demolition of interior doors, furniture, and carpets. Richards watched helplessly as the mob battered his ten-plate iron heating stove and smashed other, more fragile artifacts of his economic success. Not content with destruction of all that this middle-class black man possessed, the crowd then proceeded viciously to beat him, breaking his arm and inflicting sundry other external and internal wounds before leaving Richards lying in his own blood amidst the rubble that shortly before was his home.

The white men also stole three promissory notes, reflecting sums owned to Richards, a judgment note from the common-pleas court for the collection of yet another debt, and four dollars in cash. They took dental implements for making and cleaning teeth, broke the windows and doors of the schoolhouse Richards ran for black children, and entered the school and did further damage inside, destroying the inkstands and paper used by the students to write. Black literacy, no doubt, was also perceived by jealous white laborers as a threat to their identity, and the schoolhouse was a symbol and harbinger of further acculturation by racial outsiders.[28]

According to the newspaper, the triggering cause of this outburst was "the reported recent marriage of a black man to a white woman, which rekindled the smouldering ashes of former popular madness and afforded an opportunity to evil-disposed individuals to reenact past occurrences of disorder and destruction." In other words, the black community was partly to blame for the riot—one man for racial amalgamation and the rest for

tolerating his presence in their midst. As the newspaper noted in its de-
nunciation of the mob, the violence "did not stop when they had punished the object of their wrath, but spent the residue of it upon others
who had committed no fresh acts which called for punishment."[29]

The victims perpetrated no "fresh acts," that is, except embodying the
characteristics of wealth, race, and presence in the community that drove
the white working class to distraction. The "reported" interracial marriage
was a rumor that bore no basis in fact; it was spread for the purpose of
inciting a riot against a select group of victims, whose property and standing in Columbia symbolized the amalgamation that seemed an imminent
threat to working-class whites and their gentlemen supporters.

The crowd dispersed after the initial round of violence against four
exemplary African-American homes. White families who lived near Tow
Hill could return to bed after the streets emptied and things quieted
down. The rioters themselves were probably too agitated to fall asleep
quickly. Perhaps they were drunk, maybe still angry, but certainly the
experience left them emotionally, and perhaps physically, drained. I wonder about their dreams, how soundly they slept, and their condition the
next morning when it was time to get up for work.

It would be harder for African-Americans to rest. Even those whose
possessions, homes, and bodies remained undamaged by white wrath must
have had a difficult time dozing off. Some, of course, poked their heads
through doorways after the danger was past. A few of the more curious
and brave ventured out to see for themselves the consequences of bigotry
that afflicted their town. Neighbors comforted the victims after the damage was done—helped sift through the rubble, bandaged the wounds, and
provided shoulders to cry on for those who had lost so quickly what they
had worked decades to achieve. And what about the rest of Tow Hill?
Anger, fear, and depression are a likely mix of emotions after a catastro-
phe such as this—relief and guilt are often felt by those spared the fate of
good friends.

Neither black nor white residents of Columbia borough could have
been long asleep when shouts of "FIRE!" catapulted them from their beds.
Someone had set a carpenter's shop ablaze, and the flames "reflected from
the walls of the neighboring houses in excessive brightness, while the sky
was illuminated with the conflagration." The building burned to the ground;
several valuable sets of tools were lost, as was the finishing work for a
"new and extensive" house. No other property was damaged and the ar-
sonist(s) were never caught.[30]

Did the shop belong to an African-American or a white man building
a fine house for a black? The records do not say. The fire was set, of this

the newspaper was sure. Was it just a disgruntled worker, fired from a job and seeking revenge; or was there some link between the violent acts that combined to rob the town of a decent night's sleep? Perhaps it was a coincidence, or maybe the mob inspired the burning of the carpenter's shop. Maybe the fire was started by blacks in reprisal for the destructiveness of the mob—an act of guerrilla warfare by people who, unlike the white working men, required stealth to avoid the retribution of the law. Violence breeds violence, as the citizens of Columbia knew; destruction feeds flames of anger and fear. Race relations were bad, violence seemed rampant, and this night made them worse.

Nine men were caught and charged for the crimes against James Smith and James Richards. Since no one had been arrested for the riots in mid-August or early September, this was a start, a recognition by at least some members of the white community that the race of victims did not necessarily forgive such violence; although we should remember that riots against members of the *white* middle class were never ignored or allowed to pass unpunished by this community. Those indicted for the riots of October 2 included John Lightner—a laborer charged as the first actor in the affray—four other laborers, a miller, a blacksmith, and a "gentleman."

So there was a class mix to the crowd that reflected wider support for working-class violence. If these nine were deemed "leaders" or leading actors in riots by twenty to fifty men, we are probably safe in concluding that active, personal support for violent methods did not include many men from outside the working class. One "gentleman" is a very light seasoning for a mob of such size; and, after all, a laborer is listed as the prime mover, and "laborers" outnumber all others among the "leaders" of the riot. During the eighteenth century, the court would have assumed that the "gentleman" was the "leader" of the violence and would have acted accordingly; during the nineteenth century, such an assumption no longer informed the actions of the court.

Bonds of five hundred dollars were secured for each of the accused, which were among the highest set for rioting by a Lancaster County court before the Civil War. The judges, at least, were serious about prosecuting collective violence against middle-class blacks and sending a message that riots were not tolerated by this community. As usual, the cases were continued through January, April, and into the August session of the court. Unlike the overwhelming number (85 percent) of antebellum defendants charged with riot, however, these nine pressed for a trial. The jury found them innocent of all charges; and, in an almost unprecedented move, the county—rather than the defendants—paid the court costs.

So John Lightner and his fellow defendants were released with no cost in the eyes of the community, innocent men who should not be forced to bear any expenses. These trials were exceptions to every rule about the way that courts responded to collective violence at this time. Over a period of approximately 130 years in Lancaster County, these are the only men charged with riot against property-owning members of the community who got off scot-free. Class defined the seriousness of riots, *except* when the victims were members of the black middle class. Race transcended class in antebellum Lancaster County in a way that gender and ethnicity did not. It was the joker in the deck played by Lancaster's courts.

The threats, intimidation, and violence across racial lines did not end in this community with the Columbia Race Riots of 1834. Stephen Smith was still carrying his advertisment for the sale of his lumber business in February 1835, when he received a letter warning him again to be gone:

> You have again assembled yourself amongst the white people to bid up property as you have been in the habit of doing for a number of years back. You must know that your presence is not agreeable and the less you appear in the assembly of the whites the better it will be for your black hide, as there are a great many in this place that would think your absence from it a benefit, as you are considered an injury to the real value of property in Columbia. You had better take the hint and save— MANY.[31]

But there were no buyers for Smith's holdings, and the project to purchase the property of the entire black middle class never got off the ground. Perhaps this reflects a split among whites, which found the most prosperous white citizens more tolerant of the African-American presence than was the white working class. In any event, six months after the original tender to sell, Smith finally withdrew his advertisement, informing the public that he intended to continue his business as usual and thanking his customers for their continued support.[32]

One week before Smith withdrew his advertisement, another riot occurred, aimed at the property of yet another African-American. White "laborers" armed with axes, hatchets, staves, and sticks dismantled the close of Daniel Reed, letting his animals loose, and then destroyed the outbuildings that were inside the fence. The mob terrorized Reed and his family by threatening to pull down the house with them all still inside. The court again rounded up four white men, identified as "laborers" in the records, and this time demanded a two hundred dollar bond for each man. When the case came to trial, the men were again acquitted and released without paying costs.[33]

So Smith and the rest of the African-American community knew that the violence was not over and that they could not expect protection from white friends or white courts. If they were to continue to live in this place, blacks would have to fight and rely on themselves. The best intentions of liberal whites would not suffice, because the white community was profoundly divided on the question of race. Even the most racially enlightened Lancastrians drew the line at including blacks within their definition of community. Wear my old clothes, sleep in my barn, or rent a separate house on my property, but do not expect to worship as members of my church. This was the message delivered by Quakers and other "friends" of the blacks.

Contemporaneous with the Columbia Race Riots of 1834–1835, the black self-protection association first appeared in the county. For obvious reasons, its origins are shrouded in mystery. The causes for its existence are more obvious; its need for the likes of William Parker, who joined some years later, are clear. We cannot know the role played by the association in exacerbating the interracial tensions of the county, but it was certainly not a *cause* of stress along lines of race or class. Before, as long after, the association was born, it was easy to find working-class whites who were eager to bang blacks on the head for fun, money, or in defense of the law.

When a posse was needed to round up some blacks in the days after the Christiana Riot, white laborers and those who shared the bigotry of their class were eager to join. Not all whites were sure this was the right thing to do, especially since the African-Americans had killed an "outsider"—a white man to be sure, but a Southerner, not a neighbor, not a member of the community. So the aftermath of the Christiana Riot would reveal, yet again, how the lines between races and classes were drawn and where the community's definition of membership along territorial lines intersected with other categories of individual and collective identity.

When racial outsiders murdered a territorial outsider, how would the community react? Class defined membership in the local community, except that blacks were excluded even when they had a stake defined by property ownership. If blacks killed a property-owning Lancastrian, they could expect to receive the full punishment of the law, but if they assaulted a working-class white that was not the same thing. If local white laborers collectively or individually attacked another working-class white man or woman, or a local black, of any class and either gender, that was generally not as serious as any physical assault across class lines within the white race.

But on a spectrum of inclusion and exclusion, where did local blacks and alien, upper-class whites fall? When one killed the other, would the community care? Or would Lancastrians leave it to other outsiders—the executive and judicial branches of the federal government—to sort it all out? Was it murder; was it riot; was it treason or no crime at all for a crowd of fugitive slaves and free blacks in Lancaster County to kill Edward Gorsuch in the course of resisting the federal Fugitive Slave Law? The courts—federal and state—gave one set of answers to such questions in the way that they handled the Christiana Riot case.

Conclusion

THE STORY OF THE CHRISTIANA TRAGEDY, OF COURSE, did not end with the decisions of the federal and state courts. Castner Hanway returned to his mill; the Parkers started anew in Canada; and the Gorsuches divided up Edward's estate. We can only imagine what happened to the four men who gained their freedom by running away from Retreat Farm—or to Cassy Harris, who once again was a slave. Life was substantially unchanged for Lancaster's African-American community, the members of which still struggled to live and still lived in a world where being poor and being black was a double social curse. Race relations had not gotten better and in some ways continued to get worse. But those are also different stories, as is the Civil War that grew in the political soil fertilized by Edward Gorsuch's blood.

Legal and illegal attempts to recapture fugitives continued in Lancaster County and throughout the nation after the Christiana Riot, as did the kidnapping of free blacks. Federal tribunals remanded over a hundred African-Americans to slavery between 1852 and 1860. The violence associated with the Fugitive Slave Law continued as well. There were at least seventeen rescues of fugitives during those years; and we know of over a hundred successful abductions of blacks in the North. As late as March 1860 a free black man who was native to Lancaster County fell victim to Maryland kidnappers.[1]

There were undoubtedly violent encounters that went unreported or that have not yet been counted by historians who quantify crime. Bloodshed disillusioned Pennsylvanians about the Fugitive Slave Law, and public support decreased significantly over a brief period of time. In Harrisburg, for example, those local officials most directly responsible for enforcing this law were voted out of office in early 1853. Although relations between the state governments of Pennsylvania and Maryland improved after 1851, masters did not find it easier to retake their escaped slaves. Violence led to additional deaths, and those caught conspiring with the wrong side fell victim to vigilante actions that included arson, tarring and feathering, beating, whipping, and the one hanging mentioned earlier in this book.[2]

The Civil War eliminated the market for kidnapped blacks, thus ending this one cause of violence. After the war, all the public-policy motives for savagery across the Maryland-Pennsylvania border were past. The eighteenth-century boundary dispute was settled; the Indians were long gone; and slavery no longer existed as an incentive for interstate mayhem. So when William Parker returned to Lancaster County for a visit twenty years after the Christiana Riot, battles against kidnappers were only stories told about the past.

Unfortunately, the passage of time had not brought improvements in the quality of life for most blacks. The percentage of African-Americans in Lancaster city's population had doubled in the two decades since Parker ran away. About half of the city's black children were not in school; more than 80 percent of African-Americans could not read or even sign their names; and in the rural environs linkages among race, poverty, and illiteracy were even more striking.[3]

As a consequence of such long-standing social problems—of the history that made African-Americans who they were in southeastern Pennsylvania—violence still plagued the black community from within its own ranks; nor had violence across racial lines become a thing of the past. African-Americans held no monopoly on ignorance, and the prejudices of race festered and spread. As the numbers of blacks in the population continued to rise and social problems worsened, tolerance for violence against African-Americans even grew.

The lynching of a black man named Zachariah Walker in 1911 suggests how things had changed—and how they had not—in southeastern Pennsylvania over the sixty years since the Christiana Riot. Walker was drunk and staggering toward home on a Saturday night—nothing new about that. He had a pistol, which he fired to frighten two Polish laborers. Perhaps Walker believed that the white men threatened him harm. A private policeman in the employ of a coal-and-iron company heard the shots and confronted the black man. They exchanged words; then they struggled when the cop attempted an arrest. Both men had guns. Walker later claimed that he fired in self-defense; in any event, the policeman fell dead.[4]

The next afternoon firemen searching for the murderer found him hiding in a tree. When they approached, Walker tried to shoot himself in the head but only wounded his jaw. Authorities placed their prisoner in a hospital to have the bullet removed from his face, tied him in a strait-jacket, and shackled one of his legs to an iron bed.[5]

The police chief put one guard on the prisoner and left the scene. Later that night, a crowd of about two thousand men, women, and children marched down the street to the hospital; a contingent of twelve to fifteen rioters broke in, brushed the guard aside, dismantled the bed, and delivered Walker to the mob. Individuals took turns dragging their prisoner down the street until they reached a small grassy area outside the town. There they stopped and tore down a fence, which they threw into a pile and then ignited with flaming straw. By this time upwards of five thousand people cheered the proceedings, straining to witness this public execution of a black man. As the "leaders" were about to throw Walker into the fire, he pleaded for his life: "I killed Rice [the policeman] in self-defense. Don't give me a crooked death because I'm not white."[6]

A witness later remembered that Walker's cries could be heard over half a mile away. Three times they threw Walker into the flames, and three times he clambered out screaming and begging to be let go. Members of the mob pushed him back a fourth time, and he died in the flames. By all accounts, no one tried to stop the horror that night; we can assume that the burning took place with the sufferance of those charged to enforce the state's laws. One newspaper commented on the politeness of the crowd—how men stepped aside to give women and children a better view. Some waited long after Walker was dead for the ashes to cool and then collected pieces of his bones as souvenirs of the event. By and large, the community's passions were spent. There was general satisfaction that "justice" was done, although the policeman's widow did complain that she was not accorded the ceremonial privilege of lighting the fire.[7]

A grand jury indicted fifteen men for the murder of Walker. Included in this group were the police chief and the officer assigned to "guard" the prisoner. Juries acquitted them all. No one served time for a public execution that the white citizenry united behind.[8]

The attitudes of whites toward African-Americans had only gotten worse since the 1850s. Public anger was greater than at the Christiana rioters; respect for the rule of law was less than that shown at the time of the "Manheim Tragedy." Seeds of racial hatred and violence sown during the eighteenth century, fertilized with nineteenth-century blood, were ripe for the twentieth-century harvest that our nation has reaped.[9]

In the same year as the lynching of Walker, Lancastrians gathered to commemorate the sixtieth anniversary of the Christiana Riot. They used the occasion to retell a story about their community's past but did not even comment on the violence that continued in their midst. It was an opportunity to re-create myths about the courage of local people and the tragedy of the Civil War. There were still people alive who remembered these events, dimly to be sure, and memory has a way of filling in gaps to serve the individual and collective needs of narrators and their audiences. The intended reconciliation was not between white and black residents of Lancaster County. The wounds that local historians hoped to heal were those still smarting among whites on either side of the Mason-Dixon Line. As W. U. Hensel wrote at the time, "that the Gorsuch runaways were not heroic and scarcely even picturesque characters; and that their owners were humane and Christian people, and not the brutal slave traders and cruel taskmasters who figured in much of the anti-slavery fiction, can no longer be doubted." The goal in 1911 was to rewrite the myth by eliminating the slave owning villain and the romantic black victim—to cut Simon Legree and Uncle Tom out of the story. Even more to the point, white citizens were undoubtedly afraid of such aggressive and competent black characters as Eliza and George Harris, who took and defended their own freedom in Harriet Beecher Stowe's novel. So the 1911 version of the Christiana Riot was primarily a story told by, to, and about whites.[10]

In 1951, when Lancastrians commemorated the one hundredth anniversary of the riot, a conciliatory hand was also extended to African-Americans. Descendants of local blacks and the Maryland Gorsuches gathered together under the same roof, and the progeny of slave owners and slaves posed together for a group portrait that showed how far they all had come over the course of a century. But some things had not changed. As the myth was retold in 1951, the villains in the story were still black. The invocation delivered by a representative from the Society of Friends asked forgiveness for those who needed to be pardoned: "Father, we come to this historic spot today, not with hearts filled with pride, but with humiliation as we realize the errors of Thy children in their efforts to obtain freedom." The heroes as well as the victims were still white, even as African-American speakers recounted the story. Dr. Horace Mann Bond thanked God for the likes of Thaddeus Stevens, who believed in "the equality of man before his creator." But Bond wanted to speak principally about another man associated with the riot:

William Parker is the tragic symbol of our Centennial, of the troubles of his generation, and of our own. This is the Centennial of the violence engendered by great passions and forces, but also by one man. It is the story of A Man Without A Country; it is the tragedy of William Parker; it is the tragedy of mankind everywhere who would be free, but must resort to violence to obtain their freedom.[11]

There is no simple or direct path to understanding the past and its influence on our own lives. Laying the blame for the Christiana Riot on the head of one man is no more helpful a way out of our nation's cycle of violence than blaming God, alcohol, or "them"—whoever "they" might be. Indeed, the search for scapegoats denies the historical and cultural dimensions of all such complex events; it ignores the social and political roots of violence in which everyone is complicit. To see any participant in the Christiana Riot as simply a victim or a victimizer is to caricature the reality that we must comprehend.

If the two hundredth anniversary of the Christiana Riot calls for an observance in the year 2051, the sponsors and participants should ask themselves why. Why remember a "tragedy"; why not let the past go? One plausible answer, which occurs to me after writing this book, is that we have yet to learn any number of lessons taught by this story. The first commemoration of the riot reconciled whites on both sides; the second "forgave" blacks for resisting the law and killing a slave owner in order to be free. Perhaps we all can someday acknowledge the continuing injustices that lead to such violence. If one child goes hungry, cannot read, or has no reason to hope, we should not be surprised by what happens next. When we define community narrowly to exclude others unlike ourselves in some sense—if we build better schools, housing, and hospitals for "us"— then we share the burden of violence committed by "them." If we beat our children "for their own good," kick our dogs when we have a bad day, or perform experiments on animals because they are genetically similar but somehow different from "us," we forge additional links in the chain that binds us to our violent past.[12]

If Dr. Bond was wrong to describe the Christiana Riot solely as "the story of A Man Without A Country," he was right to depict it as a story. This book tells one version of the story about violence that should be narrated time and again. The setting may be one rural region in a day long ago; but there is, after all, only one story, and it is about us. We must respect our stories, be true to their meanings, and learn from them what we can. They are our connection to the past and can help set us free. Telling them badly or, worse yet, not hearing them at all condemns us to live our stories over again.

Afterword

> She must be true to the story. There is one story, Grey thought, and we tell it endlessly because we must; it is the definition of our being.
>
> N. SCOTT MOMADAY, *The Ancient Child: A Novel*

THIS IS NOT, OF COURSE, the only way that I might have told this story, nor is it the only way that it has been told. Local historians and historians of the Underground Railroad have recounted aspects of the Christiana Riot as it fits within the other stories that they have to tell. The riot is not well known among academic historians, however, nor does it play a role commensurate with its historical significance in the modern literatures on violence, race relations, or the coming of the Civil War. One of my goals is to bring the riot to my colleagues' attention, while telling the story in a way that may interest readers who are not specialists in these fields.

Over a century ago, the fugitive slave experience moved one local writer to compose a novel based on his personal observations and those of his white neighbors. The novel is revealing, I think, in any number of ways that also cast light on the perspectives of historians who have written about this general phenomenon in his day and since. It helps to comprehend the meaning of race relations in antebellum Lancaster County from an elite white male point of view and something about the journey that our nation has taken since.

When Ellwood Griest sat down after the Civil War to sort out the meaning of the fugitive slave experience in his own mind, he created fictional characters and portrayed events that had never really occurred. We cannot know for certain why Griest chose fiction to get at truth, but we can be pretty sure that truth was his goal. "The following story," he told readers, "is founded on facts that came within the personal knowledge of the writer. The characters described are all real ones. . . . The narrative is founded strictly on facts."[1]

Perhaps Griest wished to avoid controversy surrounding particular episodes; or maybe he dared not risk offending neighbors, whose roles in real-life events did not always show them in the best light. It is possible, of course, that he wanted to throw off the encumbrance of excessive detail associated with the writing of history in his own day no less than in ours. Griest clearly hoped to recapture the emotional dimensions of the fugitive experience, and fiction undoubtedly gave him the sort of license that historians are sometimes denied by our sources, professional fashion, and the personality traits that lead us to the craft.

Whatever his motives, Griest spun a yarn that reveals a century later even more truth than he intended about himself, his neighbors, and the battle for freedom waged by black women and men before the Civil War. The prejudices that are obvious to us in the novel, especially in the stock characterizations of whites and blacks, were cultural norms neither self-consciously employed by the author nor remarkable to his readers. They help me to comprehend the perceptual limitations of other documents consulted for the story that I have told in this book. They encourage me to envision historical actors as they saw themselves and each other, to see their world through eyes other than my own.

It would be a mistake, according to Griest, to imagine that Lancaster County was "anti-slavery" during the decades preceding the Civil War. It was a community deeply divided over the issue but less "pro-slavery" than it might have been without the influence of the Quakers who lived there. Granted, the Quakers were clannish and were often "better 'dealers' than strict honesty or the pure spirit of Christianity would warrant." But their opposition to slavery, reaching back into the mid-eighteenth century, had much to do locally with "preventing the growth of a bitter pro-slavery sentiment." "True," Griest wrote, "there was a bitter prejudice against the negro, and a general conviction that he was better off in slavery than in freedom, if he had a 'good master,' but it was believed that there were many bad masters, and a great deal of wrong done to slaves." Even Quakers had "strong and inveterate prejudices against the colored race." African-American laborers on Quaker farms, just as those in other local households, ate at separate tables and knew their place in the community. According to Griest, the blacks were "used to this, and therefore considered it no degradation." You may recall here the role played in my story by the Quaker miller, who reported to Edward Gorsuch that his slaves had stolen some wheat.[2]

As Griest's story of the fugitives John, Mary, and their son Charlie unfolds, the reader is told that the work habits of those raised in slavery were slothful and their attitude toward the world around them was one of "stolid indifference." They are portrayed as incompetent and fearful; the women are prone to fainting and the men to incapacitating despair. A fit of maternal concern does drive Mary to a heroic escape attempt, after which she falls into a helpless and extended swoon at the feet of her white patroness. John remains a passive spectator throughout, leading a free black laborer to observe that Mary is "wuth half a dozen sich fellows as her man." The fugitives' only identity in the novel is as victims—of their pursuers, of their own ignorance, and even of other blacks, who would sell them back into bondage for a drink or a handful of change.[3]

The role of the "kidnapper" is even less developed in the novel than those of the fugitive slaves. The pursuers are archetypal villains—cowards, cheats, corrupt and corrupting by nature and profession. In fact, as the author acknowledges, the colloquial use of the term "kidnapper" in southeastern Pennsylvania bore no necessary correspondence to its meaning in law. Legislation respecting the capture of fugitive slaves was "little understood by the common people," who had a sense of justice that led them to lump all pursuers of fugitives into the same despicable category.[4]

The work of the kidnapper would have been impossible, Griest tells us, without the sufferance of the wider community and the cooperation of two classes of local residents. First, there were lower-class whites, such as the character Sam Doan, a sometime coal miner who lived in "the barrens," on the fringes between white and black society. (The character William Padgett from my story may come to mind.) Such lowlifes were always looking for ways to turn an extra dollar or two, Griest tells us, and had no compunction about trafficking in human chattel for the price of a dishonest-day's wage.

Then, there were the "wust of the blacks," who associated with the white riff-raff. Doan "runs with 'em," another character tells us, "and 'sociates with 'em, and gits 'em to drinkin' and then he'll pick out of 'em ennything he wants." True to form, it is one of these marginal blacks who betrays John and Mary at a weekend frolic. "After several potations the secret he had learned . . . began to oppress him, and he commenced throwing out vague hints that he 'know'd sumthin,' but there wasn't enny body goin' to find it out—not enny." A couple more drafts from a bottle shrewdly provided by Doan for the purpose, and the beans were spilt.[5]

By this telling, it is the calculated maliciousness of the white man and the sodden loquaciousness of the black that conspires against vulnerable fugitives. Only the heroism of white patrons, in this case a Quaker family and a lapsed pacifist who was good with a gun, saves the victims from a fate worse than death. Courage triumphs over cowardice, love over hate, good over evil, and ultimately justice is secured. The morning after the decisive battle between "conductors" on the Underground Railroad and the kidnappers who sought to return John, Mary, and their son to slavery, Doan's cabin is found burned to the ground.

> A short distance away he was discovered lying helpless, beaten almost to death. During the night a gang of blacks had visited the place, and, infuriated by his treachery, had taken summary vengeance upon him. Except for the interference of one or two, more thoughtful and humane than the rest, he would have been murdered outright. As it was, he barely escaped with his life.[6]

To my reading, Griest's novel fails as art and entertainment. It has wooden characters, scenes, and dialogue; and the plot is simplistic. Perhaps contemporaries found it lacking in similar ways. And yet, Griest drew on typologies that resonate in literature because they resonate in life. The images of good and evil, victim and victimizer, hero and coward, betrayer and betrayed: these were, and to a large extent still are, the essence of mythology surrounding the fugitive slave experience in southeastern Pennsylvania. Historians, no less than novelists, are affected by these images. Over the past century, each of the novel's characters—the passive fugitive-slave victim, the heroic Quaker, the evil Southern kidnapper, the incompetent free black, and the corrupt local slave catcher—has appeared in historical accounts, and some of them are still featured in the enduring fugitive-slave legend.

There may be kernels of truth in such stereotypes, and they certainly can be used to help us understand how contemporaries saw each other. Caricatures are no substitute, however, for analysis that both incorporates and transcends the perspectives of historical actors. More subtle, true-to-life portrayals of the "kidnapper," the "master," the "fugitive slave," the "abolitionist," and the "free black" are surely in order.

Over eighty years ago, one of Lancaster County's ablest local historians made complaints similar to mine about the stock characterizations of pro- and anti-slavery forces in the antebellum battle for black freedom and contributed much in his own right to setting the historical record straight. "There were," according to W. U. Hensel, "on either side of the border troubles of that period, men of high principle and right motive and also rowdies and adventurers, disposed to resort to ruthless violence for purposes of sordid gain." There were good men who owned slaves and bad men who sought to overturn the institution of slavery. No side in this multifaceted controversy, Hensel contended, had a monopoly on virtue or vice, good or evil, right or wrong.[7]

We also have to try harder than either Hensel or Griest did to transcend the fugitives' status as "victim," thereby crediting the agency of victimized peoples in their own lives. Indeed, William Still, the African-American chronicler of the Underground Railroad, presented an image of runaways quite different from Griest's. "As a general rule," Still insisted, "the passengers of the U.G.R.R. were physically and intellectually above the average order of slaves." The fugitives Still wrote about were intelligent, brave, assertive, and instrumental in achieving their own freedom; these were not the sullen "victims" characterized by Griest.[8]

The unflattering depiction of Northern free blacks in the novel merits reexamination for the same reason, particularly in light of the enigmatic role played by African-American vigilantes on the fringes of Griest's story— and the central role that they play in mine. The novelist offers us little insight into the world of free blacks and no clue to the character of the black "gang" that beat up Doan and leveled his home. Finally, experience and surviving documentary evidence teaches us to suspect that the white community was composed of something more than villains and less than heroes.

More than thirty years ago, Larry Gara made observations similar to these about the myths still associated with the Underground Railroad. "Strangely," he noted, "the hero of the legendary struggle for freedom was not the slave who panted for release from his chains. Indeed, the slave often received only a secondary role in the exciting drama." White abolitionists were usually the ones who retold the stories and portrayed themselves as the heroes who sacrificed much and risked all for the fugitive slave. In some accounts, the legend still pits "God-fearing and righteous New Englanders on the one side and the wicked Southerners on the other." In another version, the Underground Railroad is portrayed as principally a Quaker institution. Both variations have a stereotypical villain; "he is a mean Southerner, a term synonymous in the popular legend with slaveholder or defender of the slave system. He, too, is something other than human, in this case something less." And the myth tends to ignore the serious problems faced by fugitives who escaped to the North. As Gara suggests, "like a Hollywood movie, the legend implies a happy ending when the fugitives reached a haven of free soil."[9]

Some historians and novelists now know better and recognize that fugitive slaves drew primarily on their own resources and secondarily on the help of fellow fugitives and free blacks. Witness the recent work of such eminent local historians of the African-American experience as Leroy Hopkins, Carl Oblinger, Jean Soderlund, and Julie Winch for Pennsylvania; and Barbara Fields, Allan Kulikoff, and Jean Lee across the Maryland line. Consider the insights given into the lives and mentalities of other African-Americans by such path-breaking historians as Ira Berlin, Eugene Genovese, Herbert Gutman, and Gary Nash; and the unsettling fictional portraits of fugitive and free blacks by such gifted writers as David Bradley, Toni Morrison, and John Edgar Wideman.[10]

This is not to say that white abolitionists did not sometimes play a significant role in the lives of fugitive slaves, occasionally at genuine risk to their own safety and property, or that their stories are unworthy of retelling. To ignore relationships across lines of race, gender, and class would be to supplant one set of modern caricatures—new heroes and old villains—for those of an earlier day. Some "God-fearing New Englanders" and Quakers, among other whites, suffered physical abuse and financial losses, became estranged from their neighbors, and had their barns burned by pro-slavery activists. Some played instrumental roles on a regular basis in the resettlement of escaped slaves. But the agonies and risks associated with the fugitive slave experience were endured primarily by African-Americans, who acted individually and in concert to protect themselves, their families, friends, and even people they had never before met from the lash of Southern masters, Northern bigots, and the force of the law. Again, as Gara reminds us, "in many cases it was the slaves themselves who took things into their own hands, planned their escapes, and during the greater part of their journeys arranged for or managed their own transportation." And, as is still frequently forgotten, "free Negroes contributed much to the success of whatever organized aid was offered to fleeing slaves."[11]

These are some of the ruminations that inform this book. They are some of the lessons that I learned in the course of my research and writing and some of the intellectual debts that I have to the writers—historians and novelists—who have preceded me in our collective endeavor to discover truth through our minds and our hearts. There are other influences as well that have come to me through personal encounters, and I want to acknowledge them also at this point.

Over the past five years, I have incurred a number of debts while researching and writing this book. At Oxford University Press, Sheldon Meyer's early interest, his wide-ranging advice about writers, readers, and books, and his specific suggestions about this manuscript were most valuable. The editorial work of Scott Lenz has also made this a better book. Rutgers University has provided institutional support of various kinds, including a two-year term as a Henry Rutgers Research Fellow, two summer research grants, and ongoing funds for travel and research. Both the past dean of the Faculty of Arts and Sciences, Tilden Edelstein, and his successor, Richard L. McCormick, have supported my scholarly endeavors during this period.

The American Council of Learned Societies also provided financial assistance for research through a grant-in-aid. A fellowship from the Shelby Cullom Davis Center at Princeton University gave me time under conditions that enabled me to finish writing the book. I am most grateful to the director of the Center, Lawrence Stone; the Center's manager, Joan Daviduk; the chairman of Princeton's History Department, Daniel Rodgers; and others among the faculty and graduate students who made my year at Princeton such a productive one. I thought that I had learned everything I could at Princeton when I was a graduate student there, but somehow I missed a few of Lawrence's lessons, which I am extremely fortunate to have had the opportunity to make up during his last year as director of the Davis Center.

I am indebted to historians who took the time from extraordinarily busy lives to write letters in behalf of my applications for financial assistance and a fellowship leave. Joyce Appleby, John Brewer, Philip Greven, Stanley Katz, John Murrin, Gary Nash, Lawrence Stone, and Michael Zuckerman provided indispensible help of this kind and a morale boost by endorsing my proposal. Audiences at Columbia University, the University of Delaware, Harvard University, the Library Company of Philadelphia, the University of Maryland Baltimore County, the University of Pennsylvania, and Princeton University gave me opportunities to formulate my thoughts at various stages and shared ideas that made this a better book.

My favorite talk, I must admit, was from the floor of Mike Zuckerman's living room. Partly, that represents a personal preference for informality, but it also is a measure of the helpfulness of the discussion. The intellectual community connected to the Philadelphia Center for Early American Studies and the late, great Transformation Project is the most constructively critical of any in my experience, and I highly value what I hope will be an ongoing association with that group.

All historians are dependent to one extent or another on the generosity of the research institutions where we do much of our work. I feel particularly fortunate to have had the opportunity to work one summer as a fellow at the Library Company of Philadelphia. James Greene, Mary Anne Hines, Philip Lapsansky, and John Van Horne made my research much easier and more enjoyable than it might have been, and the unsurpassed Afro-Americana collection of the Library Company led me to cast the project more broadly than I would have without it. The staff at the

Afterword

Lancaster County Historical Society, where I have spent a good many days and weeks over the past five years, were likewise unfailingly helpful and, dare I say it, fun to be around. The president of the Society, John W. W. Loose, encouraged my research through correspondence at an early stage; and Salinda Matt, Debra Smith, and Randall Snyder made an immense research task possible by giving me access to the entire run of county court records, most of which had not been unpacked since the day the case papers were tied into bundles a century or two ago. I will always remember my days at the Historical Society fondly and the generosity of the staff in sharing their facilities with me, even when I got in the way.

I also want to thank the research staffs at the Lancaster County Court House, the York County Court House, the Historical Society of York County, the Historical Society of Pennsylvania, the Pennsylvania State Library, the Bucks County Historical Society, the New Jersey State Library, Firestone Library (Princeton), the Baltimore County Historical Society, the Baltimore County Court House, the Baltimore County Office of Planning and Zoning, the Maryland Historical Society, the Enoch Pratt Free Library, the Maryland State Archives, the Library of Congress, the National Archives, the American Antiquarian Society, the Friends House Library (London), the Friends Historical Library (Swarthmore), the British Museum, the Ohio Historical Society, and the Buffalo and Erie County Historical Society.

Several colleagues in the History Department at Rutgers have taken time to read and comment on the manuscript that became this book. I am grateful to Paul Clemens, Philip Greven, and James Livingston for stimulating conversations, encouragement, and good advice. Paul's multiple close readings have saved me from several flat-out mistakes. His willingness to read the manuscript at least three times that I know of (without even being asked) is a testament to his generosity as a colleague and friend. As Phil Greven knows, his impassioned belief in the power of the written word to reform society has influenced me, as has his conviction that domestic violence is responsible for many of the gravest threats to our planet. No one has had a greater impact on the course of my scholarship since I left graduate school than Phil, and I thank him for sharing his book manuscript with me while this one was in progress. Conversations with Jim Livingston have not improved my golf game, but they did help me focus on my central story line and to see some of the larger analytical complexities of the historian's task.

Students at Rutgers are also a continuing source of inspiration. Undergraduates listened patiently to much of the material in this book and helped hone my story-telling skills. Graduate students in my reading colloquia and research seminars have likewise played a role in shaping the philosophical and methodological perspectives that inform the book. There is no more talented group of graduate students than those I have been blessed to teach during the past five years; I am honored to have shared a classroom and Patti's bar with some of them. Jacquelyn Miller helped check some newspapers one summer and thus played an important role in my research.

Two gluttons for punishment who helped me so much with my first book offered their services again. Douglas Greenberg and Louis Masur are still two of my toughest, most perceptive critics. I greatly appreciate the time they took to read and critique the manuscript as closely as they did; and then, in Lou's case, go another couple of rounds with a very combative author. No Verbedian ever had a better Gossage than I have in Lou, and I hope that some of the evidence of my gratitude is reflected in the revisions I have made since he read the manuscript. The book is structurally different as a consequence of his reading, and it is also shorter by about 25 percent partly because of his impatience with long books.

Jean Soderlund gave the manuscript a particularly close reading and saved me from a number of mistakes. She also shared some of her research notes, statistical compilations, and an unpublished (at that time) book manuscript. I greatly appreciate the help and such exemplary collegiality. So, too, did Edward Ayers take time from his own manuscript to give this one a careful reading and to make suggestions that led me to alter the text substantially.

Finally, and most of all, I have the great good fortune to be married to my best friend and the best editor that any writer ever had. Denise Thompson knows this manuscript as well as I do, has made countless editorial suggestions, collated information from the newspapers, compiled the index, and still loves me (I hope) just the same. In what has undoubtedly been the roughest year of her life, Dennee found the time and energy to help me more than I can acknowledge in words, making this the paragraph of this book in which I feel most frustrated by an inability to express what is in my heart.

Trenton, New Jersey   T. P. S.
September 1990

Abbreviations
Used in the Notes

AAS	American Antiquarian Society
AHR	*American Historical Review*
AJLH	*American Journal of Legal History*
BCCH	Baltimore County Court House, Towson, Maryland
BCOPZ	Baltimore County Office of Planning and Zoning, Towson
BECHS	Buffalo and Erie County Historical Society, Buffalo, New York
BHS	Baltimore County Historical Society, Cockeysville, Maryland
EHR	*English Historical Review*
FHL	Friends House Library, London
HSP	Historical Society of Pennsylvania
HSYC	Historical Society of York County
JAH	*Journal of American History*
JIH	*Journal of Interdisciplinary History*
JLCHS	*Journal of the Lancaster County Historical Society*
JNH	*Journal of Negro History*
JSH	*Journal of Social History*
LC	Library of Congress
LCHS	Lancaster County Historical Society
LCP	Library Company of Philadelphia
LCQS	Lancaster County Court of Quarter Sessions
LMC	Lancaster City Mayor's Court
MdHM	*Maryland Historical Magazine*
MdHR	Maryland State Archives, Annapolis
MHS	Maryland Historical Society, Baltimore
NA	National Archives
NEQ	*New England Quarterly*
OHS	Ohio Historical Society
PA	*Pennsylvania Archives*

Abbreviations Used in the Notes

PAH	*Pennsylvania History*
PASL	Pennsylvania State Library, Harrisburg
PMHB	*Pennsylvania Magazine of History and Biography*
PPAS	Papers of the Pennsylvania Abolition Society, HSP
Pratt	Enoch Pratt Free Library, Baltimore
VMHB	*Virginia Magazine of History and Biography*
WMQ	*William and Mary Quarterly*
WPHM	*Western Pennsylvania Historical Magazine*

Notes

Introduction

1. Stanley W. Campbell, *The Slave Catchers: Enforcement of the Fugitive Slave Law, 1850–1860* (Chapel Hill, 1970), 3–25; James M. McPherson, *Battle Cry of Freedom: The Civil War Era* (New York, 1988), 78–91.
2. Jonathan Katz, *Resistance at Christiana: The Fugitive Slave Rebellion, Christiana, Pennsylvania, September 11, 1851; A Documentary Account* (New York, 1974); Katz, *Inquest at Christiana*, performed on WBAI-FM, New York; Margaret Hope Bacon, *Rebellion at Christiana* (New York, 1975); John W. W. Loose, "Bloody Dawn: A Play," *JLCHS*, 83 (1979): 212–17; David R. Forbes, *A True Story of the Christiana Riot* (Quarryville, Pa., 1898); W. U. Hensel, *The Christiana Riot and the Treason Trials of 1851; An Historical Sketch*, 2d and rev. ed. (Lancaster, 1911); Paul Finkelman, "The Treason Trial of Castner Hanway," in Michal R. Belknap, ed., *American Political Trials* (Westport, Ct., 1981), 79–100.

Chapter 1. The Escape

1. Karen Riddlebaugh, "An Early American Farm . . . Gorsuch Farm, Glencoe, Maryland," report for the Baltimore County Office of Planning and Zoning, 1965; Baltimore County Register of Wills (Inventories), 65, MdHR 11, 718–1, pp. 420–27, Edward Gorsuch, 20 Oct. 1851.
2. Frederick Douglass, *My Bondage and My Freedom* (1855; New York, 1969), 189. On slave thievery, see Eugene D. Genovese, *Roll Jordan, Roll: The World the Slaves Made* (New York, 1974), 599–612.
3. Hensel, *Christiana Riot*, 20–21, gives the ages and character of the slaves based upon his interviews with members of the Gorsuch family and others who lived on the farm at the time of the escape.
4. On the relationship between labor and crop production in a Maryland setting,

see Paul G. E. Clemens, *The Atlantic Economy and Colonial Maryland's Eastern Shore: From Tobacco to Grain* (Ithaca, 1980); Barbara Jeanne Fields, *Slavery and Freedom on the Middle Ground: Maryland During the Nineteenth Century* (New Haven, 1985).

5. On Gorsuch genealogy, see [James F. H. Gorsuch,] *Genealogy and Biography of Leading Families of the City of Baltimore and Baltimore County* (New York, 1897); Gaddess Papers, MHS, MS 1946, "Genealogy of Gorsuch Family, 1721–1759"; Rider Family Papers, MHS, MS 2522; File A, MHS; J. H. P., "Genealogy: The Gorsuch and Lovelace Families," *VMHB*, 24–29 (1916–1921); Thomas W. Griffith, *Annals of Baltimore* (Baltimore, 1824), 5, 7; Brantz Mayer, *Baltimore As It Was and As It Is* (Baltimore, 1871), 13; Vertical File, "Gorsuch," Pratt; J. Thomas Scharf, *History of Baltimore City and County,* 2 vols. (Philadelphia, 1881; rpt. ed. in one vol., Baltimore, 1971), 880–81; Baltimore County Wills, Book I, 418–19, 439–40; Book VI, 479; Book XLII, 339–403; Baltimore County Inventories, no. 3, p. 543, BCCH. The fact that Gorsuch was a "class leader" of his church is from the *Pennsylvanian*, Sept. 18, 1851, p. 1.

6. Fields, *Slavery and Freedom on the Middle Ground,* 24. There is some confusion among the secondary sources about the number of slaves emancipated by Gorsuch and the manner in which that was accomplished. The inventory of his estate indicates clearly that provision had been made for eight slaves remaining in his possession in 1851 to be freed when they reached the age of twenty-eight years. Provision had also been made in his Uncle John's will for the manumission of several of the slaves inherited by Edward in 1845. These included Jarret Wallace, who was freed according to the terms of the will in 1849. The adult males who escaped in 1849 would also have been manumitted when they reached age twenty-eight. The exact age of each at the time of escape is not known. U.S. Federal Census, Population, 1850, Maryland, Slave schedules, Slave Inhabitants in 1st District in County of Baltimore, Nov. 3, 1850, p. 485, shows that Edward Gorsuch owned seven slaves. Baltimore County Register of Wills (Inventories) 65, MdHR 11, 718–1, pp. 420–27, Edward Gorsuch, 20 Oct. 1851, lists eight slaves at the time of Gorsuch's death, their ages at the time of the inventory, and the comment that each was to be released upon reaching age twenty-eight. It is unclear where Gorsuch picked up the additional slave between the time the census was taken and his death, especially since one of the slaves listed on the 1850 census was twenty-seven years old and due to be released the following year. Indeed, that particular slave woman was not on the estate inventory, so Gorsuch actually had two slaves at the time of his death who were not listed on the 1850 census, while he had lost only one from a manumission.

7. Fields, *Slavery and Freedom on the Middle Ground,* 17–19, 24–25, 83.

8. Riddlebaugh, "An Early American Farm"; "Old Gorsuch Homestead on Patapsco Neck Prominent in the Battle of North Point," *The Jeffersonian* (Towson, Md.), June 30, 1933; Mary B. M. Mitchell, *A History of Retreat Farm* (Baltimore, 1954).

9. Hensel, *Christiana Riot,* 3. Hensel's account draws on oral sources that are essential for reconstructing events from the various perspectives of white and

black residents of the farm. Katz, *Resistance*, also draws on interviews with descendants and on a modern recording of oral traditions. Myles Jackson, producer, and Dr. Florence Jackson, associate producer, "Two Man War At Christiana, 1851," *Viewpoints on American Abolition* (New York, 1971). See also, W. U. Hensel, "Aftermath Supplementary to Christiana Riot, 1851," *LCHS Papers*, 16 (1912): 133–41. Unless otherwise noted, these are the basic sources for my reconstruction of events in the fall of 1849.

10. William Francis Allen, Charles Pickard Ware, and Lucy McKim Garrison, comps., *Slave Songs of the United States* (New York, 1867), 68, 78.

11. Information about the barn is from Riddlebaugh, "An Early American Farm"; "Gorsuch Stone Barn," BCOPZ.

12. Information on the theft and the unraveling of the story is drawn from, J. S. Gorsuch to Hon. Wm. F. Johnston, Governor of Pennsylvania, Washington, Sept. 18, 1851 (copy), LCP; Edward Gorsuch to Philip Thomas, Gov. of Md., Nov. 29, 1849, Gorsuch to Thomas, Jan. 22, 1850, Exec. Papers, Misc., MdHR; Hensel, *Christiana*; Katz, *Resistance*.

13. Epistles Received by the London Yearly Meeting, Friends House Library, London; Stephen B. Weeks, *Southern Quakers and Slavery: A Study in Institutional History* (Baltimore, 1896); David Brion Davis, *The Problem of Slavery in the Age of Revolution, 1770–1823* (Ithaca, 1975); [Anonymous,] *Life of Elisha Tyson, the Philanthropist By a Citizen of Baltimore* (Baltimore, 1825), LCP. The number of Quakers in the state of Maryland was extremely small, about 700 by one estimate in 1843, so their ability to act effectively for change was necessarily limited. By comparison, there were 8,686 in Philadelphia. See John Chandler, "Letters on America, no. VI," *The British Friend* (Glasgow), 1 (1843): 117, FHL.

14. Baltimore to London, Oct. 31–Nov. 3, 1842, Epistles Received by the London Yearly Meeting, FHL. Joseph Gurney, an English Quaker, also commented on the public attitude of Maryland Quakers toward the slavery that existed in their midst. Gurney visited Baltimore's slave market and reported his horror to the Baltimore Yearly Meeting. The Maryland Friends responded, according to Gurney, that they saw "no way for action" against the sale of slaves in their state. Joseph John Gurney to J. H. and Anna Gurney, Nov. 9, 1839, Gurney MSS 3/735 a.b., FHL. Individual Quakers, however, acting secretly and without the formal endorsement of their meetings, did provide heroic aid to fugitive slaves in Maryland and throughout the South. See Weeks, *Southern Quakers and Slavery*. Weeks specifically excludes discussion of the Baltimore Yearly Meeting, because its constituent monthly meetings "lie only in part in Maryland, and extending into Pennsylvania, where the emancipation sentiment was strong, there was not the same heroism implied in opposition to slavery as in the more southern yearly meetings (vii)." Quaker involvement in Underground Railroad activities in the North is documented in a host of primary and secondary sources. See, for example, Thomas E. Drake, *Quakers and Slavery in America* (New Haven, 1950); William Still, *The Underground Rail Road* (Philadelphia, 1872); Wilbur H. Siebert, *The Underground Railroad from Slavery to Freedom* (New York, 1898). On the seventeenth- and eighteenth-century origins of Quaker opposition to slavery,

see Jean R. Soderlund, *Quakers and Slavery: A Divided Spirit* (Princeton, 1985); Jack D. Marietta, *The Reformation of American Quakerism, 1748–1783* (Philadelphia, 1984).

15. Epistles Received by the London Yearly Meeting, Maryland to London, Oct. 28–31, 1844, FHL; Baltimore Meeting for Sufferings to London Meeting for Sufferings, Oct. 26–31, 1844, Casual Correspondence, London Yearly Meeting, FHL.

16. Edward Gorsuch to Philip Thomas, Nov. 29, 1849. Johnson's name was also spelled "Johnston" and "Jonston" in the records.

17. Hensel, *Christiana*, 20–23.

18. Still, *The Underground Rail Road*, 136.

19. Ibid.; Katz, *Resistance*, 71.

20. Katz, *Resistance*, 22; Hensel, "Aftermath," 135–36.

21. Duke de la Rochefoucauld Liancourt, *Travels Through the United States of North America*, vol. II (London, 1799), 281, LCP; Fields, *Slavery and Freedom on the Middle Ground*, 34–35, 70; *Report of the Visitors and Governors of the Jail of Baltimore County* (Baltimore, 1831), LCP; *Baltimore Penitentiary Unroofed: or the Penitentiary System Illustrated, in a Letter to the Philadelphia Society for Ameliorating the Miseries of Public Prisons* (Philadelphia, 1833), LCP; *Annual Report of the Visitors of the Jail of Baltimore City to the Mayor and City Council of Baltimore* (Baltimore, 1860), LCP; *Report of the Trustees of the Alms House for Baltimore City and County* (Baltimore, 1827, 1845, 1847, 1848, 1849, 1851, 1852), LCP; *Baltimore Association for Improving the Condition of the Poor: Annual Report, Constitution and By-Laws, and Visitor's Manual* (Baltimore, 1851), LCP; *Fifth Annual Report of the Managers of the House of Refuge, Made to the Legislature of Maryland, January, 1856* (Baltimore, 1856), LCP.

22. Richard S. Dunn, "Black Society in the Chesapeake, 1776–1810," in Ira Berlin and Ronald Hoffman, eds., *Slavery and Freedom in the Age of the American Revolution* (Charlottesville, 1983), 49–82; Fields, *Slavery and Freedom on the Middle Ground*, 1, 3, 8–9, 15, 34, 70.

23. An Act Respecting Free Negroes, passed 31st of Dec. 1801, ch. 109; An Act, Entitled, an Additional Supplement to an Act, Entitled, An Act Relating to Negroes, and to Repeal the Acts of Assembly therein Mentioned, passed 25th of Jan. 1806, ch. 66; An Act to Prohibit the Emigration of Free Negroes into This State, passed 3d of Jan. 1807, ch. 56; A Further Supplement to the Act, Entitled, An Act Relating to Servants and Slaves, passed 24th of Dec. 1808, ch. 81; A Further Supplement to an Act, Entitled, An Act to Prevent the Inconveniences Arising From Slaves Being Permitted to Act as Free, passed Feb. 6, 1823, ch. 115; A Supplement to the Act, Entitled, An Act to Prohibit the Emigration of Free Negroes into this State, passed Feb. 21, 1824, ch. 161; An Act Relating to the Trustees of the Poor and Judges of the Orphans Courts of the Several Counties in this State, passed Feb. 4, 1825, ch. 87; An Additional Supplement to the Act Relating to Negroes, and to Repeal the Acts of Assembly Therein Mentioned, passed Mar. 2, 1826, ch. 16; An Additional Supplement to the Act Concerning Crimes and Punishments, passed Mar. 12, 1827, ch. 229; An Act Relating to Free Negroes and Slaves, passed Mar.

14, 1832, ch. 323; An Act to Amend the Constitution and Form of Government of the State of Maryland, passed Mar. 10, 1837, ch. 197; An Act Entitled, a Further Supplement to an Act, passed at Dec. session eighteen hundred and thirty-one, chapter three hundred and twenty-three, passed Mar. 7, 1842, ch. 272; An Act to Prohibit the Formation and Assemblage of Secret Societies of Negroes, passed Mar. 9, 1843, ch. 281; An Act Entitled a Supplement to an Act Relating to Free Negroes and Slaves, passed at Dec. session, eighteen hundred and thirty-one, passed Feb. 18, 1846, ch. 94; An Act Entitled, a Further Supplement to an Act Entitled, An Act Relating to Negroes and Slaves, passed Mar. 9, 1848, ch. 244, MdHR. The laws are also available on the microfilm series of early state records. See *A Guide to the Microfilm Collection of Early State Records* (Washington, D.C., 1950).

24. J. S. Gorsuch to Hon. Wm. F. Johnston, Sept. 18, 1851, LCP; Edward Gorsuch to Philip Thomas, Nov. 29, 1849, MdHR; Hensel, *Christiana Riot*, 20, 22; James J. Robbins, *Report of the Trial of Castner Hanway for Treason* (Philadelphia, 1852), testimony of Dickinson Gorsuch. (Hereafter cited as Robbins, *Report.*) On contemporary theories of slave passivity and violence see, for example, Jeffrey Rossbach, *Ambivalent Conspirators: John Brown, The Secret Six, and a Theory of Slave Violence* (Philadelphia, 1982).

25. Gorsuch to Thomas, Nov. 29, 1849, MdHR; Gorsuch to Thomas, Jan. 22, 1850, MdHR.

26. As Larry Gara points out, "after 1850, the pursuit of fugitive slaves became, like the Fugitive Slave Law itself, more a symbolic than a practical matter. The recovery of a slave under the new law often cost many times the market value of the runaway, and each rendition was potentially a source of public controversy which might well end in violence" (*The Liberty Line: The Legend of the Underground Railroad* [Lexington, Ky., 1961], 141). Of course, masters very well may have projected additional expenses arising from a successful escape. If one slave got away, that would certainly increase the possibility that others would try. One demonstration of the master's vincibility might reasonably be expected to undermine his ability to extract labor from his other slaves. So the calculation of costs should be construed more broadly than the market value of the fugitive slave. In addition to pecuniary concerns and the ethic of personal honor, there was also certainly an ideology of social responsibility that is only partly explained by "honor." The master shared responsibility for upholding the slave system, a duty that incorporated, but transcended, his personal interests and honor. I thank Louis Masur for this observation.

27. Gara, *Liberty Line*, 141.

28. Bertram Wyatt-Brown, *Southern Honor: Ethics and Behavior in the Old South* (New York, 1982), 373, 40, 375, 5.

29. Edward L. Ayers, *Vengeance and Justice: Crime and Punishment in the 19th-Century American South* (New York, 1984), 131. On the capacity of slavery to "tame" Africans, see George Fredrickson, *The Black Image in the White Mind: The Debate on Afro-American Character and Destiny, 1817–1914* (New York, 1971), 53–56, and Ayers's discussion of the same point, *Vengeance and Justice*, 130. On Southern "honor," see also Kenneth S. Greenberg, "The

Nose, the Lie, and the Duel in the Antebellum South," *AHR*, 95 (1990): 57–74; Dickson D. Bruce, *Violence and Culture in the Antebellum South* (Austin, 1979).

30. Douglass, *My Bondage and My Freedom*, 163–264, 90–91, 272.

31. Willie Lee Rose, "The Domestication of Domestic Slavery," in Rose, *Slavery and Freedom*, edited by William W. Freehling (New York, 1982), 1836.

32. Bertram Wyatt-Brown, "The Mask of Obedience: Male Slave Psychology in the Old South," *AHR*, 93 (1988): 1228–52.

33. Douglass, *My Bondage and My Freedom*, 333.

34. Wyatt-Brown, "The Mask of Obedience," 1248; Eugene D. Genovese, *From Rebellion to Revolution: Afro-American Slave Revolts in the Making of the New World* (Baton Rouge, 1979), 49, 50; Genovese, *Roll Jordan, Roll*, 648; Fields, *Slavery and Freedom on the Middle Ground*, 16.

35. Fields, *Slavery and Freedom on the Middle Ground*, 16; Robert L. Hall's "Slave Resistance in Baltimore City and County, 1747–1790," *MdHM*, 84 (1989): 305–18, is based on a study of advertisements for runaway slaves a century before the four men ran away from Gorsuch's farm. During the period examined by Hall, there were advertisements for 182 runaways, of whom 84 percent were men. He estimates that 75.8 percent of males and 60 percent of female fugitives during the eighteenth century were between the ages of fifteen and thirty-four (306–7). According to Hall, "as early as 1785, James Hutchings, a Baltimore slaveholder, complained that his Ned, whom he believed had joined forces with 'that long and old offender, and rape-committing villain, known by the name of Smith's Sam,' had 'taken asylum in the Pennsylvania State, under the cover of a law, fraught with great mischiefs and inconvenience to her sister states' " (p. 313). On the eighteenth century, see also Lorena S. Walsh, "Rural African-Americans in the Constitutional Era in Maryland, 1770–1810," *MdHM*, 84 (1989): 327–41; Jean Butenhoff Lee, "The Problem of Slave Community in the Eighteenth-Century Chesapeake," *WMQ* 3d ser., 43 (1986): 333–61.

36. *Liberator*, Oct. 3, 1851; Katz, *Resistance at Christiana*, 72–73.

Chapter 2. Black Images in White Minds

1. "An Act for the Gradual Abolition of Slavery" (1780), was the first legislative enactment of its kind in the United States, but far from the quickest. Those who were already slaves at the time were to remain slaves for life. Black and mulatto children born after adoption of the law were to be freed after serving their mother's master until the age of twenty-eight. See A. Leon Higginbotham, Jr., *In the Matter of Color: Race and the American Legal Process: The Colonial Period* (New York, 1978), 299–303.

2. U.S. Census, Population; Jean R. Soderlund, "Black Importation and Migration into Southeastern Pennsylvania, 1682–1810," *Proceedings of the American Philosophical Society*, 133 (1989): 144–53; Carl Douglas Oblinger, "New Freedoms, Old Miseries: The Emergence and Disruption of Black Communities in Southeastern Pennsylvania, 1780–1860," Ph.D. diss., Lehigh University, 1988, pp. 67, 73, 79. In 1790, Lancaster and Dauphin together (the

two had separated in 1785) had the fourth largest slave population in proportion to total population in the state. This helps to account for the opposition of eight of Lancaster's eleven assembly delegates to the state's gradual abolition act ten years earlier. The county's slave population had grown eightfold between 1759 and 1780. Gary B. Nash and Jean R. Soderlund, *Freedom By Degrees: Emancipation in Pennsylvania and Its Aftermath* (New York, 1991); Jerome H. Wood, Jr., *Conestoga Crossroads: Lancaster, Pennsylvania, 1730–1790* (Harrisburg, 1979). See also Paul Erb Doutrich, "The Evolution of an Early American Town: Yorktown, Pennsylvania, 1740–1790," Ph.D. diss., University of Kentucky, 1985; Owen Ireland, "Germans against Abolition: A Minority's View of Slavery in Revolutionary Pennsylvania," *JIH*, 3 (1973): 685–706; Arthur Zilversmit, *The First Emancipation: The Abolition of Slavery in the North* (Chicago, 1967); Edgar McManus, *Black Bondage in the North* (Syracuse, 1973).

3. Alexis de Tocqueville, *Democracy in America*, vol. I (1835; New York, 1945), 359, 360; Captain [Frederick] Marryat, *A Diary in America*, vol. I (London, 1839), 294, LCP.

4. Tocqueville, *Democracy in America*, I, 360.

5. This is not to say that whites were absolutely free to brutalize African-Americans in colonial Pennsylvania, but a complaint against a white man for assaulting a black would have to come from a white man and be based on information from white witnesses. In fact, there is no record of a master in Lancaster County ever being tried for assaulting a slave or any master in the colony ever being prosecuted for killing a slave, although there is one case mentioned in 1770 in which a master was apparently advised by friends to leave the area before coming to trial "as otherwise they could not avoid taking him prisoner, and that he would be condemned to die according to the laws of the county [*sic*], without any hope of saving him." Peter Kalm, *Travels*, I, 391–92, as quoted in Higginbotham, *In the Matter of Color*, 307.

6. Higginbotham, *In the Matter of Color*, 269, 282–85. By comparison, poor white male children under the care of the county were bound to the age of twenty-one, females to eighteen. Of course, the legal status of slaves was comparatively better in Pennsylvania than in the Southern colonies. See Nash and Soderlund, *Freedom By Degrees*, Chapter 1.

7. Merle G. Brouwer, "The Negro As a Slave and As a Free Black in Colonial Pennsylvania," Ph.D. diss., Wayne State University, 1973, pp. 109, 112, 137, 139, 144, 145, 149, 155, 160, 170, and passim. See also Darold D. Wax, "The Negro Slave Trade in Colonial Pennsylvania," Ph.D. diss., University of Washington, 1962. The traditional portrayal of Pennsylvania slavery as comparatively benign is apparent in Edward R. Turner's classic book *The Negro in Pennsylvania* (Washington, D.C., 1911), as well as in other, more recent scholarly literature on the black experience in eighteenth-century Pennsylvania. Nash and Soderlund point out that by comparison with the colonial laws of South Carolina and Georgia, "the Pennsylvania code was positively enlightened." *Freedom By Degrees*, Chapter 1.

8. According to Merle G. Brouwer, "Marriage and Family Life Among Blacks in Colonial Pennsylvania," *PMHB*, 99 (1975): 368–72, "the materials available for an assessment of black family life in colonial Pennsylvania are rather lim-

ited." Jean R. Soderlund, "Black Women in Colonial Pennsylvania," *PMHB*, 107 (1983): 49–68, also notes that "not very much is known about the economic status of free blacks in the late colonial period" (64), but in this essay and "Black Importation and Migration into Southeastern Pennsylvania, 1682–1810," *Proceedings of the American Philosophical Society*, 133 (1989): 144–53, she does as good a job as I can imagine anyone doing with the surviving documentation. On general questions about the lives of African-Americans see, for example, Herbert G. Gutman, *The Black Family in Slavery and Freedom, 1750–1925* (New York, 1976), and Berlin and Hoffman, eds., *Slavery and Freedom in the Age of the American Revolution*. The best book-length study of African-American life in Pennsylvania during this period is Gary B. Nash, *Forging Freedom: The Formation of Philadelphia's Black Community, 1720–1840* (Cambridge, Mass., 1988).

9. On violence in eighteenth-century Lancaster, see Thomas P. Slaughter, "Crowds in Eighteenth-Century America: Reflections and New Directions," *PMHB*, 105 (1991): 3–34; and Slaughter, "Interpersonal Violence in a Rural Setting: Lancaster County, Pennsylvania in the Eighteenth Century," *PAH*, 58 (1991): 98–123.

10. On slave suicides in Philadelphia, see Nash, *Forging Freedom*, 12. On slave escapes in Pennsylvania, see Billy G. Smith and Richard Wojtowicz, *Blacks Who Stole Themselves: Advertisements for Runaways in the* Pennsylvania Gazette, *1728–1790* (Philadelphia, 1989).

11. Brouwer, "The Negro as Slave," 144. On runaway-slave advertisements, see Gary T. Hawbaker, ed., *Runaways, Rascals, and Rogues: Missing Spouses, Servants, and Slaves*, vol. 1, *Abstracts from Lancaster County, Pennsylvania Newspapers*, Lancaster Journal, *1794–1810* (Hershey, 1987); Richard Wojtowicz and Billy G. Smith, "Advertisements for Runaway Slaves, Indentured Servants, and Apprentices in the *Pennsylvania Gazette*, 1795–1796," *PAH*, 54 (1987): 34–71; Gerald W. Mullin, *Flight and Rebellion: Slave Resistance in Eighteenth-Century Virginia* (New York, 1972); Daniel E. Meaders, "South Carolina Fugitives as Viewed Through Local Colonial Newspapers with Emphasis on Runaway Notices 1732–1801," *JNH*, 60 (1975): 288–319; Lorenzo J. Greene, "The New England Negro as Seen in Advertisements for Runaway Slaves," *JNH*, 29 (1944): 125–46; Hall, "Slave Resistance in Baltimore City and County."

12. Acting Committee Minute Book, 1784–1788, 7 (Apr. 24, 1784), 28 (Nov. 27, 1784), 42–43 (Apr. 23 and May 20, 1785), PPAS, reel 4. Cited in Nash, *Forging Freedom*, 93.

13. Alan Tully, "Patterns of Slaveholding in Colonial Pennsylvania: Chester and Lancaster Counties, 1729–1758," *JSH*, 6 (1973): 285. The use of tax assessments as measures of wealth can be misleading because not all kinds of property were counted, and assessments were not necessarily at market values. For example, a slave was rated at about £4. I thank Jean Soderlund for this clarification.

14. Oblinger, "New Freedoms, Old Miseries," 19, 20–21, 25, 27, 28; Tully, "Patterns of Slaveholding," 284–305; Jerome H. Wood, Jr., "The Negro in Early Pennsylvania: The Lancaster Experience, 1730–90," in Elinor Miller and Eugene D. Genovese, eds., *Plantation, Town, and County: Essays on the Local*

History of American Slave Society (Urbana, 1974), 441–52; Soderlund, "Black Importation and Migration Into Southeastern Pennsylvania"; Wax, "Negro Slave Trade"; Brouwer, "The Negro as Slave." According to Nash and Soderlund, the percentage of the colony's slaves who labored in the countryside—by which they mean outside the city of Philadelphia—rose from 66 percent in 1750 to 75 percent in the 1760s and to over 90 percent in 1780 and 1790. By 1790 the rural counties bordering Maryland had 44 percent of the state's population but 66 percent of its slaves. In 1810, with about the same proportion of the population, these counties held 94 percent of the state's slaves (*Freedom by Degrees*, Chapter 1, Table 1-1).

15. Quoted in Brouwer, "The Negro as Slave," 71, 74. On the Quakers, see Henry J. Cadbury, "Negro Membership in the Society of Friends," *JNH*, 21 (1936): 151–213; Soderlund, *Quakers and Slavery*; Marietta, *Reformation of American Quakerism*; Thomas E. Drake, "Joseph Drinker's Plea for the Admission of Colored People to the Society of Friends, 1795," *JNH*, 32 (1947): 110–12; Drake, *Quakers and Slavery*. On Franklin and Quakers, see Jacquelyn C. Miller, "Franklin and Friends: Benjamin Franklin's Ties to Quakers and Quakerism," *PAH*, 57 (1990): 318–36.

16. Brouwer, "The Negro as Slave," 112, 137; Nancy Slocum Hornick, "Anthony Benezet and the Africans' School: Toward a Theory of Full Equality," *PMHB*, 99 (1975): 399–421; George S. Brookes, *Friend Anthony Benezet* (Philadelphia, 1937).

17. "Germantown Friends Protest Against Slavery, 1688," facsimile edition (Philadelphia, 1880), LCP; "The First Printed Protest Against Slavery in America," *PMHB*, 12 (1889): 265–70; Society of Friends, Pennsylvania and New Jersey Yearly Meeting (Sept. 9, 1754), *An Epistle of Caution and Advice, Concerning the Buying and Keeping of Slaves* (Philadelphia, 1754), LCP; Society of Friends, *Rules of Discipline and Christian Advices of the Yearly Meeting of Friends for Pennsylvania and New Jersey* (Philadelphia, 1797), LCP; *Rules of Discipline of the Yearly Meeting of Friends, Held in Philadelphia* (Philadelphia, 1806), LCP; Soderlund, *Quakers and Slavery*; Marietta, *Reformation of American Quakerism*; Drake, *Quakers and Slavery*; J. William Frost, "The Origins of the Quaker Crusade against Slavery: A Review of Recent Literature," *Quaker History*, 67 (1978): 42–58; Donald Brooks Kelley, "Friends and Nature in America: Toward an Eighteenth-Century Quaker Ecology," *PAH*, 53 (1986): 257–72. Noah Dixon is quoted in Oblinger, "New Freedoms, Old Miseries," 37.

18. Cadbury, "Negro Membership in the Society of Friends"; Drake, "Joseph Drinker's Plea"; Winthrop D. Jordan, *White Over Black: American Attitudes Toward the Negro, 1550–1812* (Chapel Hill, 1968), 196, 419–23.

19. John Chandler, "Letters on America, no. II," *The British Friend* (Glasgow), 1 (1843): 55, FHL. See also the other five letters of Chandler published in the same number and the replies defending American Friends against such charges in the same journal the following year. See also "Epistles Received by the London Yearly Meeting," FHL; "Letters to and From Philadelphia," 2 vols., FHL.

20. Leroy T. Hopkins, "The *Negro Entry Book*: A Document of Lancaster City's Antebellum Afro-American Community," *JLCHS*, 88 (1984): 147.

21. Jordan, *White Over Black*, 409–10.
22. Ibid., 179.
23. The focus here is on African-American images, but portrayals of blacks in African and Caribbean settings played a significant role in this process as well. See, for example, Alfred N. Hunt, *Haiti's Influence on Antebellum America: Slumbering Volcano in the Caribbean* (Baton Rouge, 1988). Of course, we would like to know how readers perceived these images, but such information does not survive for Lancaster at this time. The chapters that follow supplement the newspaper images with others from court records, newspapers, and other public documents. It might also be useful to know more about the editors who printed the stories; but prosopographical research of this kind is not only difficult for Lancaster, it is not obviously relevant to the limited use of the newspapers in this chapter. The images of blacks in Lancaster's papers were drawn primarily from newspapers in other cities, and the images transcended the known editorial perspectives of newspaper editors. What is more, although the images presented changed over time, there is no direct relationship between the timing of changes and editorial personnel. So, as stated in the text, the selection and printing of stories about blacks provide clues to Lancaster's place in the larger culture of which it was a part and to how attitudes were changing in Lancaster, but they do not enable us to pin down such amorphous cultural transformations in any definitive sense.
24. During the thirty years between 1796 and 1835, for example, the number of negative characterizations of blacks in the *Lancaster Journal* outnumbered articles containing positive portrayals by more than ten to one. Over time, the number of negative characterizations increased dramatically, so that during the ten-year period ending in 1835 there were thirty-nine articles that contained negative portraits of blacks and only three that showed them in a positive light. There were 138 articles in the *Lancaster Journal* from 1796 through 1835 that portrayed blacks negatively: 1796–1805—27; 1806–1815—15; 1816–1825—57; 1826–1835—39. Articles portraying blacks positively appeared as follows: 1796–1805—10; 1806–1815—4; 1816–1825—15; 1826–1835—3. Articles depicting black violence appeared as follows: 1796–1805—32; 1806–1815—10; 1816–1825—64; 1826–1835—41.

    Clearly, a wider array of images was available from the larger culture right through the Civil War. The writings of Frederick Douglass and Harriet Beecher Stowe, for example, circulated in Lancaster, as elsewhere in the North. The selections made by newspaper editors who, during the antebellum era represented competing mainstream political parties—for example, Democrats and Whigs—generally rejected images from the cultural fringes, such as radical abolitionism and pro-slavery racism, with which their readership was generally out of sympathy. So, what we find in the *Lancaster Journal* and *Lancaster Intelligencer* are the middle range of opinion most widely shared in this county. Despite the divergent political views of the two newspapers, especially from the 1830s onward, the depictions of African-Americans were not so diverse as one might expect. It was possible to be more sympathetic to the plight of fugitives—as the Whigs were—but to have no greater respect for the mental capacity or character of black people in the community. Most local "liberals" on racial questions favored colonization of African-Americans during the antebellum era, which left blacks increasingly on their own from the 1820s onward. The historical literature about the small minority of extremists on both sides is perhaps more fully developed than that on mainstream beliefs. Most useful for my purposes here are Leon F. Litwack, *North of Slavery: the Negro in the Free States, 1790–1860* (New York, 1961); David Brion Davis, *The Problem of Slavery in Western Culture* (Ithaca, 1966); Jordan, *White Over Black*; Fredrickson, *The Black Image in the White Mind*; David Brion Davis, *The Problem of Slavery in the Age of Revolution*; Lawrence W. Levine, *Black Culture and Black Consciousness: Afro-American Folk Thought from Slavery to Freedom* (New York, 1977); David Brion Davis, *Slavery and Human Progress* (New York, 1984); Sterling Stuckey, *Slave Culture: Nationalist Theory and the Foundations of Black America* (New York, 1987); and Turner, *The Negro in Pennsylvania*. Radical abolitionists from the Garrisonian wing of the movement did not, of course, support colonization.

25. Between June 17, 1796 (the earliest surviving issue of the *Lancaster Journal*) and June 21, 1800, there were four stories that portrayed a black servant as loyal, faithful, or brave in the service of a white master—Feb. 3, 1797, p. 3; July 26, 1797, p. 3; Mar. 2, 1799, p. 3; and June 21, 1800, p. 2. There was only one additional positive characterization of that sort in the *Lancaster Journal* and the *Lancaster Intelligencer* through Dec. 31, 1856. And the slant of that story—in the *Lancaster Journal* of Oct. 19, 1818, p. 2—was not the bravery of a black man for saving a white child from a rabid puppy but about him as a victim of hydrophobia. Twenty years earlier, he would have been praised as a hero, but by the second decade of the century, black heroism was not one of the images that appeared in the papers. The statements about L'Ouverture are taken from the *Lancaster Journal*, Aug. 22, 1801, p. 2.

26. *Lancaster Journal*, July 1, 1796, p. 3; July 8, 1796, p. 3; Sept. 23, 1796, p. 4; June 3, 1797, p. 3; Oct. 28, 1797, p. 1; Dec. 30, 1797, p. 3; July 25, 1801, p. 3; June 12, 1802, p. 3; July 16, 1803, p. 3; Oct. 11, 1803, p. 1; Apr. 18, 1806, p. 2; Oct. 2, 1807, p. 3; Mar. 11, 1811, p. 3; Aug. 7, 1812, p. 3; Feb. 10, 1815, p. 3; Apr. 5, 1816, p. 2; Mar. 17, 1817, p. 3; Mar. 28, 1817, p. 3; Dec. 19, 1817, p. 3, and passim. There is no discernible change in the images of escaped slaves over time. The number of different advertisements for escaped slaves in the *Lancaster Journal* were distributed over time as follows: 1796–1805—63; 1805–1815—98; 1816–1825—109; 1826–1835—49. Advertisements offering slaves for sale occurred as follows: 1796–1805—9; 1806–1815—24; 1816–1825—29; 1826–1835—4. Advertisements were generally repeated, sometimes for a year or more, so the total number of ads for escaped slaves, including repeats, was significantly higher than the figures given above.

27. *Lancaster Journal*, July 1, 1796, p. 3; Aug. 12, 1797, p. 3; Aug. 12, 1798, p. 4; Feb. 4, 1801, p. 1; June 13, 1801, p. 2; Nov. 14, 1809, p. 3; Jan. 6, 1817, p. 3; Jan. 4, 1819, p. 3; Aug. 10, 1819, p. 2; Nov. 23, 1819, p. 3; Apr. 20, 1820, p. 2; May 4, 1821, p. 3.

28. *Lancaster Journal*, Sept. 9, 1796, p. 2 (story about a woman throwing herself and her children down a well in Savannah, Georgia); July 25, 1801, p. 4 (confession of "Negro Chloe").

29. *Lancaster Journal*, Oct. 7, 1797, p. 3; July 30, 1803, p. 3; June 9, 1804, p. 2; Apr. 25, 1806, p. 2; May 19, 1809, p. 2; Nov. 17, 1815, p. 3; May 22, 1816,

p. 2; Oct. 27, 1817, p. 3; Apr. 6, 1818, p. 2; May 13, 1818, p. 2; May 29, 1818, p. 3; June 1, 1818, p. 3; July 8, 1818, p. 3; July 22, 1818, p. 3; Aug. 12, 1818, p. 2; Nov. 16, 1818, p. 3; Jan. 13, 1819, p. 3; June 29, 1819, p. 1; May 18, 1821, p. 3; June 15, 1821, p. 3; and passim.

30. *Lancaster Journal,* May 5, 1797, p. 3 (carelessly kept fireplace); June 21, 1811, p. 3 (board blows off roof, killing black woman); Nov. 13, 1815, p. 2 (caught in chimney); May 7, 1817, p. 3 (playing with gun); May 21, 1817, p. 2 (loses control of wagon); July 16, 1817, p. 1 (playing with gun); Oct. 10, 1817, p. 3 (road-building accident); June 8, 1821 (swallows pins); *Lancaster Intelligencer,* June 13, 1824, p. 2 (accident at Philadelphia almshouse); Aug. 23, 1825, p. 2 (accident involving black boy who foolishly tied horse's halter around his own neck).

31. *Lancaster Intelligencer,* Jan. 15, 1820, p. 3 (Norfolk, Virginia).

32. *Lancaster Journal,* Sept. 9, 1796, p. 2; Sept. 12, 1809, p. 2.

33. *Lancaster Journal,* July 1, 1796, p. 3; July 8, 1796, p. 3; Sept. 23, 1796, p. 4; Feb. 3, 1797, p. 2; Mar. 24, 1797, p. 2; May 5, 1797, p. 3; Aug. 12, 1797, p. 3; Oct. 28, 1797, p. 1; Dec. 30, 1797, p. 3; Mar. 2, 1799, p. 3; June 21, 1800, p. 2.

34. *York Recorder,* Jan. 19, 1803, p. 2; Jan. 26, 1803, p. 2; Feb. 9, 1803, p. 2; Aug. 31, 1803, p. 2; Sept. 4, 1803, p. 2; Oct. 5, 1803, p. 2; Dec. 7, 1803, p. 2; Dec. 21, 1803, p. 3; *Lancaster Journal,* Mar. 27, 1802, p. 2; May 29, 1802, p. 2; May 28, 1803, p. 2; June 9, 1804, p. 2, and passim.

35. *York Recorder,* Jan. 19, 1803, p. 2; Mar. 2, 1803, p. 2; Mar. 9, 1803, p. 3; Mar. 16, 1803, p. 3; Mar. 23, 1803, p. 3; May 25, 1803, p. 2; W. C. Carter and A. J. Glossbrenner, *History of York County From Its Erection to the Present Time; [1729–1834]* (Harrisburg, 1930), 139–42; George R. Prowell, *History of York County Pennsylvania,* vol. I (Chicago, 1907), 788; Oyer and Terminer case papers related to arson trial, May 1803, HSYC; "Rules to be observed by the Capt. and his Guard," Mar. 17, 1803, HSYC.

36. In addition to violent, African-Americans were portrayed throughout the antebellum period as fools. Apocryphal stories, in which blacks are the butt of jokes, were printed in the newspapers. Such characterizations are also visible in Lewis Miller's paintings and in advertisements for minstrel shows. Litwack, *North of Slavery,* 99; Robert P. Turner, ed., *Lewis Miller: Sketches and Chronicles* (York, 1966).

37. Litwack, *North of Slavery,* 69, 75, 97; *An Appeal of Forty-Thousand Citizens, Threatened with Disfranchisement, to the People of Pennsylvania* (Philadelphia, 1838); *Opinion of the Hon. John Fox . . . Against the Exercise of Negro Suffrage in Pennsylvania* (Harrisburg, 1838); S. B. Weeks, "History of Negro Suffrage," *Political Science Quarterly,* 9 (1894): 671–703; Gen. W. W. H. Davis, "How the Word 'White' Became Inserted in Our Constitution of 1838," *A Collection of Papers Read Before the Bucks County Historical Society,* II (1909): 595–600; Emil Olbrich, *The Development of Sentiment on Negro Suffrage to 1860* (Madison, 1912); Charles H. Wesley, "Negro Suffrage in the Period of Constitution Making, 1787–1865," *JNH,* 32 (1947): 143–68; Charles McCool Snyder, *The Jacksonian Heritage: Pennsylvania Politics 1833–1848* (Harrisburg, 1958); Lyle L. Rosenberger, "Black Suffrage in Bucks County:

The Election of 1837," *Bucks County Historical Society Journal,* I (1975): 28–36.

38. *Lancaster Intelligencer,* Jan. 29, 1820; *Lancaster Journal,* Mar. 24, 1820; Hopkins, "Negro Entry Book," 144, 148.

39. Hopkins, *"Negro Entry Book";* Hopkins, "Bethel African Methodist Church in Lancaster: Prolegomenon to a Social History," *JLCHS,* 90 (1986): 205–36.

40. Hopkins, "Bethel African Methodist Church in Lancaster"; Oblinger, "New Freedoms, Old Miseries," says that the black middle class had incomes between $400 and $750 at this time, with a median of $530. Only 15 percent of this group owned their homes in Columbia, but Oblinger suggests that the percentage was higher in Lancaster city.

41. Litwack, *North of Slavery,* 103. On chronologically parallel developments in a very different setting, see Julie Winch, *Philadelphia's Black Elite: Activism, Accommodation, and the Struggle for Autonomy, 1787–1848* (Philadelphia, 1988).

42. Carl D. Oblinger, "In Recognition of Their Prominence: A Case Study of the Economic and Social Backgrounds of an Antebellum Negro Business and Farming Class in Lancaster County," *JLCHS,* 72 (1968): 70.

43. Ibid., 65–83; Oblinger, "New Freedoms, Old Miseries," 222.

44. Litwack, *North of Slavery,* 94, 165; Oblinger, "New Freedoms, Old Miseries," 175. According to Litwack, the disproportionate percentage of African-Americans in Pennsylvania's jails can be accounted for, in part, because of the following facts: (1) they were more often picked up for vagrancy and other minor crimes; (2) they found it more difficult to obtain counsel; (3) judges sentenced blacks to longer terms; and (4) it was more difficult for them to get pardons or pay fines.

45. Oblinger, "New Freedoms, Old Miseries," 181, 185, 193, 199.

46. Ibid., 213–16.

47. See, for example, Bruce G. Laurie, *Working People of Philadelphia, 1800–1850* (Philadelphia, 1980); Sean Wilentz, *Chants Democratic: New York City and the Rise of the American Working Class, 1788–1850* (New York, 1984); Howard B. Rock, *Artisans of the New Republic: The Tradesmen of New York City in the Age of Jefferson* (New York, 1979); Graham Russell Hodges, *New York City Cartmen, 1667–1850* (New York, 1986).

48. Fredrickson, *The Black Image in the White Mind,* 101; *Lancaster Intelligencer,* Feb. 20, 1838, p. 4; Mar. 6, 1838, p. 2; Mar. 20, 1838, p. 3; Apr. 3, 1838, p. 2; May 22, 1838, p. 3.

49. Fredrickson, *The Black Image in the White Mind.*

50. Jordan, *White Over Black,* 20.

Chapter 3. The Chase

1. Maryland Historical Trust, "Inventory Form for State Historic Sites Survey, Gorsuch Tavern," 1979, BCOPZ; "Ye Old Tavern at '19-Mile Stone' on York Road One Hundred and Twenty Years Old," *Jeffersonian,* Dec. 26, 1931. On

the weather in 1851, see *The Planter's Advocate and Southern Maryland Advertiser*, Oct. 15, 1851, p. 2; *The North American*, Oct. 1, 1851.

2. Forbes, *True Story*, 10–12.

3. Ibid., 9. According to Hensel, *Christiana Riot*, 15–16, the Gap Gang hung out north of the Mine Ridge, which ran westward from Gap across Lancaster County, and engaged in general raids and robberies on citizens of both races in addition to kidnapping blacks. One reason that the line between legal and illegal "kidnappings" was so unclear in Lancaster County was that members of the Gap Gang engaged in both types of enterprise.

4. Forbes, *True Story*, 8. According to Hensel, *Christiana Riot*, 14, the ethnic mix and long-term history of different parts of Lancaster County also contributed to the nature and locale of race-related violence:

> In its citizenship Lancaster County represented all the principal elements which enter into our composite commonwealth. The more numerous and important strain of blood, occupying the wider and richer upper domain, was composed very largely of the so-called Pennsylvania German sect and church people, who had little fellowship with the negro race, little interest in or sympathy with its cause and very slight personal contact with its members. In the lower townships the principal elements were the so-called Scotch-Irish Presbyterian and the Friends; between them there was considerable friction, if not antagonism; they had for nearly a century represented different views of society and government. Their variance was very distinct in their respective early attitudes toward "the Indian question."

According to local custom, the Gap Gang was largely composed of men whose ethnic origins were Irish and Scots-Irish, but the individual identities and birthplaces of members are not known. The Quakers who lived in the "lower end" of the county, where most of the race-related violence occurred, were predominantly Hicksites, which tended to be the more actively anti-slavery branch of the Society of Friends. Again, according to Hensel, the lines of conflict on the fugitive slave issue were generally drawn with the "disreputable" sort who kidnapped blacks, on one side; and farmers, artisans, and tradesmen who found the frequent attacks on their African-American employees unsettling, on the other (pp. 14–15, 18). On kidnapping in Philadelphia, see Julie Winch, "Philadelphia and the Other Underground Railroad," *PMHB*, 111 (1987): 3–25. On the kidnapping of blacks in the South, see Ira Berlin, *Slaves Without Masters: The Free Negro in the Antebellum South* (New York, 1975), 99–101, 160–61, 309.

5. *Lancaster Intelligencer*, Apr. 1, 1851, p. 2.

6. Ibid., Jan. 24, 1851, p. 2; Feb. 1, 1851, p. 2.

7. Lottie M. Bausman, "The General Position of Lancaster County on Negro Slavery," *Historical Papers and Addresses of the Lancaster County Historical Society*, 15 (1911): 5–21; [William Parker,] "The Freedman's Story," *Atlantic Monthly*, 17 (Feb.-Mar. 1866): 161. It is clear from Parker's narrative that the self-protection society was formed some years before the federal Fugitive Slave Act became law, but continued its work, perhaps even stepped up its activity, during 1850 and 1851 with no regard for the authority of the federal law. It is also apparent that Parker did not write this narrative by himself and that

although it reflects his perspective, there is a tendency toward exaggeration for effect and some falsification or mistaken memory on some of the facts. Where these mistakes are relevant to the issues discussed here, they are indicated in the text or notes. See Roderick W. Nash, "William Parker and the Christiana Riot," *JNH*, 96 (1961): 24–31.

8. Robert C. Smedley, *History of the Underground Railroad in Chester and the Neighboring Counties of Pennsylvania* (Lancaster, 1883), 99, 108, 113; Thomas Whitson, "The Early Abolitionists of Lancaster County," *LCHS Papers*, 15 (1911): 33, 71; Katz, *Resistance*, 28–34.

9. [Parker,] "Freedman's Story," 154.

10. Ibid., 157.

11. Ibid. According to Hensel, *Christiana Riot*, 27, Parker was born in Anne Arundel County, Maryland, to Louisa Simms, who died when he was quite young, which left him to the care of his grandmother: "His mother was one of the seventy field hands of Major William Brogdon, of 'Rodown' plantation; and six years after the old master died, when his sons David and William divided his plantation and slaves, William Parker fell to David and to his estate 'Nearo.'"

12. [Parker,] "Freedman's Story," 160. According to Hensel, *Christiana Riot*, 28, Parker worked on a farm near the town of Lancaster for $3 per month when he first arrived in the county, then later went to work for Dr. Obadiah Dingee, "a warm sympathizer, who lived near Smyrna. . . . While there Parker had access to anti-slavery periodicals and he heard William Lloyd Garrison and Frederick Douglass speak; he caught inspiration from them to organize his fellows, fugitive and free, in that community to resist recapture and repel assaults upon their race."

13. The term "maroon" is an English modification of the Spanish word "cimarron," which originally referred to bands of escaped slaves in the West Indies and Guiana. During the seventeenth and eighteenth centuries, the word "maroon" was applied more generally to communities of fugitive slaves living on the fringes of settlement in English North America.

14. On the original Cimarrons, see Edmund S. Morgan, *American Slavery, American Freedom: The Ordeal of Colonial Virginia* (New York, 1975), Chapter 1.

15. Genovese, *Rebellion to Revolution*, 51, 54–55, 57, 68, 81, 100.

16. Ibid., 7.

17. [Parker,] "Freedman's Story," 162.

18. Ibid., 161–63. Smedley, *History of the Underground Railroad*, 96–97, in discussing this episode does not mention the two fatalities.

19. [Parker,] "Freedman's Story," 162–63.

20. Ibid., 164–66; Hensel, *Christiana Riot*, 17. For a fuller account of the kidnapping of John Williams, see Smedley, *History of the Underground Railroad*, 98–99. The brutal kidnapping of John Williams came to be known as "the outrage at Chamberlain's," and was an issue during the treason trial of Castner Hanway, which is the subject of Chapter 7.

21. [Parker,] "Freedman's Story," 165–66.

22. Campbell, *The Slave Catchers*, 79, 91, 102. Associate Justice of the Supreme Court Robert C. Grier and Judge John K. Kane, of the federal district court

for eastern Pennsylvania, petitioned the President of the United States for federal troops to help in the enforcement of the Fugitive Slave Law in the fall of 1850. See, Grier and Kane to the President [Millard Fillmore], Oct. 22, 1850, U.S. Attorney General's Papers, Letters Received, President, 1814–1852, NA.

23. In some sources "Pierce" and "Hutchings."

24. It was apparently at this point that Kline picked up a passenger, a man named Gallagher, who was probably the driver of the second wagon and who had nothing more to do with the slave-catching enterprise. He is mentioned by Kline only in passing and was not in evidence the next day when the riot occurred. Robbins, *Report*, Kline's testimony, 57.

25. [Parker,] "Freedman's Story," 281–82.

26. Ibid., 282.

27. Ibid.

28. Hensel, *Christiana Riot*, 26, writes with certainty that the guide was Padgett. Since Hensel interviewed descendants of the posse members, family tradition is probably the source for the information. At the trial, all the members of the Gorsuch party denied knowing the identity of the guide, but perhaps that was to protect him from retribution.

29. [J. Franklin Reigart,] *A Full and Correct Report of the Christiana Tragedy . . . On the Hearing and Examination, as the Same was Presented in Evidence, Before Alderman Reigart, September 25th* (Lancaster, 1851), 2–3. (Hereafter cited as *A Full and Correct Report*.)

30. Forbes, *True Story*, 12; Robbins, *Report*.

31. [Parker,] "Freedman's Story," 283.

32. Katz, *Resistance*, 82; Frederick Douglass, "Freedom's Battle," *Douglass Paper*, Sept. 25, 1851; Smedley, *History of the Underground Railroad*, 115.

33. [Parker,] "Freedman's Story," 283; J. S. Gorsuch letter, dated Sept. 17, 1851, printed in *Pennsylvania Freeman*, Sept. 25, 1851, p. 1; Hensel, *Christiana Riot*, 20–23; Katz, *Resistance*, 71. Gorsuch identifies the black man surprised by Gorsuch's posse as Nelson Ford. There is much confusion in the sources about the names and identities of the African-Americans who took part in the riot. It is not even certain how many of the fugitives from Gorsuch's farm were at Parker's on Sept. 11, 1851. It seems likely that three of the fugitives were there that day—two in the house whom Parker called Kite and Thompson, and Noah Buley who arrived on a horse as the riot began. And it is not clear to me whether the man identified by Gorsuch as Ford was known by two different names in freedom—Kite and Beard—or whether the man's actual identity is a matter of dispute or confusion in the primary sources. According to the surviving Gorsuches, the fugitives in Parker's house were "Nelson" and "Josh." So if Nelson Ford was one of them (and was known in Lancaster as John Beard or Joshua Kite), then "Nelson" could have been the man known in freedom as Samuel Thompson. As if things are not confusing enough, that means that Kite had adopted Thompson's first name from when he was a slave!

Chapter 4. The Riot

1. [Parker,] "Freedman's Story," 283; J. S. Gorsuch letter, dated Sept. 17, 1851, LCP; Robbins, *Report,* Kline testimony, 58.
2. Robbins, *Report,* Kline testimony, 58.
3. Ibid.
4. [Parker,] "Freedman's Story," 160, 163, 165, 286; Katz, *Resistance,* 29–30.
5. *A Full and Correct Report,* Kline testimony, 3; [Parker,] "Freedman's Story," 283.
6. [Parker,] "Freedman's Story," 283; J. S. Gorsuch letter, dated Sept. 17, 1851, LCP.
7. [Parker,] "Freedman's Story," 285; Hensel, *Christiana Riot,* 30, identifies the fish "gig." According to *The Random House Dictionary* (New York, 1980), a gig is "a spearlike device for fishing."
8. Although the sources contradict each other on the point, on balance it does not appear that this was the same Abraham Johnson (or Johnston) who was involved with the stolen grain back in Maryland. In light of Gorsuch's animosity toward the Maryland Johnson, we might expect a clearer identification at this point if it were the same man. [Parker,] "Freedman's Story," 284–85; J. S. Gorsuch letter, dated Sept. 17, 1851, LCP; Hensel, *Christiana Riot,* 29.
9. Hensel, *Christiana Riot,* 29; Robbins, *Report,* testimony of Dickinson Gorsuch, 84.
10. [Parker,] "Freedman's Story," 284.
11. Ibid; J. S. Gorsuch letter, dated Sept. 17, 1851, LCP.
12. J. S. Gorsuch letter, dated Sept. 17, 1851, LCP; Robbins, *Report,* Dr. Thomas Pierce [Pearce] testimony, 74; J. M. Gorsuch testimony, 81.
13. [Parker,] "Freedman's Story," 285.
14. *A Full and Correct Report,* Kline testimony, 6; Robbins, *Report,* Kline testimony, 58; Pearce testimony, 74; Dickinson Gorsuch testimony, 83; Nicholas Hutchings [*sic,* Hutchins] testimony, 85; Nathan Nelson testimony, 86.
15. Robbins, *Report,* Nathan Nelson testimony, 86; Hensel, *Christiana Riot,* 31.
16. Katz, *Resistance,* 328n.20, explores the contradictory estimates of the number of whites at the riot. He believes, based on contemporary evidence, that there might have been local kidnappers there, perhaps upwards of thirty, hoping to take Parker, who interfered in their business. [Parker,] "Freedman's Story," 286, claimed that the posse included a large number of white men, who were "coming from all quarters" as the riot began. Hensel, *Christiana Riot,* 31, found "no satisfactory proof" that there were any whites on the grounds except for the six-man posse and "residents of the vicinage attracted to the place by the commotion." Almost certainly, Hensel is correct and Parker exaggerated for dramatic effect, misperceived, or misremembered the number of whites engaged in the battle. Surely, had local kidnappers sympathetic to the posse's business been present, they would have been called by the government as witnesses in the treason trial resulting from the riot. Certainly, had such experienced kidnappers been on the scene, the marshal would have tried to recruit their help rather than that of the unarmed miller and shopkeeper, as he did. The six-man posse fought alone. See note 20

(below) for a discussion of the number of African-American participants in the riot.

17. Robbins, *Report*, statement of defense attorney, Theodore Cuyler, 108–9; Elijah Lewis testimony, 120; Henry Birt [Burt] testimony, 125.

18. Robbins, *Report*, Henry Birt [Burt] testimony, 125.

19. Ibid.; *A Full and Correct Report*, testimony of Jacob Woods, 22.

20. Katz, *Resistance*, 94–95; 330 n.7, estimates that there were between fifteen and twenty-five black rioters, which he bases on the guess by W. A. Jackson, *History of the Trial of Castner Hanway and Others for Treason* (Philadelphia, 1852), 36–37. Jackson based his estimate on the fact that only about two hundred blacks resided within eight miles of the scene of the riot and a hundred within four miles. He reasoned from such information that it would be impossible to gather more than thirty within an hour's notice. Jackson thus dismissed the testimony of every witness to the event, both those of Kline and other members of the posse who had reasons to estimate on the high side the numbers of rioters they faced and of those on the other side who had reasons to minimize the size of the riot. The lowest estimate by a witness is fifty black rioters; the highest is 150. All the rest of the estimates fall between seventy-five and 150. Allowing for the confusion of the moment, it seems improbable that all the witnesses were off by a factor of ten or more. Jackson also overlooked the fact that in light of the previous day's warning about the arrival of kidnappers, the black community was prepared for battle. We know from testimony that some blacks slept in the fields around the Parkers' house the night preceding the riot rather than in their usual residences miles away. It is possible that a large proportion of the African-American community of Lancaster County, perhaps a majority of adults, participated in the riot. It seems likely that the estimates of seventy-five to a hundred rioters is in the correct range. Jackson's motives in offering a low estimate of the number of rioters are no less suspect than the posse's for estimating quite high. Jackson was the junior counsel for the defense in the treason trial of Castner Hanway and a dedicated anti-slavery reformer. He was attempting to minimize the numbers who resisted the law, to portray the posse as cowards and liars and the black community of Lancaster as generally law-abiding, with a few exceptions.

If Katz is correct that there were upwards of thirty whites at the riot at least tentatively supporting the posse and only half as many blacks, the outcome of the riot—the blacks blowing the posse away without suffering a single major injury themselves—is quite baffling. More likely, the six members of the posse fought alone and were outnumbered by at least ten to one. See note 16 (above) for a discussion of the number of white men engaged in the riot.

21. J. S. Gorsuch letter, dated Sept. 17, 1851, LCP.

22. *A Full and Correct Report*, Kline testimony, 6–7; Robbins, *Report*, Kline testimony, 58–59.

23. Robbins, *Report*, Kline testimony, 58–59; Robbins, *Report*, Lewis testimony, 120.

24. Robbins, *Report*, Pierce [Pearce] testimony, 74.

25. Ibid. Nathan Nelson testimony, 86; Lewis testimony, 120; Kline testimony, 58–59; *A Full and Correct Report*, Kline testimony, 6–7.

26. *A Full and Correct Report,* Kline testimony, 6–7.
27. Robbins, *Report,* Kline testimony, 59; *A Full and Correct Report,* Kline testimony, 7.
28. Robbins, *Report,* Pearce testimony, 74–75.
29. [Parker,] "Freedman's Story," 287. According to Hensel, *Christiana Riot,* 35, who interviewed Edward Gorsuch's relatives decades after the event, the family believed that he was unarmed on the day of the riot. Their beliefs in this regard were based, Hensel wrote, on "his habits of life and temperament." Other witnesses to the event testify to his use of a pistol, which Frederick Douglass claimed was later presented to him by William Parker. See Chapter 5.
30. Hensel, *Christiana Riot,* 35; J. S. Gorsuch letter, dated Sept. 17, 1851, LCP; Robbins, *Report,* Dickinson Gorsuch testimony, 83–84.
31. J. S. Gorsuch letter, dated Sept. 17, 1851, LCP.
32. Ibid.; Robbins, *Report,* Dickinson Gorsuch testimony, 84.
33. Robbins, *Report,* Hutchins testimony, 85; Lewis testimony, 120.
34. Ibid., Lewis testimony, 121.
35. Ibid., Pearce testimony, 75.
36. Ibid., J. M. Gorsuch testimony, 81.
37. Ibid.; Robbins, *Report,* Pearce testimony, 75.
38. [Parker,] "Freedman's Story," 287.
39. Ibid., 287; Robbins, *Report,* Pearce testimony, 75; J. M. Gorsuch testimony, 81.
40. Robbins, *Report,* Kline testimony, 60.
41. Ibid.
42. Ibid.
43. [Parker,] "Freedman's Story," 288; Hensel, *Christiana Riot,* 33.
44. *Lancaster Examiner,* Sept. 17, 1851, p. 2; Roderick W. Nash, "The Christiana Riot: An Evaluation of Its National Significance," *JLCHS,* 65 (1961): 65–91; *Daily News* (London), Sept. 25, 1851, p. 5, draws on Baltimore and Philadelphia newspapers for its account of the riot; *Manchester Guardian,* Sept. 27, 1851, p. 5; *Planter's Advocate, and Southern Maryland Advertiser* (Upper Marlboro, Md.), Sept. 17, 1851, p. 2; *American* (Baltimore), Sept. 12, 1851, p. 3; Sept. 15, 1851, p. 2; Sept. 17, 1851, p. 2; Sept. 18, 1851, p. 3; Sept. 24, 1851, p. 2; *The Cecil Whig* (Elkton, Md.), Sept. 20, 1851, pp. 2–3; Hensel, *Christiana Riot,* 33; Maryland State Documents, 1852, Document A, "Annual Message of the Executive to the General Assembly," 36, MdHR.
45. The Philadelphia Vigilance Committee was interracial between 1838 and 1844, but it was run by African-American members. After 1844, William Still, a black man, became chairman of the group's Acting Committee. There were both African-American and white "conductors" on the Committee's "Underground Railroad." Some of the more famous black ones were Harriet Tubman, Leonard Grimes, and Josiah Henson.
46. On the general question of African-American leadership and abolitionist expectations for blacks, see David M. Potter, "John Brown and the Paradox of Leadership Among American Negroes," in *The South and the Sectional Conflict* (Baton Rouge, 1968), 201–18; Rossbach, *John Brown, the Secret Six, and a Theory of Slave Violence.*

Chapter 5. Aftermath

1. *North American,* Oct. 1, 1851.
2. [Parker,] "Freedman's Story," 288; Robbins, *Report,* testimony of Dr. Augustus Cain, 99–100. Dr. Cain identified the two men whom he treated after the riot as Henry C. Hopkins and John Long. His testimony about the nature and seriousness of the wounds conforms with Parker's.
3. According to George Steele, a black man interviewed many years after the riot, Parker and Pinckney left on their journey from the house of Parker's landlords, the Pownalls. So, as Steele told the story, during part of the evening after the riot both the wounded Dickinson Gorsuch and two of the principal rioters were under the same roof. The Pownalls then put some food in a pillowcase for the fugitives and sent them on their way under cover of night. See "George Steele's Account," in Bacon, *Rebellion at Christiana,* 119–21.
4. Frederick Douglass, *The Life and Times of Frederick Douglass: Written by Himself* (Boston, 1892; New York, 1962), 281; [Parker,] "Freedman's Story," 290.
5. Douglass, *Life and Times of Frederick Douglass,* 281–82.
6. Ibid., 282.
7. Ibid., 282, 280. On the general question of the African-American struggle for freedom, see, for example, Frederick Douglass, *Oration, Delivered in Corinthian Hall, Rochester* (Rochester, 1852).
8. [Parker,] "Freedman's Story," 290–91.
9. Ibid., 291.
10. Ibid., 292.
11. The story of Cassandra Harris is reconstructed from newspapers, which reported different aspects of the case and took different slants on its meaning. One of the fullest accounts was printed in the *Philadelphia Bulletin* and reprinted with elaboration in the *Planter's Advocate,* Oct. 1, 1851, p. 2. For a different perspective, also incorporated into the present account, see the *Pennsylvania Freeman,* Sept. 25, 1851, p. 2; the *Liberator,* Oct. 17, 1851; Smedley, *History of the Underground Railroad,* 125–26. Katz, *Resistance,* 127–28, discusses Harris's case using only the abolitionist perspective, which seems to me just as suspect as the retelling by pro-slavery and pro-Compromise newspapers. The part of the story that puts Cassandra Harris on the streets of Philadelphia tapping Commissioner Ingraham on the shoulder strikes me as a creative embellishment of the story, as does the interview by the abolitionist reporter. It seems unlikely that the court and police officials would have given a reporter for the notorious *Liberator* access to their prisoner. Katz, *Resistance,* 271–76 and passim, writes about the Parkers' settlement in Buxton, Canada, and even spoke with some of their descendants but does not pick up the story of Eliza's mother. [Parker,] "Freedman's Story," 292–93, is the principal source of information about his family's life after their escape to Canada, although Katz very creatively located several others not previously identified.
12. *Pennsylvania Freeman,* Sept. 25, 1851, p. 1, described the local scene after the riot as a "reign of terror."
13. *Planter's Advocate,* Oct. 1, 1851, p. 2 and passim; *North American,* Sept. 18,

1851, p. 1; *Pennsylvania Freeman,* Sept. 25, 1851, p. 2; *New York Times,* Sept. 18, 1851, p. 3.

14. *Pennsylvania Freeman,* Sept. 25, 1851, p. 2; Oct. 2, 1851, p. 1.
15. *Pennsylvania Freeman,* Oct. 2, 1851, pp. 2–3. The episode involving the fugitives from Virginia occurred in that state, and the story was reprinted from the *Wytheville Gazette.* The other two incidents took place in Dauphin County, Pennsylvania.
16. *Lancaster Intelligencer,* Sept. 16, 1851, p. 2; Katz, *Resistance,* 124; *Liberator,* Oct. 3, 1851; Forbes, *True Story,* 36; Hensel, *Christiana Riot,* 137; *Pennsylvania Freeman,* Oct. 23, 1851, p. 1; "List of persons who assisted in the arrest &c of the murderers of Edward Gorsuch," Maryland State Papers, 1851, Executive Papers, 1851 Miscellaneous Papers, folder 1, 12 Sept. 1851, MdHR.
17. Hensel, *Christiana Riot,* 137.
18. Ibid., 40–41; Katz, *Resistance,* 123; Still, *Underground Rail Road,* 349.
19. Hensel, *Christiana Riot,* 42.
20. Robbins, *Report,* testimony of J. Franklin Reigart, 93.
21. Ibid.
22. Members of the Gorsuch party apparently were the original source for the story that Hanway had "inspired" the blacks to resist the federal posse. Not only did Dr. Pearce testify to that effect in the preliminary hearings, but J. S. Gorsuch offered the same interpretation in his letter dated Sept. 17, 1851, which was widely reprinted in newspapers. See, for example, *Pennsylvania Freeman,* Sept. 18, 1851, pp. 2–3. Kline clearly blamed Hanway and Lewis for their refusal to help and even accused the two men of encouraging the blacks to attack, but the accusations that the blacks inside the house were about to surrender before Hanway rode up and that he was the "leader" of the rioters were not originally parts of Kline's recounting of the riot scene.
23. *A Full and Correct Report,* Kline testimony, 2–8, 12, 15–16.
24. Ibid., G. W. Harvey Scott testimony, 13–14; Katz, *Resistance,* 132; Forbes, *True Story,* 22–23, 26–27; *Lancaster Examiner and Herald,* Sept. 17, 1851.
25. *A Full and Correct Report,* Pearce testimony, 10–11; Hutchins testimony, 12; William Proudfoot testimony, 14; Henry Cloud testimony, 14; Miller Knott testimony, 14.
26. Ibid., John Carr testimony, 18–19; John Cochran testimony, 19; Benjamin Elliot testimony, 19; and Jesse J. Morgan testimony, 19–20.
27. Ibid., John Carr testimony, 18; John Cochran testimony, 19; Benjamin Elliot testimony, 19; and Jesse Morgan testimony, 19.

Chapter 6. Stratagems

1. See Chapter 4, notes 42 and 43; Hensel, *Christiana Riot,* 38; [Parker,] "Freedman's Story," 288. Corn cutters reputedly used on Edward Gorsuch's body are preserved in the museum of the Lancaster County Historical Society.
2. Charles L. Blockson, *The Underground Railroad in Pennsylvania* (Jacksonville, N.C., 1981), 95.

3. *Planter's Advocate*, Sept. 17, 1851, p. 2; D. F. Magee, "The Christiana Riot: Its Causes and Effects from a Southern Standpoint," *LCHS Papers*, 15 (1911): 193–208; Nash, "The Christiana Riot," 65–91. Nash's essays are among the most perceptive and reliable of the modern writings on the riot. The *Planter's Advocate*, Oct. 15, 1851, p. 2, condemned Northern newspapers for reporting that a member of the Gorsuch party fired the first shot. Clearly, such a suggestion—which very well may have been true—presented problems for Southern concepts of honor and Southerners' visions of the fighting competence of Southern white men. If the Gorsuches had been in a position to fire first, then Southerners were certain that they would have defeated the blacks in battle. Only an ambush would explain how they could fall in defeat to their African-American opponents.

4. *Pennsylvania Freeman*, Sept. 18, 1851, p. 3; Sept. 25, 1851, p. 1, reprinted from the *New York Independent*.

5. *Pennsylvanian*, Sept. 13, 1851, p. 2. This newspaper carried the initial report of the riot that was quoted verbatim by the *Planter's Advocate* in the passage cited above. See the *Pennsylvanian*, Sept. 12, 1851, p. 1; Sept. 13, 1851, p. 1.

6. Among contemporary sources, the Whig's ·*North American*, Sept. 27, 1851, p. 2; and Oct. 3, 1851, p. 2, attempted to demonstrate that the portrayal of Governor Johnston as responsible for the Christiana Riot was a campaign strategy based on desperation.

7. William Freame Johnston, Annual Message to the Assembly—1849, *PA* 4th ser., VII (Harrisburg, 1902), 336.

8. *Pennsylvanian*, Sept. 8, 1851, p. 1; *North American*, Sept. 27, 1851, p. 2; Oct. 3, 1851, p. 2.

9. William C. Armor, *Lives of the Governors of Pennsylvania* (Philadelphia, 1873), 403–12; *PA* 4th ser., VII, 491–95; *Pennsylvanian*, Sept. 4, 1851, p. 2; Sept. 6, 1851, p. 2.

10. "To the Senate Vetoing an Act to Repeal the Sixth Section of an Act, Entitled An Act to Prevent Kidnapping . . . ," Jan. 8, 1852, *PA* 4th ser., VII, 491–96; Armor, *Lives of the Governors of Pennsylvania*, 410–12. Pennsylvania's anti-kidnapping law was a direct response to Justice Joseph Story's dictum in the Supreme Court case of *Prigg* v. *Pennsylvania* (1842). On the consequences of the *Prigg* decision and the legal dimensions of the fugitive-slave question in general, see Robert M. Cover, *Justice Accused: Antislavery and the Judicial Process* (New Haven, 1975); Campbell, *The Slave Catchers*; Paul Finkelman, "*Prigg* v. *Pennsylvania* and the Northern State Courts: Anti-Slavery Uses of a Pro-Slavery Decision," *Civil War History*, 25 (1979): 5–35; J. C. Burke, "What Did the *Prigg* Decision Really Decide?" *PMHB*, 93 (1969): 73–85; Thomas D. Morris, *Free Men All: The Personal Liberty Laws of the North, 1780–1861* (Baltimore, 1974); Paul Finkelman, *An Imperfect Union: Slavery, Federalism, and Comity* (Chapel Hill, 1981).

11. *Pennsylvanian*, Sept. 13, 1851, p. 2.

12. Ibid.

13. Ibid., Oct. 9, 1851, p. 2. This article quotes a number of Southern newspapers to prove the point, including the New Orleans *Picayune*, the Richmond *Republican*, the Warrenton, N.C., *News*, the New Orleans *Delta*, the Wil-

mington, N.C., *Commercial,* the Richmond *Examiner,* the Louisville *Democrat,* and the Columbus, Ga., *Times.*

14. *PA* 4th ser., VII, 479–80; Wm. F. Johnston to Mr. John Cadwalader, and others, Philadelphia, Sept. 14, 1851, Cadwalader Collection, Correspondence of Judge John Cadwalader, HSP. [Jackson,] *History of the Trial of Castner Hanway . . . for Treason,* 40–42, who reprinted this letter, believed that the governor was genuinely misinformed and issued the proclamation and reward for capture of the escaped murderers of Edward Gorsuch as soon as he received the accurate information. In light of Johnston's presence on the scene, his proximity to Lancaster County over the next several days, the availability of more accurate information to any who sought it over the weekend, and Johnston's political self-interest in these events, it seems to me more likely that he either did not want better information or that he purposefully ignored the information that he had until political exigencies dictated that he take another course.

15. *Pennsylvanian,* Sept. 16, 1851, p. 2. On the politics of the 1850s, see Daniel Walker Howe, *The Political Culture of the American Whigs* (Chicago, 1979); Michael Holt, *The Political Crisis of the 1850's* (New York, 1978); Eric Foner, *Free Soil, Free Labor, Free Men: The Ideology of the Republican Party before the Civil War* (New York, 1970); Foner, "Politics, Ideology, and the Origins of the American Civil War," in George M. Fredrickson, ed., *A Nation Divided: Problems and Issues of the Civil War and Reconstruction* (Minneapolis, 1975), 15–34; Richard L. McCormick, "Ethno-Cultural Interpretations of Nineteenth-Century American Voting Behavior," *Political Science Quarterly,* 89 (1974): 369–71; John F. Coleman, *The Disruption of the Pennsylvania Democracy, 1848–1860* (Harrisburg, 1975); James L. Huston, "Economic Change and Political Realignment in Antebellum Pennsylvania," *PMHB,* 113 (1989): 347–95; William E. Gienapp, "The Republican Party and the Slave Power," in Robert H. Abzug and Stephen E. Maizlish, eds., *New Perspectives on Race and Slavery in America: Essays in Honor of Kenneth M. Stampp* (Lexington, 1986), 51–78; Stephen E. Maizlish, "Race and Politics in the Northern Democracy: 1854–1860," in Abzug and Maizlish, eds., *New Perspectives on Race and Slavery in America,* 79–90.

16. *North American,* Sept. 16, 1851, p. 2; *Pennsylvanian,* Sept. 18, 1851, p. 2; John Campbell, *Negro-Mania: Being an Examination of the Falsely Assumed Equality of the Various Races of Men* (Philadelphia, 1851), HSP.

17. *Pennsylvanian,* Sept. 18, 1851, p. 2.

18. *Pennsylvania Freeman,* Sept. 25, 1851, p. 1; *Pennsylvanian,* Sept. 26, 1851, p. 2; *North American,* Sept. 26, 1851, p. 1. This is yet another point at which the facts are extremely difficult to ascertain. There is no evidence in the sources that anyone was arrested for a crime related to these alleged events. It seems, based largely upon reports from politically less interested newspapers closer to the scene of the action, that a shot was fired but that it was not clear whether it was purposefully aimed at the governor or anyone else. The *Pennsylvanian* quotes the Pottsville *Journal* (date not given) to this effect. So, the Whigs were apparently trying to milk this incident for much more than the demonstrable facts warranted.

19. Broadside, Philadelphia, Oct. 6, 1851, Ferdinand J. Dreer Autograph Collec-

tion, vol. 17:2, Governors of States II, p. 83, HSP; J. S. Gorsuch, Washington, Sept. 18, 1851, to William F. Johnston, Governor of Pennsylvania, LCP. The letter was reprinted in numerous papers, including the *Lancaster Intelligencer*, Sept. 30, 1851, p. 2. The copy in the Library Company of Philadelphia is accompanied by a note from its author to J. F. Reigart, requesting the letter's publication. See also J. S. Gorsuch, Washington, Oct. 6, 1851, to Pa. Attorney General Franklin, *Lancaster Intelligencer*, Oct. 14, 1851, p. 2.

20. Broadside, Philadelphia, Oct. 6, 1851, Dreer Collection, HSP; *North American*, Sept. 23, 1851, p. 2.
21. Armor, *Lives of the Governors*, 413–23.
22. Hensel, *Christiana Riot*, 51–54; *Lancaster Intelligencer*, Oct. 14, 1851, p. 2; Oct. 21, 1851, p. 2. Bigler received 186,499 votes to Johnston's 178,034.
23. Baltimore County Resolution in relation to the Murder of Mr. Gorsuch by a Mob in Pennsylvania, signed by W. H. Freeman, Towson, Sept. 13, 1851; W. H. Freeman, Baltimore, Sept. 14, 1851, to Thomas H. O'Neal, Secretary of State, Maryland State Papers, Executive Papers, 1851 Miscellaneous Papers, folder 1, MdHR; announcement and resolutions of Baltimore meeting, reprinted in the *Pennsylvanian*, Sept. 17, 1851, pp. 1–2; *Planter's Advocate*, Sept. 24, 1851, p. 2.
24. Governor E. Louis Lowe, Annapolis, Sept. 15, 1851, to His excellency, the President of the United States, Governor and Council Letterbook, 1845–1854, pp. 253–55, MdHR.
25. Ibid.
26. Ibid.
27. "Human Heart," to President Fillmore, Sept. 22, 1851; John Evans to Fillmore, Sept. 20, 1851, the Papers of Millard Fillmore, BECHS.
28. J. J. Crittenden, Acting Secretary, Department of State, to John W. Ashmead, Attorney of the U.S. for the Eastern District of Pennsylvania, Sept. 27, 1851, Gratz Collection, case 15, box 24, HSP. A letter from an under-Secretary of State to Maryland governor Louis Lowe, dated Sept. 16, 1851, asserted that the federal prosecutor had been instructed "to ascertain whether the facts would make out the crime of treason against the United States, and if so, to take prompt measures to secure all concerned for trial for that offence" (Maryland State Papers, Executive Papers, 1851, folder 1, MdHR). This would indicate that Ashmead had gotten at least some "advice" and that if he wanted more direction it might have taken the form of a request for help in interpreting the law and applying it to the evidence that he had before him. Of course, it is also possible that federal officials lied to Governor Lowe. The letter from Crittenden specifically denied Ashmead's request to come to Washington for the purpose of consulting with the attorney general, and the decision to prosecute for treason had been made before the Sept. 27 date of the letter. The letter was not necessarily a blanket refusal to offer advice, but it reads that way, and subsequent correspondence indicates that Ashmead understood that he was on his own, at least he did *until* he was reprimanded for his correspondence with Maryland's attorney general.
29. W. S. Derrick to the governor of Maryland, Sept. 16, 1851, MdHR.
30. Daniel Webster, Speech to the Young Men of Albany, delivered May 28, 1851, *The Works of Daniel Webster*, II (Boston, 1853), 577–78.

31. On the question of costs, see Alexander H. H. Stewart, Secretary of the Interior, to Ashmead, Oct. 29, 1851, Nov. 6, 1851, and Nov. 14, 1851, Gratz Collection, case 15, box 22, HSP. Letters of support from Washington include, J. J. Crittenden to Ashmead, Oct. 23, 1851, Gratz Collection, case 15, box 24, HSP.
32. Telegram, Stewart to Ashmead, Nov. 21, 1851, HSP.
33. Thomas H. O'Neal, Secretary of State, to Robert J. Brent, Sept. 18, 1851; Lowe to Hon. James Cooper, Oct. 4, 1851, Governor and Council Letterbook, 1845–1854, MdHR.
34. Brent to Ashmead, Oct. 18, 1851, Society Misc. Collections, case 19, box 17, HSP. A copy of the letter is also in Governor and Council Letterbook, 1845–1854, MdHR. Neither Brent's original letter to Ashmead nor Ashmead's initial response survives with the rest of the correspondence. Brent quotes from Ashmead's letter in the note of Oct. 18. James Cooper's objections are registered in his letter to Governor Lowe dated Nov. 11, 1851, Maryland State Papers, Executive Papers, 1851 Miscellaneous Papers, folder 1, MdHR.
35. Lowe to Fillmore, Nov. 6, 1851, with accompanying correspondence, Governor and Council Letterbook, 1845–1854, MdHR.
36. Webster to Lowe, Nov. 8, 1851; Webster to Ashmead, Nov. 8, 1851; Lowe to Webster, Nov. 11, 1851; Thomas H. O'Neal to Brent, Nov. 11, 1851; Ashmead to Lowe, Nov. 13, 1851; O'Neal to Ashmead, Nov. 14, 1851, Governor and Council Letterbook, 1845–1854, MdHR. The original of the Nov. 14 letter is in the Gratz Collection, Misc. Letters, case 15, box 22, HSP.
37. [Md.] Secretary of State Scott to Henry May, [Md.] Deputy Attorney General, Nov. 22, 1851, marked *"not* for Record," Maryland State Papers, Executive Papers, 1851 Misc. Papers, folder 1, MdHR.
38. Bills of Indictment, RG 21, U.S. District Courts, Pennsylvania, Eastern District Court, Criminal Cases, 1791–1911, 1850–1851, Boxes 4 and 5, NA, Philadelphia Branch.
39. In Hensel, *Christiana Riot*, 142–43.

Chapter 7. The Trial

1. *Planter's Advocate*, Oct. 1, 1851, p. 2. Readers interested in learning more about the American law of treason after the Revolution, as opposed to the politics of law in this particular case, might consult James Willard Hurst, *The Law of Treason in the United States* (Westport, Ct., 1971); Bradley Chapin, *The American Law of Treason: Revolutionary and Early National Origins* (Seattle, 1964); and Thomas P. Slaughter, "The Law of Treason in the 1790s," in Ronald Hoffman and Peter C. Albert, eds., *Launching the "Extended Republic": The Federalist Era* (Charlottesville, forthcoming).
2. *North American*, Sept. 13, 1851, p. 2. The *New York Times*, Dec. 15, 1851, p. 2, reminded its readers that it had predicted the outcome of the treason trial for these reasons months earlier.
3. *New York Times*, Oct. 1, 1851, p. 2.
4. Ibid., Oct. 1, 1851, p. 2; Oct. 3, 1851, p. 3; Oct. 9, 1851, p. 5; Oct. 18, 1851, p. 2; Oct. 22, 1851, p. 2; Nov. 6, 1851, p. 4; *Pennsylvania Freeman*, Oct. 9,

1851, p. 2; Oct. 16, 1851, p. 2; Oct. 23, 1851, pp. 2–3; *National Era*, Nov. 27, 1851, p. 2; *North American*, Sept. 13, 1851, p. 2; *Planter's Advocate*, Sept. 24, 1851, p. 2; Oct. 1, 1851, p. 2; Oct. 8, 1851, p. 3. The same debate was carried on in the pages of the *New York Tribune, Richmond Enquirer, Baltimore Sun, Baltimore American, Cecil Whig* (Elkton, Md.), *Lancaster Intelligencer, Lancaster Examiner,* and *Philadelphia Bulletin.*

5. See the same issues of the newspapers listed in note 4 above.

6. Ashmead to Derrick, Acting Secretary of State, Sept. 26, 1851, Miscellaneous Letters of the Department of State, Nov. 1–Dec. 31, 1851, microfilm publications, M. 179, roll 128, NA.

7. RG 21, U.S. District Courts, Pennsylvania, Eastern District, District Court, Criminal Cases, 1791–1911, Box no. 4, NA, Philadelphia Branch.

8. Ashmead to Stuart [Stewart], Secretary of the Interior, Oct. 18, 1851, NA, R. G. 60, chronological files, Eastern Pennsylvania Accounts, 1849–1861, Box 636; Ashmead to Fillmore, Oct. 1, 1851, Papers of Millard Fillmore (blank copy of indictment form enclosed), BECHS.

9. Hensel, *Christiana Riot,* 59–60.

10. Ashmead to Stuart [Stewart], Secretary of the Interior, Nov. 4, 1851, NA, R. G. 60, chronological files, Eastern Pennsylvania Accounts, 1849–1861, Box 636.

11. Ashmead to Stuart [Stewart], Oct. 11, 1851, Nov. 4, 1851, Nov. 10, 1851, Nov. 21. 1851, Feb. 14[?], 1852, June 3, 1852; John L. Thompson to Stewart, Dec. 5, 1851, Dec. 22, 1851; James Cooper to Stewart, Dec. 6, 1851; Ashmead to Stuart, Nov. 21, 1851; J. Franklin Reigart to Secretary of the Interior, June 4, 1853; Ashmead to Interior, Sept. 11, 1854, NA, R. G. 60, Box 636. Reigart to Millard Fillmore, June 10, 1852, NA, Attorney General's Papers, Letters Received, President, Christiana Riot. The Attorney General's Papers have substantial additional correspondence related to the expenses of this case, which continued for years after the trial. The responding letters are in NA, Letters Sent By the Department of Justice Concerning Judiciary Expenses, 1849–84, R. G. 60, M 700, reels 1 and 2. See, in particular, Stuart to George W. *[sic]* Ashmead, Oct. 29, 1851; Stewart to Ashmead, Nov. 6, 1851, Nov. 14, 1851, Nov. 22, 1851; Stewart to Francis Wharton, Dec. 23, 1851; Stewart to John L. Thompson, Feb. 3, 1852, Feb. 13, 1852. On the question of the court reporters, see also Robert M. Lee to Governor Lowe, Nov. 20, 1851, Executive Papers, MdHR.

12. *New York Times,* Nov. 11, 1851, p. 1; Nov. 13, 1851, p. 2. The story was, of course, reported in other newspapers, many of which used the same source. See, for example, the *North American,* Nov. 12, 1851, p. 1. For Southern suspicions, see, for example, *Report of Attorney General Brent to His Excellency, Gov. Lowe, in Relation to the Christiana Treason Trial* (Annapolis, 1852), 4–5 (hereafter, Brent, *Report). Report of the Select Committee Appointed to Consider so Much of the Governor's Message as Relates to the Murder of Edward Gorsuch, and the Trial of the Treason Case in Philadelphia* (Annapolis, 1852) (hereafter, Committee, *Report),* Maryland State Documents, 1852, Document 0, pp. 10–13, MdHR.

13. *A Full and Correct Report,* 18, 19; Katz, *Resistance,* 81–82; Hensel, *Christiana Riot,* 60.

14. *Pennsylvania Freeman,* Dec. 4, 1851, p. 3.
15. The Gorsuch diary is quoted in Hensel, *Christiana Riot,* 97.
16. *New York Times,* Oct. 21, 1851, p. 4.
17. *North American,* Nov. 25, 1851, p. 1; Nov. 27, 1851, p. 1; Nov. 29, 1851, p. 1; Dec. 1, 1851, p. 1; Dec. 2, 1851, p. 1; Dec. 3, 1851, p. 1; Dec. 4, 1851, p. 1; Dec. 5, 1851, p. 1; Dec. 6, 1851, p. 1; Dec. 8, 1851, p. 1; Dec. 9, 1851, p. 1; Dec. 10, 1851, p. 1; Dec. 11, 1851, p. 1.
18. *Pennsylvania Freeman,* Nov. 27, 1851, p. 3; *North American,* Nov. 27, 1851, p. 1; Nov. 29, 1851, p. 1.
19. Robbins, *Report,* 9–11.
20. Brent, *Report,* 4; James Cooper to E. Louis Lowe, Nov. 12, 1851; and Cooper to Lowe, Nov. 26, 1851, Maryland State Papers, Executive Papers, 1851, folder 1, MdHR. On the process of jury selection in this case, see Robbins, *Report,* 20–45. On the jury, see Hensel, *Christiana Riot,* 65–74. One of the jurors was from Philadelphia and one each from Carbondale, Pike, and Montgomery counties; two were from Perry, three from Adams, and three from Lancaster County. Newspaper reporters detected a pattern to challenges made by the defense. According to the *North American,* Nov. 27, 1851, p. 1, "the jurors summoned from Philadelphia city and county are generally challenged by the prisoner. . . . This may arise from the supposition in the mind of his counsel, that people in Philadelphia have been more affected . . . by the elaborate reports . . . of the primary hearing which took place in Lancaster County. . . ."
21. Grier was a Pennsylvanian, who was appointed to the Supreme Court by President Tyler in 1844. He served until Feb. 1870. Kane had served previous to his appointment to the federal court as a district attorney in Pennsylvania and as the state attorney general under Governor Shunk during 1845–1846. Hensel, *Christiana Riot,* 57–58; Katz, *Resistance,* 181–82; Robbins, *Report,* 12. The defense team included, in addition to Congressman Stevens, a "Woolly Headed Whig" serving his second term in Congress; John M. Read, who was a Democrat; Joseph J. Lewis, from Chester County; and the Philadelphia lawyer Theodore Cuyler. These men were, by general agreement among commentators, "four of the most prominent lawyers of the State." They were joined at the defense table by their junior counsel W. A. Jackson, who later wrote his own "history" of the case in response to Brent's *Report,* and abolitionist lawyer David Paul Brown, who represented several other defendants in the Christiana Riot case. Seven lawyers sat at the prosecution table— John W. Ashmead, the federal district attorney; Robert J. Brent, the Maryland attorney general; Pennsylvania's U.S. senator James Cooper, who was also retained by the state of Maryland to represent its interests in the trial; George L. Ashmead, the prosecutor's cousin, who helped prepare the case; R. M. Lee, the Philadelphia city recorder; District Attorney Z. Collins Lee of Baltimore; and James R. Ludlow, a Philadelphia lawyer. Jackson, *History,* 54–55, 57; Katz, *Resistance,* 178–81.
22. While continuing to denounce slavery publicly and often, Stevens had announced his dedication to the Constitution and, thereby, his commitment to enforcement of the Fugitive Slave Law. See, for example, *Speech of the Hon. Thaddeus Stevens, of Pennsylvania, on the Subject of the Admission of Slav-*

ery in the Territories, Delivered in the House of Representatives, at Washington, Wednesday, February 20, 1850 (Harrisburg, 1850), Papers of Thaddeus Stevens, box 17, Manuscript Division, LC. Also of interest, in the same archival location, is Stevens's copy of Maryland governor Lowe's letter to the Secretary of State, Sept. 15, 1851, in which Stevens has underlined passages for his preparation of this case.

23. Cooper to Lowe, Nov. 29, 1851, Maryland State Papers, Executive Papers, 1851, folder 1, MdHR.
24. Robbins, *Report*, 45, 48.
25. Ibid., 53.
26. Ibid., cross-examination of Kline, 63–73.
27. Ibid., cross-examination of Pierce [sic], 78–80; quotation, 79.
28. Ibid., cross-examination of Nelson, 87–88.
29. Ibid., 97–98. The defense produced witnesses who testified that the blowing of horns was a local custom used to call workers to breakfast. See also, *New York Times*, Dec. 5, 1851, p. 2.
30. Robbins, *Report*, 98.
31. Ibid., 110, 107, 109.
32. Ibid., 112, 113.
33. Ibid., 109, 107.
34. Ibid., 131–35.
35. Ibid., 135–40.
36. Ibid., 144–46.
37. Ibid., 119.
38. Ibid., 146–58.
39. Ibid., 148.
40. Ibid., 166. The additional details about George Washington Harvey Scott's life are from Oblinger, "New Freedoms, Old Miseries," 174.
41. *North American*, Dec. 1, 1851, p. 1.
42. Brent to Lowe, Dec. 4, 1851, Executive Papers, MdHR; Robbins, *Report*, 159–62.
43. Brent to Lowe, Dec. 4, 1851.
44. Robbins, *Report*, 244, 247; Hensel, *Christiana Riot*, 90.
45. Robbins, *Report*, 249–61.
46. Bacon, *Rebellion at Christiana*, 179–80; Forbes, *True Story*, 131. The *Pennsylvania Freeman*, Nov. 20, 1851, p. 2, reported that money was being raised to pay the expenses of the defendants in the Christiana case.
47. Commonwealth v. H. Kline, LCQS, case papers, January session, 1852. See also, Commonwealth v. Jacob Woods, riot, LCQS, November session, 1851; Commonwealth v. Elijah Lewis, C. Hanway, J. Morgan, H. Clemens, and others, riot and murder, LCQS, January session, 1852; Commonwealth v. Elijah Lewis and Castner Hanway, warrant; Commonwealth v. John Morgan, Henry Sims, Charley Valentine, Lewis Clarkson, Charles Hunter, Lewis Gales, George Williams, Alson Pernsley, Light Stewart (colored men), warrant; Commonwealth v. Hezekiah Clemens, George Wells, Walter Harris, Abraham Clinch, Nelson Carter (colored men), warrant; Commonwealth v. Jacob Philips (colored), warrant; Commonwealth v. Jacob Moore (colored), warrant; Commonwealth v. Joseph Scarlett (white), William Brown, Ezekiel Thomp-

son, Daniel Caulsbury, Isaiah Clarkson, Benjamin Pendergrast, Elijah Clark, Henry Green, William Williams, John Holliday, George Reed, Benjamin Johnston, John Jackson, Thomas Butler, Collister Wilson, arrest record, Quarter Sessions case papers, box for 1852–1853, LCHS.

48. Maryland State Documents, 1852, Document A, "Annual Message of the Executive to the General Assembly," 38–39, MdHR.

49. Cooper to Lowe, Dec. 11, 1851, Executive Papers, MdHR. Cooper was paid $1,000 by the State of Maryland for his work on the case. See Cooper to Lowe, June 2, 1852, Governor and Council Letterbook, 1845–1854, MdHR.

50. O[liver] Johnson to Joshua R. Giddings, Giddings papers, microfilm 7, reel 3, OHS; Hensel, *Christiana Riot*, 55, 94; Stephen S. Foster to Abigail Kelley Foster, Sept. 24, 1851, Abigail Kelley Foster Papers, Mss. box F, AAS. See also J. Miller McKim to William Lloyd Garrison, Dec. 31, 1852, quoted in Gara, *Liberty Line*, 134. On the general questions raised here, see Bertram Wyatt-Brown, "John Brown, Weathermen, and the Psychology of Antinomian Violence," *Soundings*, 58 (1975): 417–41; Jane H. Pease and William H. Pease, "Confrontation and Abolition in the 1850s," *JAH*, 58 (1972): 923–37; Michael Fellman, "Theodore Parker and the Abolitionist Role in the 1850s," *JAH*, 61 (1974): 666–84; John Demos, "The Antislavery Movement and the Problem of Violent 'Means,' " *NEQ*, 37 (1964): 501–26; Ronald G. Walters, *The Antislavery Appeal: American Abolitionism after 1830* (Baltimore, 1976); Merton L. Dillon, *The Abolitionists: The Growth of a Dissenting Minority* (DeKalb, 1974); Dwight Lowell Dumond, *Antislavery: The Crusade for Freedom in America* (Ann Arbor, 1961); Rossbach, *Ambivalent Conspirators;* Thomas Wentworth Higginson, "Physical Courage," *Atlantic Monthly*, 2 (1858): 728–37.

51. Committee, *Report*, Maryland State Documents, 1852, Document O, p. 15, MdHR. Nicholas Hutchins and Joshua Gorsuch billed the estate of Edward Gorsuch for their expenses associated with the attempt to retake the dead man's slaves. Dr. George Gorsuch, who attended to the wounded Dickinson Gorsuch, also billed the estate $4.55 for his services. Hutchins was reimbursed $8.84 for transportation and food. Joshua Gorsuch received $20.73 for transportation, his lost pistol and hat, and medical care. See, W. U. Hensel, "Aftermath Supplementary to Christiana Riot, 1851," *LCHS Papers*, 16 (1912): 133–41.

52. Maryland State Documents, 1852, Document A, "Annual Message," 39, MdHR; Samuel May, *The Fugitive Slave Law and its Victims* (New York, 1861; rpt. ed., New York, 1970), 21; Still, *Underground Rail Road*, 368. According to Samuel May, the name of the African-American woman in question was Rachel Parker, and her case came to trial in January 1853:

> Over sixty witnesses, from Pennsylvania, attended to testify to her being free-born, and that she was not the person she was claimed to be; although, in great bodily terror, she had, after her capture, confessed herself the alleged slave! So complete and strong was the evidence in her favor, that, after an eight days' trial, the claimants abandoned the case, and a verdict was rendered for the freedom of Rachel, and also of her sister, Elizabeth Parker, who had been previously kidnapped, and conveyed to New Orleans.

Pennsylvania's Governor Bigler demanded extradition of the kidnapper, but Governor Lowe of Maryland refused to surrender him. See also, *National Anti-Slavery Standard,* July 2, 1853.

53. See, for examples, May, *The Fugitive Slave Law, and Its Victims.*

Chapter 8. Race, Violence, and Law

1. All quotations are from the trial notes of the prosecuting attorney as printed in the *Lancaster Intelligencer,* Apr. 30, 1839, p. 2.
2. Lewis Getz—the black companion of the accused murderers—supplied these details, which are entirely consistent with the testimony of John McCarron.
3. David Martin repeated the dialogue, which he said was told him by Lewis Getz several days after the event. There was also some suggestion, implied in responses to the defense attorney's questions, that Morrison said something about "whipping negroes."
4. Lewis Getz apparently witnessed the violence from a chair where he sat throughout the affray.
5. *Lancaster Intelligencer,* May 7, 1839, p. 2.
6. Complaint of Catherine McCarron, LCQS, Apr. 1834. The case was dismissed when the prosecutrix failed to appear in court. Thomas McCarron's name is listed as "James" in the docket-book entries.
7. This version is consistent with a reading of the document in the *Intelligencer,* what we know that defense witnesses said, what we have good reason to suspect that defense attorneys asked, what we know they implied in their questions from the structure and content of the answers they got, and what we have reason to believe the judge may have said in his ninety-minute instructions to jurors before they retired to consider the evidence in the case. The sources are the trial notes printed in the *Intelligencer,* comments in subsequent stories that appeared in the newspaper on May 7, 1839, p. 2; May 14, 1839, p. 2; May 21, 1839, p. 2; May 28, 1839, p. 2; stories in the *Lancaster Examiner* (referred to in note 8 below); Commonwealth v. Samuel Caldwell and Richard Weye, LCQS, Apr. 1839.
8. *Lancaster Examiner,* Apr. 25, 1839, p. 2; May 9, 1839, p. 3; May 16, 1839, p. 3; May 23, 1839, p. 3; May 30, 1839, p. 3. See the *Lancaster Journal* for this same month, which also had serious problems with the verdict reached by the jury. Readers interested in the eighteenth-century part of this story should see Slaughter, "Interpersonal Violence in a Rural Setting."
9. During three sample years—1833, 1834, 1835—violent crime constituted 53 percent, 53 percent, and 47 percent respectively of all cases before the LCQS and LMC combined. Assault and battery cases represented 93 percent, 96 percent, and 95 percent of violent crimes presented to the LCQS during those years. On violence by and against constables, see, for example, Commonwealth v. John Bohn, LCQS, Nov. 1834; Commonwealth v. James Glenn, LCQS, Nov. 1834; Commonwealth v. John Doak, LCQS, Nov. 1834; Commonwealth v. Arthur McAleer, LCQS, Aug. 1835; Commonwealth v. Peter Sulleberger, LCQS, Nov. 1835. Changing attitudes toward violence during the nineteenth century is discussed in greater detail in Chapter 9.

10. The quarter-sessions caseload seems to mirror increases in population, since the number of Lancastrians about doubled as well between 1790 and 1830. United States Census, Population, 1790, 1830; *Population Abstract of the United States*. The federal census counted 36,147 Lancaster residents in 1790 and 76,631 in 1830. So whatever role the other variables played, they do not seem to account for a rise in the number of presentments proportionate to the total population. Other factors besides population probably played a role in the changing attitudes reflected in the way assault and battery complaints were handled, in increased conviction rates, and in harsher punishments for all forms of violence during the nineteenth century. See Chapter 9.

11. Commonwealth v. Jacob Markley, LCQS, Jan. 1834; Commonwealth v. Zachariah Lovet, alias Love, LCQS, Nov. 1833; Commonwealth v. Nancy Reaff, LCQS, Aug. 1833; Commonwealth v. Andrew Shute, John Fryer, and William Spurier, LCQS, Nov. 1834.

12. Commonwealth v. George Kiehl, LCQS, Aug. 1833; Commonwealth v. Robert Hedger, LCQS, Apr. 1834; Commonwealth v. John Keenan and Michael Keenan, LCQS, Apr. 1834; Commonwealth v. Daniel Grove, Jr., LCQS, Jan. 1835. See also Commonwealth v. Daniel Grove, Jr., LCQS, Aug. 1835.

13. Commonwealth v. Abraham Green, LCQS, Aug. 1833; Commonwealth v. David Miller, LCQS, Nov. 1833; Commonwealth v. David Jeffries, David Buyers, and Christian Strawbridge, LCQS, Nov. 1833.

14. For the sample years of 1833, 1834, 1835, women constituted about 27 percent of adult complainants in assault-and-battery cases before the LCQS. Women also represented about 9 percent of defendants in such cases during those years. Violence perpetrated by women was most often aimed at other women; but women occasionally engaged in violence with and against men, although not in statistically significant numbers. One constable told the court that he neglected to serve legal papers on two women because he was afraid of them. See Commonwealth v. Peter Sulleberger, LCQS, Nov. 1835.

15. Commonwealth v. David Wagoner, LCQS, Apr. 1833; Commonwealth v. Jacob Cable (or Coble), LCQS, Nov. 1833; Commonwealth v. Christian Whitmore, LCQS, Jan. 1834; Commonwealth v. James McCarron, LCQS, Apr. 1834; Commonwealth v. John White, LCQS, Nov. 1834; Commonwealth v. Jacob Nissley, LCQS, Jan. 1835; Commonwealth v. John Gay, LCQS, Aug. 1835; Commonwealth v. Anthony Donbach, LCQS, Aug. 1835; Commonwealth v. William Ball, LCQS, Aug. 1835; Commonwealth v. Nancy Reiff, LCQS, Aug. 1833; Commonwealth v. Susanna Blocher, LCQS, Aug. 1833. In the sample years 1833 and 1834, children represented 17 percent and 29 percent of victims identified in assault-and-battery cases. There are no children identified as victims in the records for 1835. On violence against children, see, for example, Commonwealth v. Henry Walz, LMC, Nov. 1834; Commonwealth v. Joseph Stoy, LMC, Nov. 1834; Commonwealth v. Moses Ferry, LMC, Jan. 1835.

16. Even such rudimentary statistical analyses of the court records as these should be read as broad estimates rather than social "facts." It is not clear that all principals in court cases were identified by race, and the federal censuses for 1830 and 1840, which I checked against the names of complainants and defendants appearing in the LCQS and LMC for the intervening decade, are

not a lot of help because the black population was both transient and under-counted. Most of the time, most clerks noted the race of African-Americans who appeared in court ("coloured" or "cld" in parentheses beside the name), but occasionally they did not. As a consequence, the estimates are low. Throughout this chapter, my quantitative statements are based on a tabula-tion of minute-book entries, indictments, and case papers for the years 1833, 1834, and 1835, as checked against samples and impressions for other years between 1801 and 1860. I have examined every indictment, case paper, and minute-book entry for the first sixty years of the nineteenth century (and all those that survive for the eighteenth century as well). There are gaps in the minute books, but all case papers and indictments appear to be intact for quarter sessions, Oyer and Terminer (which was the quarter-sessions court meeting in special session to consider serious felony crimes), common pleas, and mayor's court (which is the quarter-sessions court for the city of Lancaster and existed for only part of the century). Some of the research in the ante-bellum court records is reflected in this chapter, more of it in Chapter 9.

I draw my statistics and examples from a three-year sample in order to avoid, as much as possible, exaggerating the nature—quantity and kind—of violence by selecting the best "stories" from across the sixty-year period and because a quantitative study of the entire sixty years seemed unnecessary to learn what I wanted to know and to make the points that I want to make. I remain convinced that quantifying court cases is a tricky and risky business, fraught with subjectivity in creating categories and labeling cases and that such statistics imply or assert a claim for precision that I am uncomfortable making on the basis of my examination of these records. The quantitative assertions are no less impressionistic than my use of stories told in the courts, and they are certainly anachronistic in the sense that no one at the time generated such statistics or grouped cases into the categories that I use. They are thus in some ways less "true" than the stories told by historical actors themselves.

17. Commonwealth v. Henry Ferguson, LCQS, Oyer and Terminer docket book, Jan. 1833; additional details from the *Columbia Spy*, Feb. 2, 1833, p. 2, re-printed from the *Lancaster Intelligencer*. Ferguson was charged with first-degree murder, but the jury apparently determined that there was a lack of premeditation in his violent act.

18. Commonwealth v. William McCork, LCQS, Oyer and Terminer docket book, Aug. 1833, continued to Nov. 1833, trial and sentence Jan. 1834; *Lancaster Journal*, Jan. 31, 1834, p. 2. McCork was charged with first-degree murder; the jury returned a conviction on the lesser charge after deliberating about six hours. See also the letter in the *Columbia Spy*, Feb. 8, 1834, p. 2, which disputes none of the facts reported in the other newspapers and adds a few additional details. The letter does contest the implication that Williams got second-rate medical care, defends the physician, and points out that the county refused to pay doctors at all for medical care extended to the poor unless it was given on the grounds of the poorhouse to an inmate of the institution.

19. H. A. Rockafield, *The Manheim Tragedy: A Complete History of the Double Murder of Mrs. Garber and Mrs. Reim; With the Only Authentic Life and Confession of Alexander Anderson* (Lancaster, 1858), 7, LCP. The quotation

is taken from the *Evening Express*. Rockafield's compilation relied heavily on newspaper articles, reproducing them in sequence to form a chronological narrative of the crime, trial, and execution of Anderson and Richards. I have checked the sources against each other and find the compilation totally reliable in this regard. Rockafield also interviewed some of the principals, and supplemented these stories with first-person accounts of the proceedings.

Anderson's "confession" is another matter entirely. Rockafield's claim to authenticity is accompanied by his description of the process by which he helped Anderson create the text. "The greater part of it," the compiler explained,

> was written down by Anderson himself, at different times, after his conviction, as he could recall the leading incidents of his life to mind. This was transcribed, the orthography corrected, and the whole then read over to the prisoner in his cell, and again revised under his direction. Of course, it could not be expected that he could recollect the dates of so many incidents as fill up the measure of his life, or even preserve their chronological order. These were therefore arranged as correctly as possible, by the compiler referring to the court and prison records, and, in some cases to incidental circumstances, by which alone the prisoner could fix facts in his mind.

Later, Anderson requested the removal of some names from the document out of concern for the reputations of his friends. Finally, two clergymen examined the text before publication and recommended additional deletions, apparently of some of the "more revolting details" of Anderson's actions (*Manheim Tragedy*, 3–4).

If we believe this story about the collaborative origins of Anderson's confession, what we have is a version of his life and crime orchestrated by and filtered through at least three white "advisors." We might suspect that the compiler's prime interest was sales, although he claims a desire for "truth" that I would not discount out-of-hand. The clergymen seem to have been concerned about public sensibilities—limiting the pornographic appeal of the violence depicted in the text—and about Anderson's soul. So we cannot take the text at face value or accept it unquestioningly as Anderson's own, but it apparently is substantially his version of his life and descent into crime, at least as he thought it would best play to an audience of whites. Anderson, too, was interested in sales, because a portion of the proceeds went to his wife and children; we might also take seriously his own concern with his soul and the accompanying belief that he had to confess the "truth" of his debauchery as guided by the clergymen in order to be saved.

20. *Lancaster Intelligencer*, Dec. 22, 1857, p. 2; Jan. 26, 1858, p. 2; Mar. 16, 1858, p. 2; Rockafield, *Manheim Tragedy*, 5–10, 12–22.

21. Rockafield, *Manheim Tragedy*, 10, 62–63; *Lancaster Intelligencer*, Dec. 22, 1858, p. 2; Jan. 26, 1858, p. 2.

22. *Lancaster Intelligencer*, Jan. 26, 1858, p. 2; Rockafield, *Manheim Tragedy*, 12–22.

23. *Lancaster Intelligencer*, Jan. 26, 1858, p. 2; Rockafield, *Manheim Tragedy*, 12–22.

24. Rockafield, *Manheim Tragedy*, 17–19; *Lancaster Intelligencer*, Jan. 26, 1858.

25. Rockafield, *Manheim Tragedy*, 17–19; *Lancaster Intelligencer*, Jan. 26, 1858, p. 2.
26. Rockafield, *Manheim Tragedy*, 18–19; *Lancaster Intelligencer*, Jan. 26, 1858, p. 2.
27. Rockafield, *Manheim Tragedy*, 17–22; *Lancaster Intelligencer*, Jan. 26, 1858, p. 2.
28. Rockafield, *Manheim Tragedy*, 22–23, 25–26; *Lancaster Intelligencer*, Feb. 9, 1858, p. 2. On the opposition to capital punishment in antebellum America and the transition from public to "private" executions, see Louis P. Masur, *Rites of Execution: Capital Punishment and the Transformation of American Culture, 1776–1865* (New York, 1989), especially Chapter 5.
29. Rockafield, *Manheim Tragedy*, 3–4, 26; *Lancaster Intelligencer*, Mar. 30, 1858, p. 3. Richards also eventually confessed, and the details he gave of the murder agree with Anderson's story. In an ironic twist, curious investigators eventually figured out that the two condemned men were half brothers—sons of the same mother by different men—which neither of them ever knew. Rockafield, *Manheim Tragedy*, 47–49.
30. Rockafield, *Manheim Tragedy*, 27. Richards also admitted under close and repeated questioning by clergymen that he was a habitual drinker of whiskey, but it is not clear that he acknowledged liquor's decisive role in his life. Ibid., 47–48.
31. Ibid.
32. Ibid., 27–28.
33. Ibid., 28–29. Richards also spent some time in prison, serving two terms in the Lancaster County jail for larceny, but those are apparently the only two times previous to this case that he was brought into court. Ibid., 47–48.
34. Ibid., 27–37.
35. Ibid., 37–42; *Lancaster Intelligencer*, Apr. 6, 1858, p. 2; Apr. 13, 1858, p. 2.
36. Rockafield, *Manheim Tragedy*, 49–56; *Lancaster Intelligencer*, Apr. 13, 1858, p. 2.
37. Rockafield, *Manheim Tragedy*, 50–56; *Lancaster Intelligencer*, Apr. 13, 1858, p. 2.
38. Rockafield, *Manheim Tragedy*, 50–56; *Lancaster Intelligencer*, Apr. 13, 1858, p. 2.
39. Rockafield, *Manheim Tragedy*, 52.
40. Ibid., 47.

Chapter 9. Race, Riots, and Law

1. On riots in Lancaster County during the previous century, see Slaughter, "Crowds in Eighteenth-Century America." For comparative crime statistics, see also Slaughter, "Interpersonal Violence in a Rural Setting." The court records begin in 1729, when Lancaster County was created as an administra-

tive entity. On the general pattern of antebellum collective actions, see David Grimsted, "Rioting in Its Jacksonian Setting," *AHR*, 77 (1972); 361–97; Grimsted, "Ante-Bellum Labor: Violence, Strike, and Communal Arbitration," *JSH*, 19 (1985): 5–28; Michael Feldberg, *The Turbulent Era: Riot and Disorder in Jacksonian America* (New York, 1980); Paul A. Gilje, *The Road to Mobocracy: Popular Disorder in New York City, 1763–1834* (Chapel Hill, 1987). On eighteenth-century crowds, see Gordon S. Wood, "A Note on Mobs in the American Revolution," *WMQ* 3d ser., 23 (1966): 635–42; Pauline Maier, "Popular Uprisings and Civil Authority in Eighteenth-Century America," *WMQ* 3d ser., 27 (1970): 3–35; Peter Shaw, *American Patriots and the Rituals of Revolution* (Cambridge, 1981); Jesse Lemisch, "Jack Tar in the Streets: Merchant Seamen in the Politics of Revolutionary America," *WMQ* 3d ser., 25 (1968): 371–407; Edward Countryman, "The Problem of the Early American Crowd," *American Studies*, 7 (1973): 77–90; Richard Maxwell Brown, "Violence and the American Revolution," in Stephen G. Kurtz and James H. Hutson, eds., *Essays on the American Revolution* (Chapel Hill, 1973), 81–120; Arthur M. Schlesinger, "Politics, Mobs and the American Revolution, 1765–1776," *Proceedings of the American Philosophical Society*, 90 (1955): 244–50; Alfred F. Young, ed., *The American Revolution: Explorations in the History of American Radicalism* (DeKalb, 1976), essays by Gary B. Nash, Edward Countryman, Marvin L. Michael Kay, Dirk Hoerder, and Ronald Hoffman.

2. Seventy-four complaints over twenty years (1834–1853) represents between three and four (3.7) riots per year. During this period there were only two years—1841 and 1842—in which no rioters came before the court. In only four years—1834, 1849, 1851, and 1853—were there as many as seven or eight separate instances of riot before the court, and those were the high watermarks of frequency for Lancaster County during the antebellum nineteenth century. Only once in the eighteenth century—1764—were there as many as eight riot complaints in one year.

Thirty-one of the seventy-four riot complaints made it to the docket, which is 42 percent and roughly comparable, in light of the size of the respective samples, to the 47 percent from the eighteenth century. The conviction rate of 4 percent for the later period is a striking change. In terms of population, the rising rate of riot complaints is in rough alignment with Lancaster's increase in population during the nineteenth century. Between 1800 and 1850 the population more than doubled, going from about 43,403 to 98,944—source: John L. Andriot, *Population Abstract of the United States* (McLean, Va., 1980). The rising rate of complaints is clearly not, however, a direct response to population increase since the prosecution-population ratio actually was declining until the mid-1830s, when it rose abruptly and then remained constant for at least twenty years. Lancaster's population in 1830 was about 76,631.

Even expressed in real numbers rather than as percentages, from a much lower base of accusations, there were more people convicted of riot in the first thirteen years of the nineteenth century than during the next forty years.

LCQS and Mayor's Court Riot Cases,
1827–1853

Ruling	Number
nol pros	8
ignoramus	2
recognizance forfeited	1
continued indefinitely	9
jury trial, not guilty	6
jury trial, guilty	3
settled by parties	2

Source: LCQS and LMC minute books and case papers.

3. The nature and consequences of riots can be identified in fifty-eight of seventy-four riot cases during the twenty years between 1834 and 1853. Thirty-five (60 percent) involved physical violence against individuals—twenty-four of these were assaults, five were simple brawls (although a number of the assaults appear to have been overflow violence from general fights), seven incorporated violence against property and persons, and four were rescues. Twenty riots (34 percent) included property damage as all or part of the complaint—the seven cases of violence against persons and property, and thirteen cases in which only property was damaged. There is nothing comparable in the eighteenth-century records to the riot charges in the thirteen property-damage cases (22 percent) where no interpersonal violence is mentioned, or to the ten cases (17 percent) in which only disorderly conduct, but no violence or damage, was charged. I have included the domestic disorder case and the elopement case in the figures for disorderly conduct, where they belong, although calling those two events riots on the basis of information provided in the court records seems to stretch the definition of "riot" beyond our modern understandings of that term. The records do not provide sufficient information to categorize the remaining ten cases.

Riots, LCQS and Mayor's Court, 1834–1853

Types	Number
disorderly conduct	10
assault	19
fighting	5
property damage	13
assault and property damage	6
fighting and property damage	1
rescue	4

Source: LCQS and LMC minute books and case papers.

4. *Lancaster Examiner,* Sept. 4, 1834, p. 3; July 17, 1834, p. 3. See also reports of riots in *Lancaster Examiner,* July 17, 1834, p. 2; Aug. 21, 1834, p. 2;

Aug. 28, 1834, p. 2; Oct. 16, 1834, p. 2; Aug. 20, 1835, p. 2; Aug. 20, 1835, p. 4.

5. *Lancaster Journal,* Aug. 15, 1834, p. 2; Aug. 19, 1834, p. 2; Sept. 5, 1834, p. 3; Oct. 3, 1834, p. 2; Dec. 19, 1834, p. 4. See also the *Lancaster Union* and the *Columbia Spy* for this period.

6. Paul A. Gilje, *The Road to Mobocracy;* Gilje, " 'The mob begins to think and reason': Recent Trends in Studies of American Popular Disorder, 1700–1850," *Maryland Historian,* 12 (1981): 25–36; Gilje, "The Baltimore Riot of 1812 and the Breakdown of the Anglo-American Mob Tradition," *Journal of Social History,* 13 (1980): 547–64; Michael Feldberg, *The Turbulent Era;* Feldberg, *The Philadelphia Riots of 1844: A Study of Ethnic Conflict* (Westport, 1975); Feldberg, "The Crowd in Philadelphia History: A Comparative Perspective," *Labor History,* 15 (1974): 323–36; Paul O. Weinbaum, *Mobs and Demagogues: The New York Response to Collective Violence in the Early Nineteenth Century* (Ann Arbor, 1979); Vincent P. Lannie and Bernard C. Diethorn, "For the Honor and Glory of God: The Philadelphia Bible Riots of 1840," *History of Education Quarterly,* 8 (1968): 44–106; Leonard L. Richards, *"Gentlemen of Property and Standing": Anti-Abolition Mobs in Jacksonian America* (New York, 1970); Linda K. Kerber, "Abolitionists and Amalgamators: The New York City Race Riots of 1834," *New York History,* 48 (1967): 28–39; Joseph G. Mannard, "The 1839 Baltimore Nunnery Riot: An Episode in Nativism and Social Violence," *Maryland Historian,* 11 (1981): 13–26; John Runcie, " 'Hunting the Nigs' in Philadelphia: The Race Riot of August 1834," *Pennsylvania History,* 39 (1972): 187–218; David Montgomery, "The Shuttle and the Cross: Weavers and Artisans in the Kensington Riots of 1844," *Journal of Social History,* 5 (1971–72): 411–46; Richard Moody, *The Astor Place Riot* (Bloomington, 1958); David Grimsted, *Melodrama Unveiled: American Theater and Culture, 1800–1850* (Chicago, 1968); Michael S. Hindus, "A City of Mobocrats and Tyrants: Mob Violence in Boston, 1747–1863," *Issues in Criminology,* 6 (1971): 55–83; Theodore M. Hammett, "The Mobs of Jacksonian Boston: Ideology and Interest," *JAH,* 63 (1976): 845–68; Roger Lane, *Policing the City: Boston, 1822–1885* (Cambridge, 1967).

7. Feldberg, *Turbulent Era,* 25; Grimsted, "Rioting in Its Jacksonian Setting," 364.

8. The charge of rioting associated with an underage elopement was against James Garret and three others (1851). Margaret Thompson was accused of riot for cursing and making an uproar outside the house of her son and daughter-in-law (1851).

9. Nine of seventy-four cases went to trial. Six resulted in acquittals.

10. It is possible that there was an actual decline in the frequency of riots during the twenty years preceding 1834. Unfortunately, a gap in the surviving court records does not permit an examination of that possibility. Such a period of relative calm would help to explain how contemporaries and the historians who take their testimony at face value came to see the collective violence of the years after 1833 as "new" in both a quantitative and qualitative sense.

11. Commonwealth v. Jacob Hoag and six others, 1833, LCQS docket book;

Commonwealth v. William Lyttle and five others, 1836, LCQS case papers. The reasons for the variation in the amounts of bond from one charge to the next is not always clear from the surviving records, and that is the case within this category of riot accusation.

12. Commonwealth v. Francis Stain (?) and eight others, 1849, LCQS case papers; Commonwealth v. John S. Shenk and two others, 1850, LCQS case papers.

13. Commonwealth v. John Shaitzer and others, 1844, LCQS case papers; Commonwealth v. David Sailor and others, 1846, LCQS case papers.

14. Commonwealth v. John W. Hart and four others, 1835, LCQS case papers; Commonwealth v. Jackson Johnston and five others, 1835, LCQS case papers.

15. Commonwealth v. David Poorman, 1834, LMC case papers; Commonwealth v. Joseph Hughes, 1851, LCQS case papers. The two other cases involving women victims were Commonwealth v. William Hunter and others, 1851, LCQS case papers, for which the records provide no details other than that the complainant, who could not sign her name, was Mary Ann Wilson; and Commonwealth v. Margaret Thompson, 1851, LCQS case papers, for creating a disturbance outside the house of her daughter-in-law, Eliza Thompson, who also signed the complaint with her mark. The resolution of neither case is revealed in the records, which probably means that they were thrown out of court. There were two women among the six revelers charged with riot in the case of Commonwealth v. William Lyttle and others, 1836, LCQS case papers, and Emily Cossia and two other black women were presented on a charge of riot in 1846 for disrupting a service in the African Church. There is no notice of what, if any, action the court took against these women rioters.

16. *Columbia Spy*, Aug. 23, 1834, pp. 2–3.

17. Ibid., Aug. 23, 1834, p. 2.

18. Ibid., Aug. 23, 1834, p. 2; Aug. 30, 1834, p. 3.

19. Ibid., Aug. 30, 1834, p. 3. On the question of the economic origins of the initial riots, see ibid., Aug. 23, 1834, p. 3.

20. Ibid., Aug. 30, 1834, p. 3.

21. Oblinger, "New Freedoms, Old Miseries," 124, 126.

22. *Columbia Spy*, Sept. 6, 1834, p. 3.

23. Ibid.

24. Ibid.

25. Ibid., Sept. 13, 1834, p. 3.

26. Freeholders books, 1815, 1826, 1836, LCHS; William F. Worner, "The Columbia Race Riots," *LCHS Papers*, 26 (1922): 175–87; Leroy T. Hopkins, "Black Eldorado on the Susquehanna: The Emergence of Black Columbia, 1726–1861," *JLCHS*, 89 (1985): 110–32. The three freeholders books show the countywide trend, which was concentrated, but not confined, to Columbia. No black freeholders are listed in 1815; twenty blacks are listed in the 1826 book, of whom fifteen were residents of Columbia; and the 1836 book lists thirty-one black men. At least fifteen of the 198 Columbia freeholders listed in 1836 were black. This list is, at best, imprecise, and underreports the real numbers of black freeholders. Not all jurisdictions reliably noted the race of each freeholder. Stephen Smith, for example, is listed in the 1836

book without a racial designation after his name. The number of freeholders identified by Leroy Hopkins relies on tax records and a fuller knowledge of the racial identities of Columbia residents.

27. *Columbia Spy*, Oct. 4, 1834, p. 2.
28. Ibid. Commonwealth v. John Lightner and others, for attack on James Smith; and Commonwealth v. John Lightner and others, for attack on James Richards, LCQS case papers, indictments, and docket book, Nov. 1834.
29. *Columbia Spy*, Oct. 4, 1834, p. 2.
30. Ibid.
31. Ibid., Mar. 7, 1835, p. 3.
32. Ibid., Apr. 10, 1835, p. 3.
33. Commonwealth v. Stephen Witt and others, LCQS case papers, Apr. 1835.

Conclusion

1. Campbell, *The Slave Catchers*, 207; May, *The Fugitive Slave Law and Its Victims*, 27–49, 64–66, 91–92, 95, 100, 109, 121, 131–34, 137, 143–46. The references to May are to Pennsylvania cases only after the Christiana Riot. The Lancaster County kidnapping of John Brown is recounted on 131–33.
2. Gerald G. Eggert, "The Impact of the Fugitive Slave Law on Harrisburg: A Case Study," *PMHB*, 109 (1985): 537–69; May, *The Fugitive Slave Law and Its Victims; Planter's Advocate*, Dec. 31, 1851, p. 2; Jan. 7, 1852, p. 2; Jan. 21, 1852, pp. 2–3; Feb. 4, 1852, p. 4; Feb. 11, 1852, p. 2; Apr. 28, 1852, p. 2; Oct. 6, 1852, p. 1; Nov. 10, 1852, p. 2; Dec. 15, 1852, p. 2; *Journal of Proceedings of the Senate of Maryland* (Annapolis, 1852), 368, MdHR; *Journal of the Proceedings of the Senate of Maryland*, "Report of Otho Scott and James M. Buchanan, Commissioners in the Case of Archibald G. Ridgely" (Annapolis, 1853), MdHR; *Laws of Maryland* (Annapolis, 1852), Resolution number 12, MdHR; *Journal of the Proceedings of the House of Delegates of the State of Maryland* (Annapolis, 1852), 827, MdHR; *Report of the Committee on Colored Population to the House of Delegates* (Annapolis, 1852), Maryland State Documents, Document L, MdHR; *Lancaster Intelligencer Journal*, Feb. 27, 1880, p. 2.
3. Thomas R. Winpenny, "The Economic Status of Negroes in Late Nineteenth-Century Lancaster," *JLCHS*, 77 (1973): 124–32.
4. Raymond M. Hyser and Dennis B. Downey, " 'A Crooked Death': Coatesville, Pennsylvania, and the Lynching of Zachariah Walker," *PAH*, 54 (1987): 85–86. Coatesville is in Chester County.
5. Ibid., 86.
6. Ibid., 86–87.
7. Ibid., 87.
8. Ibid., 88–89.
9. On race and violence after the Civil War, see, for example, Roger Lane, *Roots of Violence in Black Philadelphia, 1860–1900* (Cambridge, Ma., 1986); Herbert Shapiro, *White Violence and Black Response: From Reconstruction to Montgomery* (Amherst, 1988).
10. Hensel, *Christiana Riot*, 4; Harriet Beecher Stowe, *Uncle Tom's Cabin; or,*

Life Among the Lowly (Boston, 1852). Stowe's novel was first serialized in the *National Era* during 1851, in some of the same issues that reported the Christiana Riot. Mrs. Stowe defended her characterizations against those in her day who found them "untrue." See Stowe, *A Key to Uncle Tom's Cabin* (Boston, 1853), which relied heavily on Theodore Weld's *American Slavery As It Is* (Boston, 1839).

11. Jack Ward Willson Loose, "The Christiana Riot Anniversary Exercises," *LCHS Papers*, 55 (1951): 181–85; Katz, *Resistance*, 297. Dr. Bond was the father of Julian Bond, the Georgia state legislator.

12. On the question of modern violence, see Philip Greven, *Spare the Child: The Religious Roots of Punishment and the Psychological Impact of Physical Abuse* (New York, 1991); Elizabeth Pleck, *Domestic Tyranny: The Making of American Social Policy Against Family Violence from Colonial Times to the Present* (New York, 1988); Alice Miller, *For Your Own Good: Hidden Cruelty in Child-Rearing and the Roots of Violence* (New York, 1984); Linda Gordon, *Heroes of Their Own Lives: The Politics and History of Family Violence* (Boston, 1988); and John Demos, "Child Abuse in Context: An Historian's Perspective," in Demos, *Past, Present, and Personal: The Family and the Life Course in American History* (New York, 1986), 68–91.

Afterword

1. Ellwood Griest, *John and Mary; or, the Fugitive Slaves, A Tale of South-Eastern Pennsylvania* (Lancaster, 1873), unpaginated Preface.
2. Ibid., 28, 32, 38, 41.
3. Ibid., 60, 114–18, 128, 131.
4. Ibid., 129.
5. Ibid., 86, 121.
6. Ibid., 145. Doan disappears after recovering from his wounds. The fugitives are shuttled offstage to lead quiet, anonymous lives beyond the reader's ken. An epilogue brings Mary and Charlie back; it appears that John is long since gone. The final act takes place on a Civil War battlefield. Charlie, a soldier in the Union army, has been seriously wounded, and his mother has been summoned to attend her son. There is a maudlin deathbed reunion between them and Charlie's commanding officer, whom they all come to realize is the son of the fugitives' Lancaster County patrons.
7. Hensel, *The Christiana Riot*.
8. Still, *The Underground Rail Road*, 2.
9. Gara, *The Liberty Line*, 3, 4, 6, 7.
10. David Bradley, *The Chaneysville Incident* (New York, 1981); Toni Morrison, *Beloved* (New York, 1987); John Edgar Wideman, *Fever* (New York, 1989); Wideman, *Damballah* (New York, 1981). References to the work of historians mentioned in this paragraph are located in the appropriate places in the notes above.
11. Gara, *The Liberty Line*, 42, 91. Gara points out that William Still's *The Underground Rail Road* is the exception to his complaints about accounts of the Underground Railroad. "The focus of his book," Gara observes, "is on the

brave fugitives rather than on the abolitionists. Although he did not slight the contribution of numerous white abolitionists, Still's hero was clearly the run-away himself." Unfortunately, "despite . . . the popularity of his book, Still's emphasis has made virtually no impact on the popular legend. For it is not the fugitive whose heroism is given the spotlight, but rather the abolitionist who helped him on his way." Gara, *The Liberty Line*, 177, 178. See also, for the more recent focus on the role of African-Americans on their own quest for freedom, Rita Jean Roberts, "In Quest of Autonomy: Northern Black Activism Between the Revolution and Civil War," Ph.D. diss., University of California, Berkeley, 1988; Leonard P. Curry, *The Free Black in Urban America, 1800–1850: The Shadow of the Dream* (Chicago, 1981); Benjamin Quarles, *Black Abolitionists* (New York, 1975); Jane H. Pease and William H. Pease, *They Who Would Be Free: Blacks' Search for Freedom, 1830–1861* (New York, 1971).

Index

Abolition movement, 38, 208 n.24.
  See also Emancipation; Gradual
  abolition
  backlash against, 40–42, 165, 172
  literature, 13, 110, 115–16, 126
  Northern U.S. and, x, 20, 85, 188
  Quakers and, 9–10, 25, 188
Abolitionist newspapers, 84, 92, 97,
  102–3, 218 n.11
Abolitionists, 10, 85, 106, 144–45,
  146
  African-American, 38–39, 54
  aid fugitives, 39, 78–79, 90, 192
  blamed for riots, 96–104, 110, 129,
  171
  Christiana Riot and, xiii, 84, 87,
  110
  Christiana Riot trial and, x–xi, 120–
  22, 132, 134–35, 137
  Christiana Riot trial prosecution
  strategy and, 106, 114, 115–16,
  122, 129
  colonization and, 209 n.24
  Fugitive Slave Law and, 107
  in Lancaster County, Pa., 38, 42,
  47
  in literature, 110–11, 188, 191
  racism and, 24, 110
African-Americans. *See also* Children;
  Court records; Free blacks;

Fugitive slaves; Kidnappings;
  Mulattoes; Racism; Segregation;
  Slaves; Underground Railroad;
  Violence; Women; *specific state
  or area names*
Christiana Riot, effects on, xii, 80–
  88, 137, 180
Christiana Riot, imprisoned for, 92,
  119, 132, 134
Christiana Riot participants, 39,
  63–79, 90–97, 110, 118, 125–27,
  216 n.20
Christiana Riot trial and, 115, 120,
  122, 132–34, 139
Christiana Riot witnesses, 117–18
communities of, 49, 162–63, 170,
  173–80. *See also* Columbia;
  Lancaster
cooperating with kidnappers, 51,
  52, 189
economic status of. *See* Free blacks
education of, 176, 183
family life of, 17, 80, 82, 84, 205
  n.8
gangs of, 133, 190, 191
health of, 32, 33, 40, 80, 132
heroism and, 33, 47, 70, 75, 79,
  110, 192, 209 n.25, 239 n.11
history and fiction, in, 187–92
homelessness and, 132, 157, 159

the North and the South, but he uses legal records reaching back over a century and a half to uncover the thoughts of average people on race, slavery, and violence.

The Whiskey Rebellion, Slaughter's previous work of history, received widespread acclaim as "a vivid account" *(The New York Times)* and "an unusual combination of meticulous scholarship and engaging narrative" *(The Philadelphia Inquirer)*. It was a selection of the History Book Club, and won both the National Historical Society Book Prize and the American Revolution Round Table Award. In *Bloody Dawn*, he once again weaves together the incisive insights of a professional historian with a gripping account of a dramatic moment in American history.

Gordon L. Miller

About the Author

Thomas P. Slaughter lives in Trenton, New Jersey, and is Professor of History at Rutgers University. He is the author of *The Whiskey Rebellion: Frontier Epilogue to the American Revolution.*